BEST BACKROADS of Florida

Volume 1
The Heartland

Douglas Waitley

Pineapple Press, Inc.
Sarasota, Florida

Inquiries should be addressed to:

Pineapple Press, Inc.
P.O. Box 3899
Sarasota, Florida 34230
www.pineapplepress.com.

Library of Congress Cataloging in Publication Data

Waitley, Douglas.
     Best back roads of Florida. Douglas Waitley.
          v. cm.
     Includes bibliographical references.
     Contents: v. 1. The heartland
     ISBN 1-56164-189-8 (v. 1)
1. Florida—Tours. 2. Automobile travel—Florida—Guidebooks. 3. Scenic byways—Florida—Guidebooks. I. Title.

     F309.3.W325 2000
     917.5904'63—dc21   99-045354

First Edition
10 9 8 7 6 5 4 3 2 1

Design by *Osprey Design Systems*
Printed and bound by Versa Press, Inc., East Peoria, IL

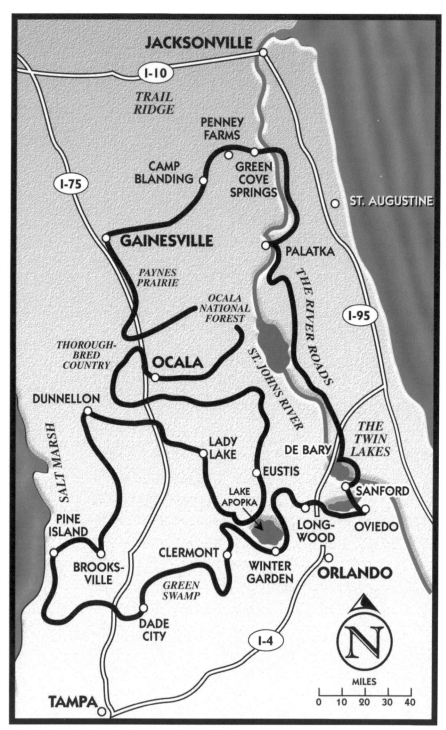

The Setting: Backroads Country, Central Florida

Contents

Introduction

Backroads have always held a fascination for me. They are a sort of refuge where I can escape the frantic hustle of modern life. I love the backroads for the friends they have not made. McDonald's, Burger King, and their rowdy crowd shun the backroads. Truckers hold them in disdain. Advertising companies, with their garish signs, snub them indignantly. And traveling salespeople and most vacationers, hot to make major destinations, ignore the backroads completely.

On the other hand, I love the backroads for their ungainliness as they twist around hills and section lines. I love them for their mean-

Leisurely backroads driving lets you pause for scenes like this sunrise near Oviedo.

ingless meanders and for their for their bumps and potholes. I love them for the people I encounter in the little restaurants, in the dusty gas stations, or just ambling along the byway. I love the cozy roadside parks and secluded streams that beckon picnickers. I love the county signs announcing the side-road names that usually commemorate an influential farmer or villager. I even love the three-digit county road numbers, which sound much more lyrical than the blunt dual digits of federal and state roads.

Backroads are casual affairs. Nobody cares if you turn onto the shoulder to enjoy the song of a mockingbird. Nobody cares if you pause to watch frolicking horses or cows just munching grass. Nobody is suspicious when you stop to ask directions. There are more smiles per county mile than on a hundred miles of expressways.

A backroad gives you time to appreciate the beauty of the commonplace. The gracefully grotesque intertwining of live oak branches. The languid dance of Spanish moss. Anglers casting their lines in clear lakes. The shadows of Gothic homes at sundown. The dew-sparkle on meadows.

On backroads you can appreciate the beauty of small waterways, such as this one near Cross Creek, quaintly called the River Styx.

On a backroad you can drive with the windows rolled down, for the clamor of speeding cars is gratefully absent. Nor are you going to be drenched with the fumes of semitrailer trucks. There is an easy quietude on a backroad that lets you enjoy the song of the highway: the soft hum of the tires; the gentle whisper of fresh country air rushing about you. The melodic call of a bird. All are enhanced by the fresh odor of life in abundance.

A backroad beckons explorers. Whereas state and federal highways have well-known destinations, a backroad can go just about anywhere. And each town and hamlet it passes through has its unique history, its own scenery; its own heroes and villains. There is drama around each bend if you know how to find it. Lives were lived, personal battles fought, victories celebrated, defeats and deaths mourned. Yes, a backroad invites exploration.

But don't take the backroads for granted, for they are under siege and their numbers diminish every day. New residents are flooding into Florida at the rate of 250,000 per year, bringing with them at least 100,000 additional cars to clog the highways. Most of these newcomers prefer suburban living, so sprawl reaches ever farther into the countryside. Thus, what yesterday was a lovely backroad is today pocked with developments and tomorrow will probably be incorporated into a town. Then the once-peaceful byway will throb to the rumble of commuters, the rattle of service trucks, and the kid-clamor of the vehicles driven by soccer moms.

A word about fishing before you set out. Florida requires licenses in many instances. The state's laws on who needs one and under what conditions are rather complex. But the licenses themselves are inexpensive and very easy to obtain. A three-day nonresident's freshwater license is only $6.50, and seven days is $16.50. A Florida resident's twelve-month license costs $13.50. However, children under sixteen need no license. Licenses, as well as information as to when they are needed, can be obtained by calling toll-free 1-888-347-4356. Have your credit card ready.

Many Floridians are concerned. In 1985 the state passed the Growth Management Act, one of the first in the nation to try to control the population surge. Each local government was required to file with the state a plan for orderly, controlled growth that would take into account the area's ability to finance the roads, schools, and other amenities accompanying each level of population increase.

However, in a way, the act aggravated one of the very problems it was intended to diminish, since it required each locality that wanted to grow to widen roads to accommodate the anticipated additional traffic. Yet the widened roads attracted even more developers, and sprawl expanded ever more rapidly. And as Wal-Mart and other chain retailers came to the suburbs, they drained away shoppers from the traditional downtowns, whose deterioration thereby worsened.

I'd like to use this opportunity to recommend the *Florida Atlas & Gazetteer* published by DeLorme Mapping, P.O. Box 298, Freeport, Maine 04032. Although at $16.95 it's expensive and I don't think you'll need it (due to my stellar directions), DeLorme's 127 pages of detailed local maps helped guide me down many of Florida's little-known byways. This is also a good place to issue a disclaimer as to the prices and hours of the attractions listed herein. They were accurate when this book was written, but prices, as well as businesses themselves, come and go.

Certain legislators have begun pushing for an amendment that would encourage a new concept called Front Porch Florida, in which developers would try to discourage the use of cars by building self-contained communities with their own elementary schools, downtowns, and homes where front porches would promote neighborliness. However, until these concepts are incorporated into legislation, the conversion of the backroads into front roads will continue.

So, with all this said, let's set out on our explorations of Florida's most choice backroads. We will travel over more than eight hundred miles of them. You'll be surprised at the richness of your experiences.

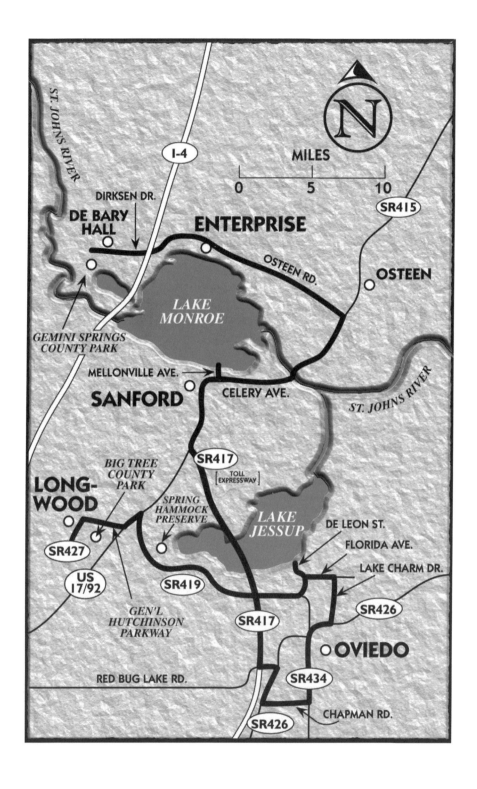

Around the Twin Lakes

DeBary to Longwood • 41 Backroad Miles

The Song of the Road: Where the Byways Lead

The first exploration will take you around two of central Florida's most interesting lakes. They are much the same size, yet completely different. Lake Monroe has been part of the American mainstream since the nineteenth century, when steamboats chugged to and from the docks at DeBary, Enterprise, and Sanford. Today the boats are largely gone from the northern shore, where the backroads pass through stands of dense trees. But the southern shore, concentrated around the active community of Sanford, is a busy place with a rich history. Here you'll want to take one of the excursion boats through the lake waters and along the scenic St. Johns River.

Lake Jessup, on the other hand, has few habitations. Alligators abound, as you'll discover if you take the airboat ride at Gator Ventures. You'll drive through the weird landscape of the Black Hammock and take the jungle-enclosed boardwalk of Spring Hammock Preserve. The chief town is Oviedo, set three miles back from the Jessup wetlands. Oviedo is a strange mixture of new bedroom developments and old communities, like the one you'll drive through when you take the single-lane road around Lake Charm.

You'll end this exploration by standing in awe beneath a magnificent 3,500-year-old cypress known as the Senator.

The Count and the Grandmother: DeBary Hall

Our backroads explorations begin at Dirksen Drive, which is off of Interstate 4 at the DeBary exit 53. Dirksen is a two-lane road that runs west along a low ridge, where on the left, just beyond some homes, is a marshy, stream-laced bayou that leads to Lake Monroe. The road is lined with deciduous trees and cabbage palms, remnants of the days when this was a dense hammock alive with deer, panthers, and black bears.

After a half mile you'll come to Mansion Boulevard, at the foot of which there was once a dock used by steamboats carrying passengers up the St. Johns from Jacksonville. Waiting at the dock were whisper-clean carriages drawn by freshly curried horses that transported the passengers up Mansion Boulevard to DeBary Hall, which rose in white majesty at the end of road. Today we can still follow Mansion to the hall, gleaming as brightly as before.

When Count Frederick DeBary constructed the hall in 1871, he intended to use it as a winter home where he and his family could live in the luxury they enjoyed in Manhattan. But the mansion was so fine, and its setting amid the Florida wilds so unusual and exciting, that the count always had a parade of distinguished guests, including former presidents Ulysses Grant and Grover Cleveland, as well as General William Tecumseh Sherman and the Prince of Wales (who later became the king of England).

The count loved to present his guests with fabulous feasts in the dining room, where a dazzling glass chandelier made the candlelight dance like fireflies. After dinner the men would retire to the billiard room for a friendly game or perhaps just for conversation over fine cigars and imported liqueurs. The women would migrate to the parlor, where they were hosted by Augusta, DeBary's daughter-in-law, to whom the duties of hostess had fallen upon the death of the count's

President Grant and other notables once enjoyed champagne cocktails on the spacious veranda of DeBary Hall.

wife several years earlier. Augusta, an accomplished musician, sere-naded the guests on a piano from New York. At other times everyone would congregate on the veranda to watch the setting sun tint the bayou saffron and rose. Then, when night came, they would retire to their bedrooms on the second floor, where refreshing breezes seemed always to curl about them.

DeBary also delighted in showing guests around his estate, where fragrant orange groves extended over many acres. Hunting was also available in the surrounding woods, which abounded with game. For fox hunts DeBary furnished highbred horses, which were housed in a stable finer than the homes of any cracker farmer. On hot days everyone could enjoy dips in the count's spring-fed swimming pool. And DeBary's parties were famous—indeed, he served so much cham-pagne that the empty bottles became decorative borders for his driveway and gardens.

Champagne was a DeBary specialty, for Frederick had begun his career in America as representative for the exclusive Mumms brand of France. He was only twenty-five when he had migrated to New York from his native Belgium. As the elite found DeBary's champagne a must for their soirées, Frederick became wealthy and eventually moved into the ritzy section of town, where he hobnobbed with the Astors and Vanderbilts.

DeBary was at the height of his success when he built his Florida mansion. Although originally it was to be a winter hunting lodge, DeBary was quick to see that significant profits could be made from growing oranges. So he planted many acres of them, and, when the trees began bearing, he shipped the fruit north on steamboats belonging to his friend, Jacob Brock, based at the nearby village of Enterprise. Business became so good that within five years DeBary purchased a boat outright from Brock and eventually formed his own steamship line.

Although Frederick DeBary died in 1898, his family kept the great hall into the mid-twentieth century, when his great-granddaughter, the young, beautiful, and quite reckless Leonie, died in a small plane crash.

With the exit of the DeBarys, the mansion led a checkered exis-tence. In the 1950s it came into use by an art group, which utilized the spacious, well-lit rooms for its galleries. But art did not pay, so the county took over. Yet neither did the county have the funds to main-tain it, and by the 1980s the once-proud home had became so dowdy that historian Arthur Francke helped found an organization for its restoration. However, not until the 1990s did the real effort jell.

It started with a simple bike ride that Peg McAllister and her husband took to visit the Hall, which by then was stumbling along as a senior citizens' center. Peg asked if there was any need for volunteers, and soon she was head of the sleepy restoration organization.

"It was very hard getting people interested in saving DeBary Hall," she told me. "At first most persons thought I was just a grandmother-type who would soon tire of making a major commitment. I found the best way to get started was to have events at the hall. So I started out with a rummage sale, although I never did one in my entire life. After that, it was one fund-raiser after another!"

Peg and her revitalized group held art shows and quilting and lace-making classes, as well as such offbeat events as barrel-making and a performance by an old-time blacksmith. Peg's group even sponsored a series of highly successful dress balls. With the seed money thus generated, they hired a historical architect, who drew up a detailed restoration plan. But then came the hard part: obtaining the really large funds for a full-scale, rafters-to-floorboards reconditioning of the old building. For that, state and county grants were essential.

"I had to convince the officials that this was my passion and I wasn't going away," McAllister confided. It often takes a bulldog to penetrate the bureaucracy, and she was just that. "There was one official who told me that what I wanted was absolutely impossible. I retorted that I would not accept such a statement. I told him that, as a taxpayer, I contributed to his salary and therefore he had to pay attention to me!" She knew when to be abrasive and when to be smooth. Thus she was all fluffy when she went before the Volusia County Council, which had to approve the master plan prior to her application for governmental grants. She took with her three children, dressed in their Sunday best, who presented the politicians with written pleadings to save the old mansion. "The council couldn't say 'no' to them," she recalled with a smile.

The funds began to come in: $250,000 from the Florida Department of Environmental Protection, plus grants from the state historical preservation agency and Volusia County. At last her group even received funds from DeBary itself, which had just become a city and had never donated money for anything before! By 1998 the restoration group had collected and spent close to $1 million—including purchasing an air-conditioning system, which at first they had planned to forgo.

So now the mansion sparkles just as it did in the days when Frederick DeBary welcomed guests with gushers of champagne. Its airy rooms again echo to the tread of awed visitors. Just don't expect champagne, for even Peg McAllister cannot restore everything.

Plans call for DeBary Hall to be a trailhead on the biking-hiking path that will run along Dirksen Drive between Enterprise and Gemini Springs County Park. Gemini, which has a $3.50-per-car entry fee, lies roughly a quarter mile west of DeBary Hall. Once the site of a large farm growing the sugar cane that thrived in the St. Johns wetlands, today it is a welcome addition to the Volusia County park system, both for its view of the DeBary Bayou and for its public swimming pond fed by the flow of the pair of freshwater springs that has given Gemini its name. A three-quarter-mile paved path weaves around the park past the springs and the swimming area. It leads to the fishing pier built out over an inlet similar to that used by Count DeBary's steamboats a hundred years ago. Anglers casting their lines told me they catch bass, sunfish, and other creatures they could not readily identify. You can see the fish swimming in the clear spring-fed water, and it is easy to dangle your bait in front of their noses—although not so easy to get them to regard it as dinner.

For a more intimate bayou experience, the park offers canoes for $7 an hour. As you paddle amid the bulrushes, arrowheads, and pickerel weeds, watch for bald eagles, ospreys, kingfishers, and river otters.

From the fishing pier the path continues across the small earthen dam that has impounded the swimming area. Then an offshoot ends beside the bayou. Looking out across the several miles of reeds and cattails, you are viewing a landscape much the same as greeted Paleo-Indian hunters nine thousand years ago. It is a little unnerving to realize that this entire tract of land was within days of being sold to a developer, the sale being prevented only by the cooperation of the West family, who owned it, and emergency purchase funds from the St. Johns River Water Management District.

A Flicker in the Flame of History:
The Village of Enterprise

From Gemini Springs head east on Dirksen Drive. Beyond Interstate 4 trees crowd in until you reach Enterprise a mile beyond. Enterprise is so minuscule that it is difficult to believe it was once of sufficient importance to be the seat of Volusia County. The reason for this honor can be summed up in two words: Jacob Brock.

Brock was a crusty individualist who grew up amid the rafts and scows on the Connecticut River. He married a New England woman, but evidently she was as flinty as he, for when Jake decided to migrate south, she sent him and their four young children on their way without her. In Charleston, Jake made enough money repairing steamboat engines that in 1853 he was able to buy his own ship, which he named the *Darlington*. Then he packed up the kids and steered for the St. Johns River, for he knew that Florida, having recently been cleared of the Seminoles, was just opening up. During the next few years Jake kept busy hauling settlers and supplies between Jacksonville and Palatka. As frontier families began penetrating deeper into the interior, Jake concluded that the hamlet of Enterprise, at the head of navigation 140 miles south of Jacksonville, would undoubtedly rise to some importance. Thus, he nosed the *Darlington* through the river's virtually uncharted narrows, where tree limbs scraped the hull, and at last reached Lake Monroe. Here a ramshackle village existed near the ruins of an army post unused since the Seminole War a decade earlier.

Brock had correctly surmised that the St. Johns would an ideal highway to the interior—indeed, it was the only way to get there, if you excluded the muddy Indian trails and abandoned army paths. Enterprise was an ideal point of disembarkation. Brock first constructed a pier into the lake to accommodate steamboats. Then he built a hotel close by the landing. It was "large and commodious," according to a reporter, and boasted cooks and waiters from the North. The two-and-a-half-story hotel stood on a slight rise broadside to the lake. Guests loved to lounge on the 110-foot veranda, which ran the hotel's entire length, where they could enjoy a magnificent view of the lake, often enlivened by the thrashing paddle wheels of gaudy steamboats, while waiters provided them with juleps and other heady refreshments.

Business was good, so in 1860 Brock built a second steamboat, naming it the *Hattie* after one of his spirited daughters. The *Hattie* was launched just in time for its own little drama during the Civil War.

Union naval strategy involved blockading Confederate ports, including Florida's. This left Jacob Brock fuming, for, even though he was born a Yankee, his sympathies were with the South. Therefore, he offered the *Hattie* to the South to patrol the St. Johns. The *Hattie* became such an irritation to Union gunboats that in the spring of 1864 the *Columbine* and *Sumter* set out from the federal base at Palatka to capture the *Hattie*. The two gunboats poked into every nook of the ragged river between Enterprise and Jacksonville, but the *Hattie* was not found. So the Union ships sailed across Lake Monroe to where the St. Johns emerged from the shallow, braided marshes. Ever so cautiously they threaded the channel until they reached Lake Harney. Here they found the *Hattie* carelessly tied up without guards. Union sailors jumped aboard, fired up the twin boilers, and then were off downstream. The *New York Tribune* told what happened next:

> The most exquisitely painful part of the downward trip occurred at Enterprise. As the fleet moved up to the landing near where the "Brock House" stands, the veritable Miss Hattie, after whom the boat was named, made her appearance on the verandah overwhelmed with astonishment, indignation, and grief as she saw that her namesake, the pride of her life, had fallen into the hands of the Yankees. The little black-eyed belle seemed like an angel angry. She was eloquent in her grief, and our marines, poor fellows, were glad to get away as soon as they had supplied their boats with fuel.

Clouds and cypress frame the cove in Enterprise, where Captain Jake Brock had his steamboat pier, pylons of which can be dimly seen on the horizon.

After the war Jake Brock and his steamers were familiar sights on the St. Johns. Jake himself served as a captain, and often the river echoed to his steam whistle, which he enjoyed blasting at unexpected moments to startle the ladies. His profanity could raise the hair of a bald man. He became almost as much a part of the St. Johns as the whispering water itself. But when railroads made river travel obsolete, Brock went bankrupt and died almost immediately thereafter. His hotel continued to attract visitors into the 1930s. Although it was torn down, its timbers survive in some of the homes in the area.

Enterprise itself was as devastated by the demise of the steamboats as Brock. The town's ultimate coup de grace came when the county seat was removed to DeLand, with its ample rail connection.

As for Hattie Brock, little is known of her, except that she married the general manager of the DeBary-Baya Steamship Line. We hope her life was sweet, but we know it was short, for she died before her father.

Today there is almost nothing to remind us of the man who once was a towering figure along the St. Johns. Only the spacious grounds surrounding the United Methodist Children's Home indicate where the captain's once famous hotel stood. All Saints Episcopal Church at DeBary Drive and Clark Street was frequented by guests of the Brock House, as well as of DeBary Hall. A dozen pylons of Brock's pier remain, and it is a moving experience to drive down Clark Street to the lakeshore and look across the water to the distant, forlorn row of wooden sentinels awaiting the steamboats that will never return.

The Enterprise-Osteen Road wends through a dense hammock on the northern shore of Lake Monroe.

Now take Main Street south to Lakeshore Drive and turn east. The road edges close to the water along a trail first formed by Indian feet nine thousand years ago. American axes broadened it in 1837 when Fort Kingsbury was built near where the Deltona Community Center currently stands. During leisure times the soldiers probably fished for large mouth bass across the road at Riverfront Park.

From here the road leaves the lakeshore and rambles through a dense, deciduous hammock before emerging from the Lake Monroe wetlands onto higher ground, where it becomes the Enterprise-Osteen Road. The carriages of Count DeBary and his frolicking guests often rolled along here on the way to New Smyrna, where everyone enjoyed champagne and cookouts on beaches throbbing to the wild Atlantic surf.

Pontooning on the Upper St. Johns River

When the Enterprise-Osteen Road ends at SR 415, turn right and you'll emerge onto the St. Johns River basin, a wide, grassy marsh. Soon you'll pass over the river on the Douglas Stenstrom Bridge, which replaced an old span that is now a fishing pier. Somehow the name intrigued me and I actually located Stenstrom, who was a distinguished state senator in the 1950s and '60s. "I worked for eighteen years to get that bridge built," he told me with pride and what must have been a surge of memories. "The old bridge was one of the most deplorable in Florida. It was actually handturned. Some people would not even go over it. There were a terrible number of accidents."

Turn right at Celery Avenue, the first street over the bridge. You'll quickly come to the road to the Sanford Boatworks and Marina. Drive down it for a hundred yards to where it ends at the Gator Landing Riverside Grill. Here you can enjoy a light meal in an open-air pavilion overlooking the river or take a narrated excursion on the St. Johns Eco Tours' pontoon boat. The cruises are two hours long and cost $14 ($10 for seniors and $8 for kids). They leave every day (except Mondays) at 11 A.M. and 1:30 P.M.

The St. Johns is an unusual river, in many ways more a channel between lakes than a true river—and for that reason the Indians called it the "river-of-lakes." Although it is several miles wide as it approaches Jacksonville, here, near its source, it is a placid stream split into innumerable bayous and backwaters as it wends through the

The St. Johns River winds through miles of exotic marsh east of Sanford.

maze of saw grass, maidencane, and pickerel weeds between Lakes Monroe and Jessup. As you glide slowly along its weaving river channels, you'll probably come upon large flocks of white ibis, sacred and magical to the ancient Egyptians. Herons and egrets often strut in the shallows, while playful coots skitter over the open water and colorful wood ducks float more casually nearby. Overhead you may glimpse an osprey, hawk, or eagle, for they nest in the large cypress trees along the marsh border. Alligators also love the marsh, and beasts up to eighteen feet long have been seen. Altogether, up to two thousand bird and animal species inhabit the vast St. Johns marsh.

Although this marsh extends southward for seventy virtually unbroken miles, it is a delicate creation. In the past segments have been altered for farms or housing developments. Once the marsh has been drained, it can never be completely restored, for the soil will have lost much of its ability to support native plants due to oxidation and subsidence. Recent plans for a condo development along the south bank of this very portion of the marsh were prevented at the last moment, when the state purchased 8,500 acres. Another seven thousand acres are still held privately and their future may be in peril.

Back on Celery Avenue, by driving west in two blocks you'll come to Cameron Avenue, upon which you can turn right if you'd like to visit an ancient Indian mound built by the Timucua, predecessors of the Seminoles. The mound whispers of endless generations who built their lodges around its base . . . who cooked their food over campfires here . . . who told and retold the legends of their great heroes, the exploits of whom they believed would live forever. A path leads to the summit, where there is a view of the St. Johns slough, with the Stenstrom bridge to the right. It's a shame that houses have been built along the road, for otherwise this would be an ideal site for a public park.

The Many Faces of Sanford

Celery Avenue continues west toward the town of Sanford past orange groves and vegetable fields. Once this rich soil supported such a vast acreage of celery that Sanford became known as Celery City. In those days a railroad spur to these fields enabled the planters to load their produce right onto refrigerated freight cars that hauled them to northern markets. Many of the planters made substantial profits, and during the 1920s their comfortable homes dotted Celery Avenue. But when outside competition captured American markets, celery production ended.

Osceola's Camp

Turn north off Celery Avenue at the Mellonville Avenue stop light. Mellonville Avenue began as an army road from Fort Mellon, one of the army's most important outposts during the Seminole War. The fort received its name after the Seminoles attacked it in 1837. Although the soldiers repulsed them, their commander, twenty-three-year-old Charles Mellon, was killed. His bones presumably still lie in a lost grave somewhere on the site.

Fort Mellon's location on Lake Monroe connected it with steamboats coming up the St. Johns River from Jacksonville. As many as forty steamers in a single week brought troops and supplies to the fort. Army operations also required boatloads of wagons and mules. One offensive into the interior involved a train of seventy mule-drawn wagons.

Osceola and several thousand followers once camped here for truce talks. Osceola was a most unusual person, for although he instigated the war when he murdered a government agent near Ocala, he was of mixed parentage and had an ambivalent attitude toward the soldiers. During the time he was here, Osceola posed amiably while an American artist drew one of the few portraits ever made of him. The fort has long since vanished, but the outline of its grounds and the village of Mellonville, which grew up around it, can be discerned in the configuration of the streets on the right side of Mellonville Avenue, ending at Seminole Boulevard on Lake Monroe. From here a strip park runs the entire length of Sanford, a city of around 40,000. The lake is four miles wide. On its distant shore you can see the Florida Power plant at Enterprise.

Now turn west on Seminole Boulevard. On the left is a rambling, three-story building constructed as a hotel in 1925 by Sanford's flamboyant mayor, Forrest Lake.

The Genial Scoundrel

Forrest Lake was a pivotal man in Sanford's development. Elected mayor eleven times in the early part of the twentieth century, he was a jaunty, confident man who virtually ran the town, as well as Seminole County, which he created almost single-highhandedly. Yet he died in disgrace, with almost no one attending his funeral. His had been, to say the least, a strange career.

When Forrest Lake arrived in Sanford at the age of seventeen, everyone was impressed by the bright, eager youngster; just seven years later he became mayor. Almost from the first he resented the fact that Orlando, not Sanford, was the seat of Orange County. So, upon entering the state legislature in 1910, he conducted a secret campaign to carve a new county out of Orange to be centered at Sanford. Lake skillfully rammed a bill through the legislature before the Orlando delegation could mount a defense. When Seminole County became a reality in 1913, Lake led a triumphant parade through downtown Sanford where he was greeted with enthusiastic hurrahs by everyone.

Having achieved this goal, Lake chose not to run again for the legislature, but instead formed the Seminole County Bank, over which he reigned as president for the next fourteen years.

By now most Sanfordites thought Forrest Lake could do no wrong, and he was elected mayor once more. This was an opportune time, for Florida was in the midst of the Roaring Twenties real estate boom, of which Forrest Lake was determined to take full advantage. In order to obtain funds for land speculation Lake, as mayor, freely borrowed from Lake as bank president. Why bother with collateral? The value of land and buildings was rising so fast that the bank would soon be amply covered. Eventually he questioned whether it was necessary to borrow at all: Why not just take a few hundred thousand and pay it back from profits? That would save his bank the useless paperwork in between. The city was another source of funds. He personally issued city bonds, then loaned himself large sums against them. Why shouldn't the city be liable? After all he was using the funds to bring in tourists. It was at this time that he built the Forrest Lake Hotel.

The hotel was a major undertaking. There was no rival for miles. It boasted 158 guest rooms, all with private baths. There were two wings, each housing a splendid dining room where floor-to-ceiling windows opened out on a grassy lawn that descended gently to Lake Monroe. Similar windows graced the magnificent ballroom that connected with the spacious lobby. A wide veranda extended along the front entryway, from which hotel patrons could enjoy afternoon tea while watching incoming guests arrive in their brass-trimmed Cadillacs.

Unfortunately for Mayor Lake, there were not enough Cadillacs, nor even Model T Fords, to cover expenses, for the hotel opened at the beginning of the devastating real estate crash that rocked speculators from Miami to Pensacola. When Lake was unable to meet the demands of his creditors, an investigation of his financial shenanigans led him to resign both as mayor and as president of the Seminole County Bank, which was forced to close. The ensuing trial found him guilty of embezzling $353,000 from the bank and of fraudulently issuing $1.3 million in city bonds. For this he was sent to state prison for three years. Since there was no special treatment offered at this time for white collar crimes, he was thrown in with the roughest criminals. It was a devastating sentence for a man of sixty-two.

Most Sanfordites probably thought it was not enough, for now the citizens themselves were forced to pay for Lake's reckless spending. As a result property taxes rose nearly 150 percent and city salaries were slashed. Yet Sanford was still so deeply in debt that it struggled for four decades before meeting its final obligations. As for Lake himself, he returned to Sanford a broken old man, as he had no place else to go. He wandered the streets, shunned and hated, until finally dying in 1939.

Lake's actions left Sanford with an attitude of defeatism that replaced the buoyancy which had been the city's trademark. This gloomy pessimism was to hamper Sanford's growth even to the present.

Five Martyrs and a Question Mark

After the demise of Forrest Lake, the hotel was purchased by the city, which promptly renamed it the Mayfair Inn. But this was during

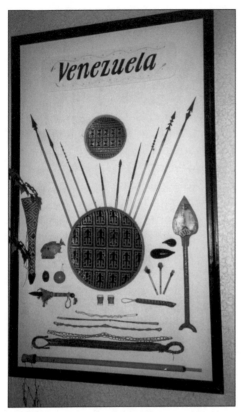

The New Tribes Mission's display boards in Sanford show arrows like those that have killed some of their missionaries.

the Depression and the hotel did not catch on. Desperate to meet at least some of the horrendous financing expenses, the city leased it to a car dealer for storage. After the Second World War, the Mayfair was finally unloaded on the New York Giants baseball team, who came to Sanford for spring training. But when the Giants moved their franchise to San Francisco, they sold the building to an academy, which went bankrupt in 1976. Thereupon the aging structure became the property of the current owner, the New Tribes Mission, a nondenominational, evangelical organization. New Tribes renovated the dowdy building and turned it into its national headquarters.

New Tribes is passionately devoted to converting tribal people around the world to Christianity. Almost all these tribes live simple existences isolated from modern civilization. Many fiercely distrust strangers. That the initial contact is fraught with danger became painfully apparent from the fate of the first five missionaries in 1943.

The five men sought out the Ayores tribe deep in the heart of Bolivia. Since there were no trails, they had to cut their way through the jungle infested with snakes, mosquitoes, and wild animals of every description. The tribe was so remote that no Bolivian even knew their language. As the missionaries approached, hidden warriors glared at them. Who were these strangers? What was their purpose? It could be nothing good. The decision was made. Arrows cut the air. In a matter of minutes all five were dead.

The five were the first martyrs, but more would follow. As late as 1993 guerrillas kidnapped three New Tribes men from a remote mission in Panama. They marched them off to a hidden location in Colombia, where they demanded millions in ransom or the men would be killed. The money was not paid, and even today the fate of the men is unknown.

New Tribes Mission welcomes visitors to its headquarters, where complimentary guided tours are conducted several times daily. For many persons the tour's most vivid moments are viewing the large display boards that present actual spears, shields, and other hand-fashioned artifacts from tribes where the organization has a mission. On one is the very arrow that killed missionary Dave Yarwood. Another tells the story of the three currently missing missionaries along with their pictures and pleadings from their wives and children.

Despite the heroism and dedication of the more than three thousand missionaries now serving in the field, New Tribes is not without its critics who claim that, by convincing the indigenous people to renounce their most sacred religious beliefs in favor of Christianity, the missionaries are destroying viable cultures. "New Tribes is a very controversial organization," one critic told me. "It is loathed by anyone who studies its effect on native peoples."

Soon New Tribes may have a new, and quite different, neighbor. Big changes may be in store for the lot immediately west. Currently a public park, it is earmarked for a major hotel and conference center, which, if built, will rouse downtown Sanford from its decades-long slumber.

Now continue west along Sanford's appealing waterfront on Seminole Boulevard. Turn right at Palmetto Avenue. Here the marina is crammed with pleasure craft and the dock across the street is home of the double-decked *Rivership Romance*, which offers excursions across Lake Monroe and along the St. Johns River. A three-hour luncheon cruise costs $35 and a dinner-dancing cruise comes to $50. Despite the expense, these are popular ways to enjoy one of Florida's most beautiful and historic waterways.

At the end of the causeway is a wide area where the Marina Inn motel, formerly part of the Holiday Inn chain, and a nearby restaurant have expansive views of Lake Monroe and the pleasant Sanford waterfront. It was here that the city's founder, Henry Sanford, constructed a pier shortly after he landed in 1870.

The Dreamer

The site was everything Henry's friend, Count DeBary, had said it was. The lake, at the head of St. Johns steamboat navigation, offered good transportation to Jacksonville, with its worldwide shipping connections. Once roads were built, the settlement would be a natural commercial center for the rich lands that were just opening up to the south and west. Henry dreamed big dreams that day. He would create a town that would blossom into one of Florida's largest and most important cities. In doing so he would not only perpetuate his name, but also his reputation for astuteness.

Henry was apparently well equipped to achieve his goal. His father had been a wealthy manufacturer in Connecticut, and Henry had inherited a goodly fortune. He knew the ways of the world, having graduated with honors from the elite German university at Heidelberg. Thereupon he entered the American diplomatic corps, where he made such a favorable reputation that President Abraham Lincoln appointed the suave, urbane young man to the important post of Union representative in Europe. When the Civil War ended, Sanford turned his talent toward America, where he purchased vast acreage along Lake Monroe.

Almost as soon as Sanford and his European-bred wife, Gertrude, stepped ashore, Henry began pursuing his plans. First, he formed the Florida Land and Colonization Company and started ballyhooing the advantages of a town he called Sanford throughout the United States

The Rivership Romance *in Sanford takes sightseers across Lake Monroe and along the St. Johns River.*

and Europe. Then he constructed the 200-room Sanford House, a three-story showplace close to the lake. Next he began experimenting with varieties of oranges and soon developed a new breed of the fruit called "Valencia," which eventually became the cornerstone of Florida's citrus industry. Stories of Sanford's successes circulated even in Scandinavia, and before long a colony of industrious Swedish farmers was thriving on Henry's gently rolling land just west of town.

As Sanford's colony began growing, steamboats lined Henry's long wharf. Such commercial activity also attracted railroads to the location, and in 1880 Ulysses S. Grant turned the first spadeful of dirt for construction of the important South Florida Railroad. Not long thereafter kingpin Henry Plant constructed a major depot in Sanford's bustling, lakefront railroad yards.

Although all was sunshine for the town of Sanford, a heavy rain was falling on Henry. He was basically a dreamer conjuring brilliant plans, but disdained nitty-gritty, hands-on management. He visited his namesake town only during the pleasant winter months, when he lived in luxury and adulation at the Sanford House. Most of the time he pursued other schemes from the residences he kept in Europe; thus, he invested in a sugar plantation in Louisiana and a cotton plantation in South Carolina. He also put a lot of money into a wild scheme to develop the Congo River in Africa. When they all went sour, he was left deeply in debt. Poor health added to his woes: he began to suffer from severe asthma as well as an eye ailment and a probable kidney disease. He was sick when he and his wife came to Sanford for their annual visit during the winter of 1890–91. Doctors advised him to go to health springs in Virginia, but he died on the way. Gertrude was left with debtors who hounded her for the rest of her life. To her the Lake Monroe venture was a hated episode. It was, she lamented, "a vampire that sucked the repose and beauty and dignity and cheerfulness out of our lives."

The First Street business district, two blocks off the waterfront, is like a museum of those yesterdays. Most of the original brick structures remain, polished up as part of the town's Main Street program. The 1923 Meisch Building at 224 East First Street stands on the site of the Sanford House, which extended back toward the lake on land also occupied by the public library. The Meisch Building housed a Piggly-Wiggly grocery that was once a downtown mainstay. The former Seminole County Bank, looted by the town's genial mayor, Forrest Lake, can be seen at 121 East First Street. The structure that housed

Henry Sanford's Land Colonization Company still stands at 108 East First Street.

Brick monuments to Sanford's steam train era also remain. There is the Pico Block at 114 West First Street and Oak Avenue, where the railroad executives had their offices. Travelers could hole up at the crowded Pico Hotel and Restaurant at 209 North Oak Avenue, today a clean and sedate office building.The passenger depot stood in the vacant area in front of it. Sometimes four trains at a time stood belching soot and cinders in the yards beside the depot.

You can pick up more information on downtown from the Greater Sanford Chamber of Commerce at 400 East First Street. To delve deeper into the city's past, visit Sanford's free historical museum at 520 East First Street in Fort Mellon Park.

In recent years Sanford has begun a long-delayed comeback. The downtown has attracted many flourishing antique and specialty shops. If the park near the New Tribes building becomes a major conference hotel, that will also help revitalize the downtown. A huge mall called Seminole Towne Center has sprung up on Sanford's outskirts. Completion of the Greeneway Toll Road (SR 417), a link-up with Interstate 4, is destined to bring even more visitors into downtown. Sanford's airport also has become so active that it offers Orlando International serious competition.

All this suits Sanfordites just fine, for many still feel that Sanford,

Sanford's downtown has been spruced up as part of its Main Street program.

not its archrival Orlando, should be central Florida's most important city. If the current leadership is any indication, perhaps someday it will.

Leave downtown Sanford on Park Avenue, which passes some of Sanford's most graceful old mansions. The bricks that sometimes show through the blacktop were probably laid by the company of Monroe "Money" Hutton, Mayor Lake's son-in-law. Hutton got virtually all the city's bricking contracts in the 1920s even though he was significantly higher than the frustrated lowest bidders. There was a pesky rumor at the time that Hutton had no choice except to bid high in order to pay for his kickbacks to Mayor Lake and his cronies.

The Causeway to Oviedo:
Six Miles of Water, Wetlands, and Wilderness

When Park Avenue merges with US 17/92, continue south and follow the signs to the Greeneway toll road, SR 417. Take the Greeneway south towards Orlando. Although a high speed expressway can hardly be called a backroad, it runs through an exotic, unpopulated area before it reaches the Lake Jessup bridge in five miles (the toll is $1.50). During this passage the Greeneway offers excellent views of an uninhabited marshland where palmettos and grasses extend for long distances. Although this is a harsh, buggy area, during the twenty-year British occupation in the late eighteenth century, plantation owners forced slaves to work the muck to grow indigo. When the

Wildflowers sometimes bloom profusely in the Lake Jessup wetlands along SR 417.

Greeneway bridge was built, a law required that funds be set aside to mitigate the wetland loss by purchasing similar land. The state used these mitigation funds to buy extensive areas on each side of the highway. Seminole County also has established a nature preserve with a three-mile trail through the wetlands. It is just west of the Greeneway at the foot of Sanford Avenue. This mitigation has helped assuage environmentalists, who vehemently opposed the Greeneway bridge, one of interior Florida's longest, which city planners regarded as a necessary Orlando bypass to help relieve congestion on Interstate 4.

Oviedo begins on the south side of Lake Jessup. The town originated as a pier called Solary's Landing. The landing's only source of supplies was by a boat that made its tedious way from Sanford across Lake Monroe, up the St. Johns a mile or so, and through an alligator channel to Lake Jessup. But Solary's Landing was low and unhealthy, so the settlers soon moved to higher land two miles south. A new name, "Oviedo," was chosen by the postmaster who wanted to emphasize the state's heritage, for Oviedo was a prestigious university town in Spain.

Turn off the Greeneway at the Red Bug Lake-Oviedo Marketplace mall exit. When Oviedo approved the mall, many citizens of the adjoining community of Winter Springs, fearing traffic problems, went to court to prevent it. As the controversy grew, Oviedoans began driving through Winter Springs with bumper stickers declaring "We Want Our Mall!" But when it was revealed that the Winter Springs litigants were receiving considerable funding from the would-be developers of a rival mall nearby, they withdrew their case. Even so, any secondary access road through Winter Springs was now impossible. Instead, the mall had to construct a costly bridge over the Greeneway.

The mall's main entrance is via Red Bug Lake Road, an unappealing name that reflects its origin as a sand path to a lake replete with troublesome chiggers, called red bugs. It seems improbable that this grubby trail would become a multilane highway with a regional mall, health center, and commercial businesses of all sorts, but development in Florida can happen anywhere.

Windows To Heaven

After turning left on Red Bug Lake Road, go about a half mile to Aloma Avenue (SR 426), then the same distance right to Slavia Road. Here you'll see the humble building that once housed Martin and Julianna Stanko's general store and filling station. In its day Stanko's was the social and economic hub of the Slavia Colony, a group of Slovaks who migrated here in 1911. Their purpose was to found a farming community where they could raise their children with a wholesome Lutheran education. They moved into crude shacks once occupied by sawmill workers who left when little remained of the dense pine forest that formerly clothed the land. Then the the Slovaks constructed their church, a small, frame structure formed from parts of the workers' shacks. Membership stood at a rousing twenty-five.

The going was tough, pioneer Paul Mikler recollected: "Running water was provided from a tank which had to be filled by hand pumps. . . . Clothes were washed by hand and boiled in iron kettles." The shack walls had large gaps that let in cold air during the winter and mosquitoes during the summer. The soil was ill drained and swampy, so the men had to dig ditches before they could raise any cash crops. Their church was about all that kept them going. "We sang hymns, folk songs, and had Bible Study and a monthly party," Mikler recalled. In the days before telephones or good roads, most of their communication with the outside world was limited to tidbits gleaned from freight men on the few trains that stopped at the open-air station across from Stanko's. But this wasn't much, since the settlers spoke Slovak.

As important as their St. Luke's Lutheran Church was, the struggling little colony could not afford to hire a full-time pastor for twenty-three years. Not until 1939 were they able to abandon the makeshift wooden shack in favor of a brick building with a real steeple. Despite the hardships, the colony began to thrive, and by 1992, when membership stood at more than 1,600, they began work on the truly noble structure that has become a showplace.

Visitors are welcome at St. Luke's on weekdays, and, of course, for the Sunday morning services at 8:15 A.M. and 10:45 A.M. You'll find the interior of the 750-pew structure to be like no church you have ever seen. It is shaped like a huge half circle, but not quite, for the walls at the apex form a slight angle that seems to embrace the congregation. At the apex there is a massive coquina column reaching from the floor to the ceiling, which soars five stories overhead. This pillar supports a twelve-foot-high, hand-carved statue of Christ as the Good Shepherd, with his arms outstretched to beckon the worshipers. The ceiling is of polished wood that, by radiating out from the pillar, enhances the feeling of Christ as a protector.

As inspiring as the Christ figure are the seven brilliantly colored windows that glow as if they were stained glass, but, instead, are a thicker, more durable type of glass called "faceted." The windows depict sheaths of wheat, bunches of grapes, and Easter lilies, each representing one of the "I ams" with which Christ characterized himself in the Book of John. These windows, each a masterpiece, are composed of some 1,700 individual glass pieces held in place by 350 gallons of epoxy glue.

The New and the Old Oviedo

Now continue on Aloma Avenue, which parallels the former railroad right-of-way, recently converted into a popular biking and hiking path called the Cross Seminole Trail. In one block you'll reach Chapman Road, where, on the southeast corner, is the old Slovak cemetery, site of the first church. Turn left on Chapman to Alafaya Trail (SR 434), then drive north, passing two shopping centers and a miscellaneous assortment of fast food outlets. This is new Oviedo, a burgeoning, bedroom community of 20,000 and growing. It is oriented toward the expanding University of Central Florida, Siemens Westinghouse, and other enterprises to the south.

By continuing on SR 434 you'll enter old Oviedo, featuring homes from the 1920s and earlier. The center of this Oviedo is at SR 434 and Broadway, where the steeple of the venerable Baptist Church rises gracefully from a small rise. When this was the heart of town, the city council met in one of the modest storefronts on Broadway—now it has moved to the modern part of town. In days of yore Oviedo got along with a single bank located in the building at the southwest corner of SR 434 and Broadway. Though small, it was important enough that late one night some persons dynamited a hole in the wall attempting to gain access. But, surprise, the explosion woke everyone up, so the incompetent crooks fled, and their names are a mystery to this very day.

The Cross Seminole Trail bisects the old business area, edging past a few once-noble industrial buildings. This was formerly a loading zone where railroad cars were stuffed with heavy cases of celery bound for Sanford. But when Oviedo's production diminished, the trains stopped coming, and a few years back the tracks were torn up.

Today the center of old Oviedo is a lot quieter. One of the main activities seems to be watching the poultry behind Popeye's Chicken. There are ten of them cackling and strutting around on the grass.

They've been there for ten years and nobody knows where they came from. At one time city officials, worried about lawsuits if the animals were responsible for motor accidents, decided to have them hauled away. But they quickly relented when they found the chickens were "wildly popular," as the Orlando Sentinel put it. The problem was resolved when it was concluded that, because they had no owners, they were wild birds, just like crows, so Oviedo could not be held responsible. Thus the officials contented themselves with the installation of several signs in official yellow warning "Caution: Chicken Crossing." That's old Oviedo.

The Lake of Charm

To reach one of the quaintest sections of old Oviedo, drive to a mile northeast from the Baptist Church on SR 426, Geneva Road. Paved today, in the 1880s it was of logs placed crosswise—a technique that prevented wagons getting stuck in the sand, but was almost guaranteed to bump a person half silly. When you round the first bend, watch for Lake Charm Drive. Turn left on it, and in a block you'll find yourself at a little body of water that is almost as pretty as when it was named Lake Charm by young Martha Gwynn just after the Civil War. Martha's father, an otherwise dour Baptist, was also so entranced by the lake that he built his home on its shore.

A single-lane road encircles Oviedo's Lake Charm. Pines frame the Whitney-Wolcott House across the water.

Soon the Gwynns were joined by Henry Foster, enjoying a sizable income from his sanitarium in New York. Dr. Foster and his learned wife, Mary (she had read and, hopefully, understood Virgil when only fourteen), built a large residence on Lake Charm's northern shore. The Fosters talked up the beauty of Lake Charm to such an extent that many of their wealthy friends also constructed homes beside its flickering waters. Although the Northerners came only during the two or three winter months, some of the homes were quite large—one had nine fireplaces. As ever more affluent visitors came to Lake Charm, a hotel was constructed on the northeast shore. Soon a store went up too. Then a railroad spur was laid out from Oviedo along the Geneva Road. The fragrance of orange trees also began to drift over the countryside, for a series of mild winters led the visitors to plant many acres of citrus, the profits from which more than paid the workers who tended the groves during the owners' long absences.

For several decades Lake Charm lived up to its enticing name. But during the winter of 1894–1895 a pair of severe freezes devastated nearly the entire state. Most of Foster's disillusioned friends sold their Oviedo homes and their now-barren groves. Although the Fosters continued to spend their winters at Lake Charm, the sparkle had vanished.

It has been more than a hundred years since the Foster era, and Lake Charm has somehow managed to survive. The rustic one-lane road continues to lope lazily along the shore, which is shaded by tall pines and occasional cypress. The Victorian Whitney-Wolcott home on the lake's southeast curve recalls departed spirits, like Gus Wolcott, who kept a six-foot alligator in the second-floor bathtub and later sold supplies to moonshiners. But Lake Charm is in transition; the north shore has fallen to suburban homes, and developers would love to send their bulldozers south. Yet for now the coziness remains, and at times it seems as if you can almost see Henry Foster putt-putting over the placid water in his little steamboat filled with festive friends.

The Black Hammock

Lake Charm Drive continues north as a dirt road into the Black Hammock. The cultivated portion of the Black Hammock is an extremely fertile area that extends a mile to Lake Jessup and several miles east and west. It is very flat and was probably part of the lake during periods of high water. The soil's dampness and fertility encouraged a thick hammock of cypress, live oaks, palmettos, and dense underbrush that over the years decayed into black humus several feet deep. When farmers in Sanford began making sizable profits from celery, Oviedoans saw that they could do the same once the hammock was cleared.

Removing the trees was muscle-wrenching work done by a crew of sixteen laborers. The cypress was the most difficult to dislodge. Sometimes thirty sticks of dynamite were required to blow up the roots. As the trees were felled and the roots removed, they were set afire. At times so many were burning that smoke rose in massive, roiling pillars seen for miles. When it was over, the hammock was dead.

But now the land had to be drained. So terra-cotta tubes three inches in diameter were set in long rows several feet deep in the muck. The water seeping into them flowed out of the hammock, leaving it moist but not saturated. This moisture enabled Oviedo farmers to grow their crops even during the dry summer months, which gave them a decided advantage over the Sanford growers. Railroads built spurs into the Black Hammock and soon Oviedo was challenging Sanford as the world's celery capital.

The celery industry reached its peak in 1960s, followed by a gradual and final decline. There were many reasons for the demise of celery in this part of Florida. One was the formation of a cooperative which set the price so high that other areas, particularly California, entered the business. Another was the periodic freezes. Whatever the reason, the sweating workers, the groaning mule wagons, and the soot-belching locomotives vanished with the celery. Now the Black Hammock waits patiently for the return of the jungle.

Lake Charm Drive ends in the Black Hammock at Florida Avenue, where Pappy's Patch Strawberry Farm invites you to pick your own. To drive further into the Black Hammock, take Florida Avenue left for a quarter mile until it ends at DeLeon Street, upon which you should turn north to Howard Avenue, then a half block left to Black Hammock Road. These are hard-packed sand roads, but they are broad and usually well graded. Black Hammock Road runs only north, passing orange groves and scrubby areas where the hammock is returning, until it reaches the Black Hammock Restaurant and Marina. This is a popular establishment on Lake Jessup, locally famous for its catfish and alligator tail, and is open Tuesday through Sunday between 11 A.M. and 10 P.M. It is also home to Gator Ventures Air Boat Rides, which will take you on an hour's zip around the lake for $20. It operates seven days a week. Beside the weathered dock of the Black Hammock Marina is a plaque commemorating Antonio Solary's Wharf where Oviedo got its start.

The Den of Alligators

Lake Jessup is named for the controversial general, Thomas Jesup (with one "s"), who captured Seminole war leader Osceola under a flag of truce. It is home to a huge colony of alligators estimated at nearly three thousand, some of which are more than thirteen feet long. For persons going out at night to fish, the water is alive with ruddy gator eyes glowing like coals from hell. The reptiles do not usually menace full-grown humans, but the rowboat of at least one fisherman heading out from the Black Hammock was attacked by an angry gator, which must have thought it was a rival during mating time. However, gators have a hankering for small dogs, which they gladly gulp down whenever the opportunity arises. Once in a very long while a gator will mistake a human toddler for a dog: a tragic news item made the local papers not long ago when a three-year-old child picking lily pad flowers for his mother at a nearby lake was snapped up by a gator. The next day, when searchers found and killed the gator, parts of the child were still in its mouth.

Tourists love to pose with this play alligator beside Lake Jessup.
Gator Ventures airboats cruise past the real thing.

A Jungle Walk

Now return to DeLeon Street and follow it south to SR 434/419, where, upon turning west, you'll pass remnants of the true Black Hammock. But these remnants will soon disappear, for the access to the Greeneway is turning this rural road into suburbia. Stay on SR 419 when SR 434 splits off, then watch for the side road to the Spring Hammock Preserve, for which there is no admission fee.

Spring Hammock, which will be a focal point of the Cross Seminole Trail, features a boardwalk that leads through a series of five hammock ecosystems. First, where the land is relatively dry, you'll come to scrub oaks. Next, as the land gets progressively wetter, are pines and ferns. Then you'll pass through the tall hardwoods, including live oaks, magnolias, and hickories. Wet soil brings palmettos and sweet gums; where it becomes downright swampy you'll find bald cypress. It is, to borrow from Joseph Conrad's *Heart of Darkness*, a "great wall of vegetation, an exuberant and entangled mass of trunks, branches, leaves, boughs, [and] festoons . . . a rolling wave of plants."

Finally you'll reach Lake Jessup with rushes, cattails, and water hyacinths. Here you can spot anhingas drying their wings and ospreys circling for food. Perhaps you'll also see a glaring alligator, but remember they are dangerous animals that, despite their often sleepy demeanor, can run faster than humans for short distances. You may feel safe on the boardwalk and want to feed a gator. But in doing so you may be signing its death warrant, for the state is concerned when a gator begins to associate humans with food. Not only is it against a state law to feed alligators, but Florida authorities are obligated to kill any gator that has received "people food." Remember, the rule is "a fed alligator is a dead alligator."

Pillar of the Sky

Continue on SR 419 less than a mile to US 17/92, then about the same distance left on that road to General Hutchinson Parkway. Despite the pompous name, which honored a chairman of the county board, the parkway is a minor road that leads west a half mile to Big Tree County Park (free admission).

You may think it strange to visit a park just to see a single tree. But what a tree! This 3,500-year-old bald cypress is taller than an eleven-story building, and its massive trunk rises like a mighty pillar supporting the sky. It is amazing that such a tree survived the logging

The huge cypress at Big Tree Park near Longwood is 3,500 years old. Notice the tiny human figures to the left.

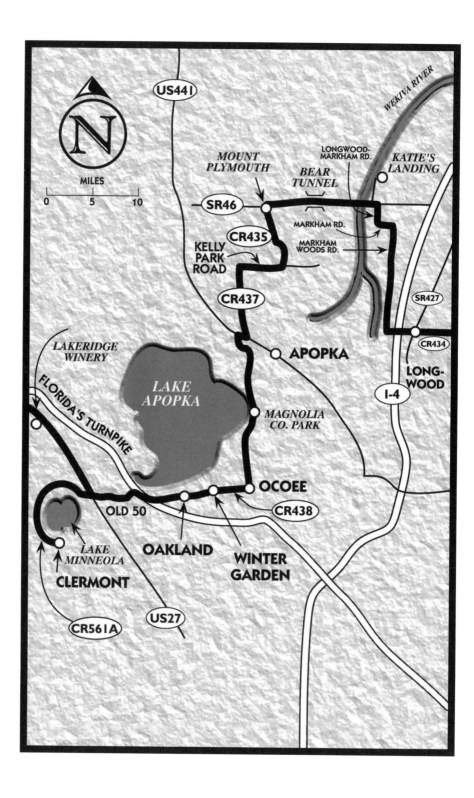

Along the Old Orange Belt Line

Longwood to Clermont • 63 Backroad Miles

The Song of the Road: Where the Byways Lead

T he second exploration will take you along the former route of the old Orange Belt Railroad, built more than a hundred years ago through what was then a virtual wilderness. After a brief tour of Longwood's recreated historic district, including a stroll down its rebricked Church Avenue, you'll follow the Orange Belt right-of-way along the Wekiva River, designated an "Outstanding Florida Waterway." You may want to pause for a canoe paddle from Katie's Landing. Then it's off through the extensive greenhouse country that has made Apopka the "indoor foliage capital of the world." Perhaps you'll want to stop and visit one or more green-houses—many specialize in one or two plants. If you like orchids, Fender's Flora will show you 100,000 plants.

Now it's southward past Lake Apopka, once known for its splendid bass fishing. Viewing the algae-green water from Magnolia Park, you'll hear the story of how the lake died and of the current, questionable attempt to bring it back to life. From there you'll travel on to Winter Garden, resurrecting its downtown around the West Orange Trail, and Oakland, with its unforgettable oak archway. Just west of Oakland you'll visit the West Orange Trail headquarters, where you can rent a bike for a spin on this popular pathway that once rocked to Orange Belt steam engines.

You'll top off this exploration with a tasty tour of the Lakeridge Winery, before enjoying the scenic trip around Lake Minneola to the town of Clermont.

Yesterday Reborn: Longwood

Longwood did a remarkable job maintaining its heritage while mushrooming from 10,000 to nearly 14,000 between 1980 and 1990.

Church Avenue, its traditional main street, has been bricked to recall the years after the town's founding in 1873 when farm wagons rolled down it, bringing produce to be loaded on the South Florida Railroad. On Sundays the farm families would don their finery, clean up the kids, and attend services at the Episcopal Church, which still stands beside the road in simple splendor. After church they would probably go for dinner at the Longwood Village Inn, on the dusty Sanford-Orlando Road, now CR 427. Today the inn has been converted into modern offices.

On weekdays farmers would come to town once more to do business at the small cluster of stores between the tracks and the road. A stop at the farm supply store was almost always on the docket, as was a visit to the post office. Often it was necessary to stop at the bank, for it held mortgages on nearly every spread hereabouts. When it shuttered its doors during the Depression, it was a severe blow to everyone. These establishments are gone today, but the buildings remain.

The merchants lived in fine homes like the Indoor-Outdoor House (so named because the wall studs are on the exterior,) which you'll find at 141 Church Avenue. Across the street is the Bradlee-McIntyre House, another of the finer residences. Although both homes originally stood in nearby Altamonte Springs, they are authentic representations of Longwood residences.

Altogether Longwood has thirty-five historic buildings clustered in its old town. Walking tour maps can be obtained at a city building at 174 Church Avenue.

Old buildings line Longwood's charming, brick Church Street.

Although memories abound in Longwood, they rarely include one of the town's most prominent early citizens: Peter Demens.

The Czar's Man

Demens was not his original name, for he had been born Pyotr Dementyev in distant Russia. The son of a distinguished nobleman, as a young man he was selected as one of the honored palace guards for the Czar himself. Tall and slim, he must have cut an imposing figure in his splendid imperial uniform. But Dementyev was a brash, outspoken individual, and his political views were too extreme for the Czar. So in 1881 he was forced to flee his homeland. Leaving his wife and his four small children, he pocketed nearly their entire life savings of $3,000 and boarded a ship bound for the New World. Arriving in New York at the age of thirty-one, he immediately bought rail passage for Jacksonville, port of entry for booming Florida. Everything was a challenge, for he spoke almost no English and had to flick through his dictionary to understand the simplest instructions.

From Jacksonville he took a steamboat up the St. Johns, not knowing exactly where he was headed, praying he could find some profitable enterprise before his funds ran out. In Sanford, the head of navigation, he learned that sawmills were booming businesses, for the growing towns and railroads had voracious appetites for lumber. So he boldly bought a sawmill in the hamlet of Longwood. Then he sent for his family.

Soon he learned English and changed his name to Demens. Next he entered politics and was even elected Longwood's mayor. He took his job as seriously as he did everything, for Longwood was a wild place when farm hands and cattle herders roared into town for drinking sprees, probably at the Longwood Village Inn. "One fine evening," Demens later wrote, "I captured a whole dozen of these cutthroats, took away their weapons, and locked them up over Sunday in an empty barn." The next day, after he heard their case as judge and jury, he clamped them in jail. When they got out, they threatened to take their revenge. But Demens had some gun-toting ruffians of his own, so nothing came of it.

Meanwhile Demens' mill converted the surrounding forest into boards for new buildings and cross ties for the expanding railroads. One of these was the Orange Belt snaking west from Sanford. In 1886, when the Orange Belt ran into trouble and could not pay Demens what it owed, he and three colleagues simply took it over. At this point the Orange Belt ran for only a few miles. Demens realized that for it ever to succeed, he must build out to Winter Garden on Lake Apopka sixteen miles west. His first order of business was to secure financing. Demens, with his polished manner, had no trouble gaining initial loans from Eastern bankers. Then he began hiring laborers and laying his track.

They Say It's There, But Where?: The Wekiva River

To follow the old Orange Belt, drive a few blocks south on CR 427 to SR 434, then take CR 434 three miles west to Markham Woods Road, just over Interstate 4. The Orange Belt had a station here called Palm Springs. From here you'll follow the Orange Belt northward for a while. It ran immediately left of the modern road as it skirted the woodlands descending to the Little Wekiva River. The road traverses surprisingly rustic territory given its location amid a high population area. Trees abound, many of them turkey oaks that turn an appealing brown during the winter. A sign warns motorists to watch for wild animals, including an occasional black bear or two, attracted by the acorns. This is countrified suburbia, with homes scattered unobtrusively on large, forested lots that are often outlined by rail fences. Housing is restricted, for this is part of the Wekiva River Protection Area, a swath of land a mile or so wide.

It is easy to imagine the wheezing, little Orange Belt trains, most purchased on a shoestring, chugging over their narrow gauge rails through a lush forest. You can see the original road bed at Long Pond Road, where it veers off toward the northeast. The rails were ripped up not many years ago, but by that time the Orange Belt's wobbly tracks had been replaced by those of its ultimate successor, the Seaboard Coast Line. The Orange Belt had stops at locations along here, one called Glen Ethel and another Island Lake—both since vanished. A third, Sylvan Lake, has become a county park.

In the Markham Maze

A portion of the former Orange Belt–Seaboard right-of-way has been earmarked to become the Seminole Wekiva Trail, which will more or less parallel Markham Woods Road for seven miles until it ends at Markham Road. Then it will continue west for a mile and a half along a later Seaboard route to a scenic overlook to be built on the Wekiva River. The bed of this abandoned line can be easily seen on the right side of Markham Road after it passes Lake Markham Road—yes, some Markham-lover actually chose these repetitious names! A sawmill once thrived at Markham, but it too has vanished, along with the pines and cypress that once bedecked the land around it.

Markham Road ends at Longwood-Markham Road, where you may wonder if the "Markhams" will ever stop. The old railroad bed continues westward into the wilderness, where it crosses the Wekiva River on a wooden trestle. When the right-of-way is converted into a biking-hiking trail, there will be a river overlook at this point. Follow Longwood-Markham Road north for two miles past recently built suburban estates to SR 46. Here you finally emerge from the Markham labyrinth.

Searching for the Wekiva River

You are still within the protection area of the Wekiva River, which has become protected to the point that it is difficult for the public to gain access to it. So don't be misled by the official brown sign opposite Longwood-Markham Road announcing the Lower Wekiva State Preserve. It may be a nature preserve, but the fifty-minute hiking trail does not offer vistas of the Wekiva. One of the few places along your route to enjoy the river is at Katie's Landing, the access road to which is reached a short distance farther west on SR 46. Katie's is about a mile up the sand road. Most of the several thousand annual visitors

A peaceful voyage awaits canoeists at Katie's Landing on the Wekiva River.

agree that it is worth the bumpy ride to enjoy a paddle along the beautiful, slow-moving waterway in one of Katie's boats. You can cruise the river, swimming if the mood strikes you, for two hours in a $14.50 rental canoe or go on a full-fledged, four-hour downstream journey for $16.50 per person (kids under twelve are half price.) The boats are available seven days a week, though on weekends you should call for reservations (407-628-1482). Hopefully Katie's, or something like it, will be there when you seek it out, as it is currently on the "for sale" market.

SR 46 crosses the Wekiva just beyond the sign for Katie's. Horse and buggy travelers were ferried over the water on a rocking scow. They had to be alert for loggers' rafts, for as late as the 1940s cypress trunks as large as forty feet in length and eight feet in diameter were being floated down to the St. Johns River and on to the huge Wilson Cypress Mill at Palatka.

Earlier, Native Americans tramped the river banks hunting for clams. Their name for it, which fortunately we've kept, meant simply THE river.

Florida vs. Florida: The People Lose

The construction of the modern bridge, cleverly built to afford as little view of the river as possible, involved a squabble between two state agencies. Because of the river's "outstanding" designation, state law prohibited the adding of pollutants. Thus, when during construction inspectors from the St. Johns River Water Management District objected that workers from the Florida Department of Transportation were permitting mud to flow into the water, SJRWMD slapped FDOT with a fine of $44,000, which FDOT begrudgingly had to fork over to the Florida Department of Environmental Protection to be used in maintaining water quality in the river. When the complicated transfer of funds within the state government was over, the net result was that the taxpayers ended up paying the lawyers and bookkeepers.

Mastodon Playground

Just across the bridge, a side road leads a mile south to the Wekiva Falls RV Resort, which encompasses the land around one of the springs that contributes to the Wekiva and helps make it so pure. The word "falls" in the resort name is a misnomer, for they were a man-made device that the state has stopped. The bones of numerous prehistoric animals have been found within the spring—so many, in fact, that it has been named Mastodon Spring.

The Million-Dollar Bear Tunnel

Although FDOT is actively widening SR 46 as part of the state's program of converting certain east-west roads into major arteries, the road still runs through mostly undeveloped land. Happily, at least three or four miles of this land from the Wekiva will remain wilderness, having been purchased by the state as part of its Conservation and Recreation Lands program. The public land extends north as far as the Ocala State Forest and south to Wekiva Springs State Park, a total of twenty miles. One reason for the acquisition of all this land was to provide a contiguous habitat for Florida's threatened black bears, who forage over many miles, particularly at night in the months before their winter hibernation. But they run into trouble when they cross SR 46, which has become one of the deadliest bear roads in a state where seventy or more bears are run down each year. Although state officials put up a series of signs warning motorists to watch for the animals, this was only partially successful; motorists complained that in the dark the animals were indistinguishable from rolling garbage bags.

To protect the bears, environmentalists convinced the state to spend $1 million constructing an overpass with the sole purpose of

State Road 46 near Mount Plymouth can be deadly for Florida's threatened black bears.

permitting bears to use the tunnel below. In order to route the animals to the tunnel, a two-mile-long cyclone fence topped with barbed wire was erected along the road. So how many bears have used the tunnel? An infrared camera within it recorded a disappointing eight bears and one strange man in a bear costume in 1996, the first full year. "Bears are slow to learn," a ranger noted laconically. Although the total slowly improved to twenty-one within several years, the annual killings on SR 46 continued to hover around seven.

Now people to the south of the tunnel are finding bears where they never had them before. There was the greenhouse grower in Mount Plymouth, which we'll drive through shortly, who in checking his plants one night actually brushed against a black bear. Fortunately, blacks are usually not aggressive, and the animal simply grunted and shambled away. It spent the next day in a tree, to the consternation of residents; then, when darkness fell, it climbed the grower's fence and was back in his greenhouse scattering plants as it grubbed for insects. Although the bear did not return after that, now the grower makes a lot of noise whenever he enters this greenhouse.

Thar's Gold In Them Thar Hills—Maybe

For you seekers of buried fortunes, it is said that during the Second Seminole War a company of soldiers carrying a payroll of gold coins was ambushed at a watering hole just north of SR 46. The soldiers either hurriedly stashed the gold in a hole or simply dumped it in the spring. They never returned, so the tale goes, and a fortune is just waiting to be discovered. Want to try your luck?

Mount Plymouth: Al Capone Sat Here

Gangster Al Capone was a frequent visitor at the Plymouth Hotel and Country Club, once located where we turn south from SR 46 onto CR 435. The Chicago murderer with the oozy smile was a popular free spender as he enjoyed the steam bath and sauna. But he feared, with good reason, that his numerous enemies would send a hit man to riddle him while in the bathroom, so he insisted on a bulletproof door as well as a direct phone line to his hoodlum bodyguards. But bullet proofing would not save him from the probing Internal Revenue Service, which was soon to pack him off to the Big House. SR 435 goes past the golf course, but the old luxurious clubhouse was burned to the ground by persons unknown and has been replaced by a much more modest building hardly larger than a caddy shack that is open to the public for light lunches.

Mount Plymouth was planned during the booming 1920s to be the region's "playground city." The central part of the million-dollar development was to be, not one, but four golf courses. Nearby would be ritzy homes, an upscale business center, and an executive airport. Famous baseball manager Connie Mack brought his Philadelphia Athletics here for spring training. Among the other big-name personalities frequenting the resort was singer Kate Smith, who was to make "God Bless America" an inspirational hit during World War II.

Incidentally, the "Mount" in the little town's name refers, with typical Florida puffing, to the slight rise that geologists termed the Mount Dora Ridge. This narrow upland extends from near the Georgia border, where it is called Trail Ridge, south into citrus country, where it is known as the Lake Wales Ridge. During interglacial times, when the oceans were much higher, the ridge's sandy beaches were the only part of Florida that remained above the water.

Orchids, Crotons, and a Whole Lot More

South from Mount Plymouth CR 435 dips and curves along the ridge, which crests just to the west. When you reach Kelly Park Road, turn left if you want to visit the park, only a mile distant, where, for $1 a person (kids under twelve are free,) you can refresh yourself with a swim in cool spring water. Otherwise, by turning right you'll enter the agricultural belt of Apopka, the "Big Potato" to the ancient Timucuan tribe. But today the potato patches have been replaced by hundreds, even thousands, of greenhouses. They are not glass, unlike up North, where protection from snow and icy winds is needed, but plastic—either sheets supported by metal frames or covered with opaque panels fashioned into Quonset huts. They go on for miles, for the Apopka area is known as the indoor foliage capital of the world. The nursery signs tell what they specialize in. Some feature bonsai plants, some aquatic plants, some ornamental bushes, some flowering shrubs, some croton. Whatever you want, if it grows in the subtropics, some Apopka greenhouse will have it. Wholesale is their principal business, and you will see large trailer trucks loading up.

There is considerable competition among the growers, as I was quick to learn when, upon visiting one greenhouse, I asked to take a photo of the multicolored crotons sparkling in the filtered sunlight. "No pictures!" the owner said vehemently. When I mentioned that

these were common plants, he just shook his head. "No pictures."
When I said that I'd put the name of his greenhouse in my book, I just
got an answer of "No pictures." Darn, and here I wanted to sell the
photo for a fortune to a foreign government! So I continued west on
Kelly Park Road two miles to Plymouth-Sorrento Road (CR 437),
where I turned south.

Most greenhouses welcome visitors and many are happy to sell
retail, and at least one advertises free "gourmet" coffee. I had a
pleasant experience at Fender's Flora, 4315 Plymouth-Sorrento Road,
where Bill and Susan Fender specialize in orchids. Their greenhouses
glow with an array of 100,000 plants. There are tall orchids with lush
arrays of pale purple blossoms. There are medium-size plants with delicious shades of oranges merging into browns. And there are small
plants, some with delicate white and some with tender yellow flowers.

"We were both school teachers in Brooksville," Susan Fender told
me. "But one day my mother gave Bill an orchid and that started the
whole thing. That was thirty years ago, and we still have her orchid!"
Not only that, but her mother, who is now seventy-eight, works with
them most mornings, for it is mainly a family business, with Bill and
Susan putting in around fifteen hours a day.

Walking among the beautiful orchids on a balmy day in winter or
early spring, it is difficult to imagine what it is like in the summer. "It
gets up to one hundred degrees in a normal summer," Susan

*Susan Fender proudly displays one of the 100,000 orchids she and her
husband, Bill, grow in their greenhouse near Apopka.*

continued. "Some summers it reaches a hundred and fifteen. We have to bear it, for the orchids must be constantly watered by hand in order to insure that the large ones get enough and the small ones not too much. Overhead sprinklers couldn't do it right and, besides, they would get the ground too wet."

"Even so," Bill noted, "many times the earthen floor gets so slippery that I'd like to have webbed feet."

But there are also cold snaps, when propane blowers are turned on to keep the precious plants from freezing. There is also constant worry about hail, which will rip the plastic roof to shreds. And the work never ceases, for each of the 100,000 plants must be transferred to larger pots every three or four years!

The Fenders love it despite the hardships. "I've even had an orchid named after me," Susan said proudly, leading me to the Potinera Susan Fender, a variety of cinnamon stick. And where do they go during the precious two weeks they take off when business is slow in the summer? "We're off to Hawaii," Susan said with a smile, "to see the orchids."

"And to buy stock of those we like," Bill added.

The reason there are so many nurseries around Apopka may go back to 1912, when Harry Ustler arrived from Ohio with a passion to grow ferns in a warm climate. Not only was the temperature friendly, but the soil and humidity also took kindly to Boston ferns. These factors, along with good railroad facilities, encouraged so many other growers to join Ustler that in 1924 Apopka proclaimed itself "Fern City." The depression, however, caused such a great curtailment of fern purchases, that the growers turned to the diverse plantings that today involve more than eight hundred separate nurseries. The Apopka region, combined with nurseries around Tampa Bay and in south Florida, produced two-thirds of the tropical foliage plants sold in the United States. Astonishingly, the industry in Florida has more workers than Disney, Universal, and Sea World combined.

Along with the greenhouses, Plymouth-Sorrento Road passes rounded fields where cattle often graze in pastures delineated by brown board fences. A gentle valley to the east follows the road much of the distance until it ends in four miles at US 441. The federal highway is abuzz with traffic, a big change from the 1920s when it was a one-lane, bricked pathway known as the Dixie Highway. Turn right on US 441 after a half block to pick up CR 437 at the sign pointing to Ocoee and Winter Garden. Make a left and resume your backroad sojourn.

The Lake of Green Pea Soup

The road passes several industrial plants, including a greenhouse that specializes in cactus, as well as a Minute Maid complex. This particular Minute Maid plant has the distinction of initiating the frozen orange juice process that completely revolutionized and revitalized the citrus industry in the early 1950s. During the next fifteen years Minute Maid gained control of 35,000 acres of citrus groves in this vicinity. But the frozen concentrate has cooled down and now the groves are gone and the plant is used mostly for research and development.

CR 437 heads due south through land that is currently unde- veloped. In the days of horse and wagon this sand road was coated periodically with pine straw to help (somewhat) keep it firm. It was a quiet farm road then, but this is certain to change, what with the Western Beltway superhighway being constructed a few miles east. For now enjoy the long, unencumbered vistas, including that of Lake Apopka shimmering like a huge plate of gelatin. Until recently the land on its northern edge consisted of rich vegetable fields, many producing Zellwood sweet corn, agreed by many to be among the most savory in the nation. The fields are gone now, and as part of a $91 million state buyout, the area is being converted back into some- thing resembling the original marsh that filtered out the pollutants that otherwise would enter the lake. You'll drive through this area in a later exploration, so continue south and get a close-up view of the lake

Although fishermen still hope for bass, Lake Apopka's murky water is no longer hospitable for these game fish.

from admission-free Magnolia County Park, which features a picnic pavilion, a short fishing pier, and restrooms. In its heyday Lake Apopka was a premier bass mecca. Fish camps dotted the lakeshore, among them Fishermen's Paradise and the Orange Lodge near the park site. But, as the lake accumulated pollutants, algae blooms turned the water into a soupy, jade-colored brew. Then the fishing camps disappeared as the bass died out, to be replaced by undesirable species such as gizzard gar.

When you stand on the fishing pier at Magnolia Park, you'll see that the water is still a sickly green that is so dense you cannot see the lake bottom, even when it is only a few inches beneath the surface. Yet slender tips of eel grass sway on the surface, indicating that the water quality is improving. "Even a few bass are returning," a fisherman told me, adding quickly, "but they still have a long way to go." Just the fact that you can see the eel grass is an inspiration to environmentalists.

Continuing south on CR 437 you'll cross the popular West Orange Trail, the precursor of things to come. This biking-hiking trail runs along the old Orange Belt right-of-way before turning north to reach the town of Apopka. It is designed to eventually reach Kelly Park. We'll pick the trail up again in Winter Garden.

Foreshadow of the Future

The Western Beltway is just beyond the bike trail. This long-planned expressway will link US 441 at Apopka with the Florida's Turnpike and eventually continue past Walt Disney World to Interstate 4. Its completion, scheduled for 2005, will change the character of the region for miles around. Already entire new towns are on the planning boards. One huge development, Horizon West, has received considerable publicity. The idea is to have nine towns of around 10,000 persons each to be spaced so that there would be ample farm and natural lands between them. As for the towns, they would have greenbelts within them and be divided into villages, each with its own elementary school and neighborhood businesses. Although it is still in the planning stage, many hope that Horizon West will become a model for the population surge destined for this part of central Florida.

Dark Shadow of the Past

As you approach Ocoee on CR 437, turn off at the Collison Funeral Home for a mental excursion back to 1920. It is the time of the November national elections and the air is tense. Black citizens are beginning to demand full voting rights and the Ku Klux Klan is worried. On Sunday before the election they don their white robes with the pointed masks and stage a silent, ominous march down the streets of Winter Garden, several miles west of Ocoee. It is a warning of violence that must be taken seriously. When a few blacks are brave enough to show up at the polls, they are roughly turned away. One of these was Mose Norman, who became so agitated that three white marshals followed him from the polling place to July Perry's house, which stood on the site of the Collison Funeral Home. As the marshals attempted to arrest Norman, the black men drew guns and fired, killing two officers. With that the Klan surrounded Perry's house and a gun battle went on most of the day. When the Klan set the building on fire, Perry was caught trying to escape. Already wounded, he was physically attacked, then strung up and hanged.

That did not stop the violence. The call went out for reinforcements from American Legion units in Orlando, Apopka, and Winter Garden. The whites went on a rampage, burning down black homes, churches, and businesses. Although the black population numbered less than thirty, at least five were killed before the rest fled Ocoee in panic.

The Ocoee race riot not only made national headlines, but affected the town's future for decades to come. Such was its reputation that development virtually stopped. Even today the town has no business section. Not until recently did things change. Now, with the opening of the Western Beltway and the West Oaks Mall on SR 50, the town has become one of the fastest growing cities in central Florida—although its black population is still a microscopic 1.3 percent of the total.

Continue into town on CR 437. When you reach the Silver Star Highway, turn east for a quarter mile to Lakeshore Drive, and there go south along Lake Starke. Watch for the roadside plaque beside a sheltered cove denoting the site where Dr. Starke, one of the town's founders, established a fish camp for Northern guests just before the Civil War. Overlooking the location is the modern Ocoee city hall, a long wooden building with a spacious veranda where chairs afford a comfortable view of the lake.

Continue on Lakeshore Drive one block to Oakland Avenue, then one block west to Bluford Avenue, where you'll find the Withers-Maguire House, one of the most handsome homes in the area when it was constructed in 1888, and once more the town's showplace after thirteen years of arduous restoration.

From the Withers-Maguire House go two blocks north to Franklin Street, quiet and narrow now, but once the town's main street. Proceed west on Franklin Street a few blocks to where it blossoms into CR 438. Keep going west and soon you'll find a railroad and the West Orange Trail on your right. The trail has a just-built station beside CR 438, known locally as Plant Street. This is an active place, for an estimated 60,000 persons enjoy the trail monthly during the cool season. From here you can peddle fourteen miles north and east to Apopka or five miles west through Winter Garden and Oakland to the trail head. The station has maps, rest rooms, and ample parking. But bikes can only be rented at the trail head.

The Resurrection of Winter Garden

Continuing along the trail on SR 438, you will enter Winter Garden's downtown. In its prime, between 1920 and 1950, it was a major citrus center as well as the hub of retail trade that extended for miles in every direction. But when freezes ruined the citrus and SR 50 bypassed the town, it sunk into a deep stupor that left buildings deserted and the main street deteriorating. By the late 1980s the business section was a virtual ghost town.

But in 1994 the opening of the West Orange Trail began a resurrection that astonished even Winter Garden's most ardent supporters. "The trail is the single most important thing in the history of the

A mural on the side of the Heritage Museum recalls an era when Winter Garden was one of the state's major citrus towns.

city—next to the invention of the orange," the city manager told a reporter. "The city today has more and varied construction projects underway than in the last fifteen years." The downtown, especially, has taken on the air of activity it has not known for years, if not decades. Although there is still a long way to go, you can see that it is in the state of renewal.

Until 1999 the railroad rumbled directly through the center of town. The recent renovation of the station of the old Atlantic Coast Railroad, a descendant of the Orange Belt Line, gives an indication of the new spirit. It is now the Heritage Museum, open Tuesday through Sunday from 1:00 P.M. to 5:00 P.M. Although it is small, the museum has some unusual (and free) exhibits. One shows all the brands that were pasted on the citrus crates shipped out of Winter Garden. There are over a hundred of them, most with colorful pictures. There is the Blue Lagoon brand showing orange trees beside a lake. Prime Brand has a grapefruit on a plate with a spoon beside it. Cool Brand has a duck and cattails. Seven large citrus packing companies handled the fruit trucked in from the endless groves fanning out from Winter Garden. Today none remain, for the industry has moved south.

Winter Garden, with its location on Lake Apopka, was also a favorite base for bass fishermen. The Edgewater Hotel at 99 West Plant Street was one of their main haunts. Boats left from the harbor five blocks north at the foot of Main Street. It's worth the drive to visit the site, now a rather extensive public park, where a pair of cement coves were constructed by the WPA in the 1930s. Once they were jammed with boats filled with poles, bait, and landing nets. Fishermen popped beer cans and joked about the colossal bass that got away. By night kerosene lamps lit the quays and seagulls squawked as they wheeled in the air and swooped low to grasp the leavings.

But the coves are empty and silent now. For Lake Apopka is dead.

Who Killed Lake Apopka?

Who killed the lake? The people of Winter Garden liked to point toward the north end of the lake where fertilizers from 14,000 acres of vegetable farms are deemed the culprit. Yet Winter Garden itself dumped effluent sewage into the water for many years. There was also a 1940s hurricane that tore the native plants from the shallow lake bottom, thereby permitting pernicious algae to take over. There was also the massive chemical spill from a plant just west of Oakland that added another destructive element. There were culprits aplenty.

Killing the lake was easy. Bringing it back will be much more difficult. The pollution flow has greatly diminished because the chemical company is closed and the plant itself dismantled. Winter Garden no longer discharges effluents into the water. The farmers are gone and their fields are being converted to a pollution-filtering marsh. But so many of the pollutants still remain in the water that it continues to show a sickly green opacity.

The state believes that the lake will clean itself over a period of five or ten years as rainwater gradually washes out the pollutants. Environmental volunteers are helping bring back the native plants by an innovative technique of placing seedlings in athletic socks filled with sand and dropping them along the shallows. The sock holds the plant in place while it roots. By the time the sock rots away the plant is growing, and the sand enables it to become attached to the lake bottom rather than being engulfed in the unstable muck.

But not everyone is impressed. "They're going to a lot of trouble and expense," an oldtimer told me, "that hardly anyone other than a few out-of-state fishermen and a bunch of them conservationist nuts care about. It won't do Winter Garden any good. Better spend the money on schools and more cops. That's what me and most folks I've talked to think."

Home of the Puffer-Bellies

West from Winter Garden SR 438 (Plant Street) parallels the former railroad, but scrubby growth obscures the actual route. The land is fairly level, for you are still in the Lake Apopka flatlands. But there are still low rises where orange trees thrive. Their days may be numbered, however, for this area has become quite appealing to developers, who are beginning to cut the groves up.

In two miles you come to the oak-lined entry to Oakland. These massive trees announce your arrival into the center of Peter Demens' planned railroad fiefdom, for in 1886 he chose this site for the Orange Belt's headquarters as he built westward. Before him now lay an immense pine forest interspersed with lakes, marshes, and the swamp-entwined Withlacoochee River. The dense forests extended to the gulf, where the projected route lay due south, across more rivers, to a broad nub of land that protruded into Tampa Bay. All in all Demens had to construct his rail line across more than 150 miles of wilderness. Even worse, he was growing short of funds.

Demens' first job now was to determine the most favorable route. For this he hired three separate surveying teams. Then he went with each of them as they plotted five, even ten, routes between two particular points. "I had to live in the woods," he wrote, "for weeks at a stretch, at times spending nights in a tent, at times under the open sky. Now and then I had to walk all day long some 40 miles, sometimes only to discard the proposed line and start all over again."

Once the route was chosen, work crews began raising the embankments and forming the bed of crushed rocks before laying the cross ties. Finally they installed the rails themselves. They worked through the torrid Florida summer, when the heat lay upon them like a heavy blanket. Mosquitoes and gnats constantly tormented them. Yet slowly the railroad was extended through the vastness of pines and wetlands.

As Demens' efforts became known in the North, wealthy persons began coming to Oakland to see what was going on, as well as to enjoy

The gnarled arms of oaks embrace the road in Oakland.

Lake Apopka's famous bass fishing. Among them was the Chicago meat packer Philip Armour. Anxious to secure an investment from Armour, Demens decided to demonstrate how successful his railroad was. So he instructed his crews to make a great show of activity on the line, even going so far as to run a nightly procession of locomotives past the window where Armour was trying to sleep. The story goes that one night the magnate leaped from bed and shouted "I'd buy this damned Russian's railroad if only to stop that noise!"

Armour did not buy into the railroad, but he did grant Demens a considerable loan. Other money sources were more hesitant, doubtful of Demens' ability to meet a payback schedule. This was unfortunate, for Demens was experiencing such severe financial difficulties that he was forced to delay payments to his suppliers. Some of them, in turn, angrily invaded the Oakland yards, chained his locomotives to the tracks and refused to release them until Demens and his partners came up with their money. One of the partners, upon witnessing the unnerving event, suffered a fatal stroke on the spot. Frantically, Demens scrounged up the funds to release his engines.

More difficult even than the creditors were the workers, whom Demens had been likewise unable to pay. In October 1887 an angry group of a hundred or more tough Italians, hungry and in rags, rumbled into Oakland on flat cars. They stormed into Demens' office, took him prisoner, and roared that they would lynch him at eight that evening unless they received their overdue wages. Only when local bankers, almost as frightened as Demens, granted hasty loans was the severely shaken Russian released.

Despite the horrendous problems, the Orange Belt pushed through the wilderness and finally reached Tampa Bay a year later. The small settlement there was renamed St. Petersburg in honor of Demens' native town in Russia. Boasting connections on both the St. Johns–Atlantic and the Gulf of Mexico, the Orange Belt was positioned to play a major role in the development of the interior. With this in mind Demens built a pier at Oakland and launched a forty-eight-foot-long ship into Lake Apopka. The vessel could freight as many as two hundred boxes of oranges and vegetables while, at the same time, offering sixty travelers passage to and from Oakland. The town braced for fabulous prosperity. But it did not happen; the Orange Belt was never a success. Barely a year after the line opened to St. Petersburg, financial problems forced Demens to sell out. Shed no tears for the plucky man, however, for he and his wife and children moved to

California, where he made a fortune in a steam laundry venture. Later he became a European correspondent for the Associated Press. He died at the age of sixty-nine, wealthy and content.

The Orange Belt Railroad did not enjoy such a happy career. Even during its prime, when trains actually ran over its rickety tracks, it was called the "comic strip line," for something was always going wrong. The locomotives themselves were a laugh: small, discarded puffer-bellies that were castoffs from other lines. The tracks, laid over the cheapest beds, wobbled as the engines swayed over them. Thus the trains seemed to chug drunkenly across the countryside, rarely getting above the speed a person could trot. Even so, they managed to disable enough of the cows that constantly disputed passage of the tracks to cause a distressing number of lawsuits.

In 1895 the line fell into the hydra-like railroad empire of Henry Plant. It was kind of an afterthought, for Plant had a huge hotel in Tampa and no interest whatsoever in the Orange Belt's main terminal in St. Petersburg. When Plant died, the Orange Belt became a stepchild of the Atlantic Coast Line. By the time autos began displacing

The West Orange Trail goes over the Florida Turnpike on a bridge reminiscent of the Orange Belt Railroad.

passenger trains, most of the original Orange Belt line had been abandoned. Finally, the rails were torn up for scrap and by the 1990s much of the right-of-way was converted into paved trails where bike riders traveled faster than the old steam trains.

As for Oakland, the town faded with the Orange Belt, its decline hurried by a fire that wiped out much of it. Today the isolated village of just 900 inhabitants has a nostalgic appeal that causes many bikers on the West Orange Trail to pause there just to enjoy the tranquility.

You can reach the center of town by turning north off CR 438 on Tubb Street. The quaint town hall is on Pete Tucker Circle beside the trail. Demens' railroad yard was one block east. Although the site is now quiet, a century ago it clanged to the hammers of the repair sheds and the puff, puff, puff of locomotives. Farther north, at 342 Tubb Street, was the Oakland Hotel, a three-story building where railroad executives once stayed. Demens' Lake Apopka pier was just west of the foot of Tubb Street.

Although the activity of Demens' day is gone, it will soon return, as Oakland is directly in the path of development. "The pressure is on," the mayor told me. Already new homes have been built around Tubb and the lake. And this is just the beginning. "In ten years," the mayor continued, "we expect to have a population of eight thousand." Now that's growth!

Rent a Bike at the West Orange Trailhead

Continuing west on CR 438 from Oakland, note on the right the old railroad bridge, now used by bikers to cross the Florida's Turnpike. When the original structure was built in the Orange Belt era, this was just a quiet valley. The West Orange Trailhead, just beyond the bridge, during the cool months is open weekdays between 12 noon and 6 P.M. and weekends between 8:00 A.M. and 6:00 P.M. But from April to the end of October the hours are 2 P.M. to 8 P.M. weekdays and 8 A.M. to 8 P.M. weekends. It offers bike rentals at $5 for the first hour, $4 for the second, and $3 an hour thereafter. In-line skates can be rented for $6 the first hour, $5 for the second, and $4 thereafter.

Through the "Apopka Mountains" on Old Highway 50

Upon leaving the trailhead, you'll pass into Lake County, where a sign indicates that the road has become Old Highway

50, distinguishing it from the bustling, multilane SR 50 less than a mile south. Old 50 is a joy to drive, for it is almost part of the landscape, not a scar across it. If there is a hill, Old 50 it goes over, not through, it. Old 50 happily curves with the slightest land contour. It leads through orange groves and thickets of wax myrtle and sand live oaks. Cows graze lazily beside small ponds.

Old 50 was once the principal migratory route west. In those horse-and-buggy days the hills seemed more formidable, and in some literature they are even called the Apopka Mountains. The roadbed consisted of loose sand overlaid with pine needles. Wild hogs, black bears, and panthers often emerged from the scrub. When Old 50 was finally paved in 1927, many persons called it the Roller Coaster Road from its playful tendency to crest every knoll and descend every dale. Old 50 paralleled the Orange Belt Railway, just out of sight to the south. The hamlet of Mohawk was a stop for a hunting and fishing lodge with the enticing name of Jolly Palms.

All too soon Clermont's famed Citrus Tower spikes the horizon and the drive is over. It was only six miles, but they were quality miles. As it crosses US 27, and enters Minneola, proud Old 50 becomes just a humble town street.

Once There Was a Sawmill

Now you are in the hushed heart of Minneola, population 2,000. Turn right on Main Avenue and proceed north through town. When George Hull arrived here from Duluth, Minnesota, in the 1880s, the settlement had no name and the body of water was unceremoniously called Cow House Lake. At the insistence of his wife, Hull, who was a surveyor, named the lake Minneola, from the Minnesota Sioux word meaning many waters. Later, pioneers adopted the lake's name for their town.

Minneola was centered around a squealing lumbermill that extended from the middle of town down to the lake. But when the mill chewed up the last of the primeval trees, it vanished—leaving the village in an economic backwater from which it is just emerging.

Main Avenue ends at CR 561A, where you should turn right onto US 27 and continue north three miles to the Lakeridge Winery. (Or, if wine is not on your menu, turn left on 561A, for you'll will be returning here from the winery anyway.)

A Bubbly Adventure: The Lakeridge Winery

Despite the rumble of the federal highway, the drive to Lakeridge is not unpleasant, for the way is over rolling hills that were furrowed with long rows of orange trees until the freeze of 1989 abruptly ended their careers. Some groves have been replanted, the owners gambling that they can squeeze in some good harvests before the next inevitable freeze. Where the citrus has not been replanted, the land is reverting to pines, which themselves will eventually be displaced by housing as metro Orlando inexorably expands this way.

The winery building was obviously constructed to resemble a Spanish mission or a French monastery—it is very European or, dare I say it, Californian—with its squat tower and arched walkways. Grape vines extend down the hillsides on three sides. The soil is quite sandy, and this suits the plants quite well, for they thrive on good drainage. On one side of the winery is a picnic area with a good view of the vineyards and of a small lake cupped in the valley.

The winery is open Mondays through Saturdays between 10 A.M. and 5 P.M. and Sundays between 11 A.M. and 5 P.M. There are regular free tours that lead past the large vats and mysterious array of tubes and conduits. It is topped off with a visit to the tasting counter, where

The Lakeridge Winery near Clermont offers vintage wines from Florida grapes.

complimentary samples of Lakeridge's various products are offered. Many of these wines are excellent, and the Blanc du Bois recently placed in the top two percent in competition with more than two thousand wines from around the world. If you want to purchase any or all of the various wares, the friendly personnel will be more than glad to accommodate you.

Around Lake Minneola With Billy and Silly

After enjoying the tasty hospitality of Lakeridge, go back on US 27 to the junction with CR 561A. Driving west on 561A you'll quickly come to Lake Minneola. On the right is the Palisades district, which had its roots back in the post–Civil War era when husband and wife William and Sylvania Smith constructed their log domicile near here. The Smiths were evidently considered a quaint couple, for they have come down to us as Uncle Billy and Aunt Silly.

Billy and Silly sold out around 1880 to Cyrus and Lida Wilson, Yankees from New York. The Wilsons cleared the native pines, selling their logs to the sawmill nearby, and planted extensive citrus groves. At harvest time Cyrus and his workmen would load barges with the fruit, then tow them across Lake Minneola by means of Wilson's sputtering, steam-driven launch to the Orange Belt railroad yards at Clermont.

Billy and Silly's land eventually came into the possession of investors who, in the late 1920s, converted it into the Palisades Golf Course. The clubhouse was a large two-story wooden structure on a hilltop with a vista of many miles. The course ran over the hills and down close to the lake—so close, in fact, that during high water early foursomes had to fight off gar with their putters—or so the fish stories went. The golf course is still there, but now the gar have had to find new battle grounds, since the surrounding land has been converted into upscale housing.

From the Palisades the road arches around the lake and in a mile or so comes to a bridge over the Palatlakaha River, at this point less a river than a shallow channel. Westward is Wilson Island, site of one of Cyrus Wilson's most productive groves.

At the junction with CR 565A keep left as the road continues along Lake Minneola past homes on the water side and scrub oaks on the other. Soon you'll come to another small bridge—the Palatlakaha River again. Beyond is a sandy area between the road and Lake Minneola along which Peter Demens' trains staggered on their

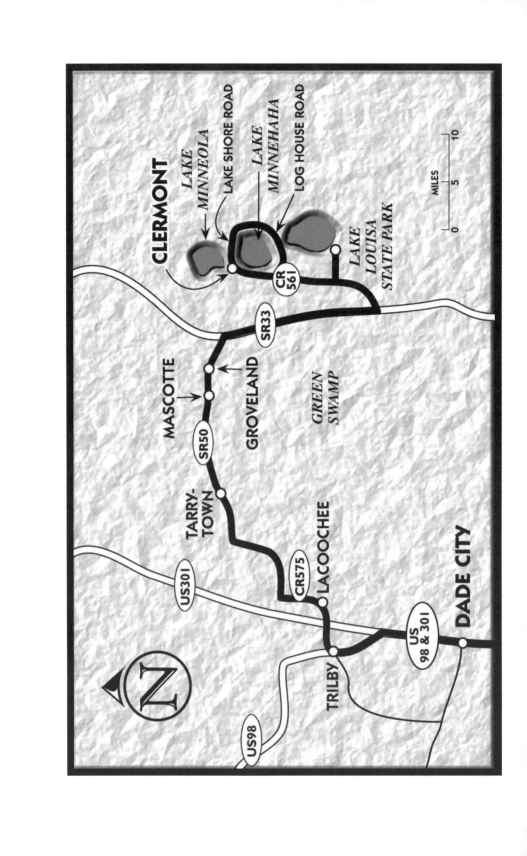

Cypress Lakes and Haunting Swamps
Clermont to Dade City • 51 Backroad Miles

The Song of the Road: Where the Byways Lead

This exploration begins in Clermont, with its appealing sand beach. From the town center head south around some pocket-size lakes to Cypress Cove, which many regard as one of the loveliest mile drives in the state. For fishing or just plain sightseeing, boats are available here, as well as at the nearby Lake Susan Lodge, which also serves meals. Then you'll continue southward, amid hills laden with citrus, to Lake Louisa State Park, where a cypress-studded beach offers a delightful setting for another swim.

Now you'll leave the hills to drive across the mysterious Green Swamp, an extensive mixture of bogs and cypress intermingled with citrus groves where the land is higher. The liquid here seeps down to the great Florida aquifer, from which most of the state obtains its drinking water. Upon reaching SR 50 you'll turn west, perhaps stopping to hike along a portion of the Van Fleet Trail, once a railroad route across the Green Swamp. Then you'll pass Tarrytown, where you can watch timber being stripped of its bark and deposited over several acres waiting to be hauled off and fashioned into utility poles.

Next it's across the Withlacoochee River wetlands, which once confounded de Soto and his avaricious Spanish army. Beyond the river you'll turn south to pay a brief visit to the village of Lacoochee, with its deserted downtown and with the monstrous shell of what was once one of the state's largest sawmills. If you care to linger in graveyards to read the inscriptions, you'll find a nice musing place here. More exciting than the graveyard is a paddle down the Withlacoochee River in a rental canoe.

The village of Trilby comes next. It was formerly an active railroad crossroads, but is somnolent now, except for the "Little Brown Church of the South," one of the cutest tabernacles you'll find anywhere.

As you approach Dade City, you'll want to visit the Pioneer Florida's Museum, where an early twentieth-century village has been partially reconstructed on part of the museum's twenty-acre grounds. Nearby is the Withlacoochee River Park, with a self-guided nature trail and picnic areas.

At last you'll reach Dade City, where you'll see the renovated old railroad station and the county courthouse, as well as hear stories of the days when courthouse square was the hub of doings in Pasco County.

The Gem of the Hills: Clermont

Clermont has the unique attribute of being founded twice: based once on fantasy and once on reality. The fantasy began in 1884 when Tom Hooks, as agent for a Sanford company, sold several hundred acres of choice land to four gentlemen from New Jersey. The New Jerseyites, duly impressed by the setting amid rolling hills and sparkling lakes, promptly incorporated as the Clermont Improvement Company, the name being a tribute to the French birthplace of the general manager, Arthur Wrotnowski, who had Polish ancestry. Not coincidentally the name agreeably connoted French beauty and European culture.

Then the company began advertising in northern markets that Clermont's lands were "in the healthiest and most picturesque region of the state and are very fertile, being high pine land . . . suitable for raising oranges, lemons, bananas, pineapples, strawberries and early vegetables." The promotion emphasized that Florida real estate was rocketing in value, and virtually guaranteed that anyone could expect wealth as well as health from an investment in wondrous Clermont.

To prove that they believed what they were preaching, Wrotnowski and the company's wealthy president, William A. House, along with their families, moved to the location, where House constructed a grand three-story mansion accented by a five-story tower. He named the main street, Montrose, after the town in Pennsylvania where he grew up.

Although sales were brisk, newcomers did not find the "model town" (as company literature called Clermont) quite as advertised. In the warm season mosquitoes thronged the air. The streets were of loose sand, frustrating to humans but appealing to the numerous hogs who rutted nearly wild. The hogs carried with them busy colonies of fleas that tormented everyone, but were particularly bothersome to the ladies, whose voluminous petticoats provided the bugs with agreeable nesting places. There was no sewer system, so the outhouses behind the buildings along Montrose Street constantly fouled the atmosphere.

Yet all this could be endured when land prices continued to rise and almost everyone was making good money from citrus crops. Clermont's economic situation improved even more with the arrival of Peter Demens' eastward-running Orange Belt Line in 1887 and the Tavares & Gulf Line, not too affectionately nicknamed the Tug and Grunt, a few months later. With the town's future seemingly assured, the male citizens crowded into William House's law office at Seventh and Minneola Avenue to formally adopt a town charter.

But the fantasy ended abruptly in 1895 with the big freeze of February 7th to 10th. Clermont was largely dependent on citrus production, and after the mercury plunged into the teens for four nights in a row, the trees died by the thousands. When it was all over, the ground was littered with rotting fruit.

To William House, Arthur Wrotnowski, and most of the others, the dream was over. With regret and empty wallets they abandoned the town. House's fine mansion was eventually turned into a rooming home. Such was the general discouragement that the charter was abolished and Clermont operated without a municipal government for the next two decades.

The little town's revitalization began with the arrival of C.O. Roe in 1899. Roe's vivid memoirs describe Clermont as he first found it. He, his wife, Belle, and their nine-year-old son, got off the Orange Belt train as a cold night wind gusted about them. They tramped up a sandy street to the home of Widow Jones at 782 Montrose. She gave them rooms in her chilly attic, then, somewhat reluctantly, hustled them up a supper of fried potatoes and biscuits.

The next day they found only slightly more agreeable lodging in a small house unoccupied while the owner was away. Since there was no meat market in town, they purchased a pork ham from a farmer. After one meal, they stored the pork in their "refrigerator," which consisted of a box with a burlap curtain covering one side. The burlap hung in a dishpan of water and, because it was wet, kept the meat moderately cool. It also allowed the wafting odor to attract a neighbor's dog, which snatched the meat and scurried off for a jolly feast of its own.

Despite their rather unsatisfactory introduction to Clermont, the Roes took a liking to the place and eventually bought the former residence of Archibald Gano. Located on Montrose, it was in the center of activity, which was just the way C.O. liked it. In 1912 he and his cousin, C.W. Roe, constructed the town's first "modern" structure. At the corner of Eighth and Montrose, it was a substantial two-story brick building with the letters "ROE" proudly emblazoned on the front. Here they opened the First State Bank, the only lending institution between Clermont and Tavares, the county seat twenty-five miles north.

C.O. became mayor when Clermont was reincorporated in 1916. His first task was a major one: get the numerous free-roaming cattle off the streets, particularly Montrose. To do this he hired a marshal and gave him a horse to help with his roundup. Evidently the marshal, galloping through town after strays, did the job, for council records show the expenditure of $500 for a corral to hold the wayward cattle until their owners claimed them.

As Clermont became the trading center for the farming communities nearby, other men decided it was time for a new bank to share in the Roes' bonanza. Thus, in 1921 the First National Bank opened at the corner of Seventh and Montrose, just one block from the First State Bank. The new bank had an even more impressive headquarters, with a pair of Greek pillars buttressing the entryway.

In 1950 Clermont's population stood at 2,100, and the town entered into what local historians Miriam Johnson and Rosemary Young call its "liveliest" period. During this time a sand beach was begun along Lake Minneola. Then, in 1956, work was completed on the Citrus Tower, an impressive shaft that rose more than two hundred feet above US 27. The tower, which commanded a magnificent view of the surrounding hills adorned with countless orange trees, gave Clermont nationwide recognition.

But by the mid-1960s downtown Clermont was on a slide as, one by one, the most prestigious companies moved to shopping centers on the more active state and national highways that bypassed Montrose. Perhaps the greatest blow was when the Publix supermarket relocated in 1965. The fact that company president George Jenkins donated the building to the city for use as an auditorium was little consolation for the loss of the hundreds of grocery shoppers who no longer frequented the downtown.

Clermont's economy was further damaged in 1989, when a deep freeze completely wiped out the orange groves. After this, the vaunted Citrus Tower was put up for sale—but no takers were immediately found. Since then Clermont has tried many things to lure people back to the old business district. A streetscape was done along Montrose between Seventh and Eighth Streets, with the planting of elm trees and the addition of public benches along the sidewalk. And many storefronts have been upgraded with the addition of stone or wood facades. The results have been good, but the Downtown Partnership, a group of private business people, is still searching for a real revitalization formula. They feel that the downtown needs something unique. Sanford and Mount Dora have antiques. Clermont needs to find its own specialty.

A chamber of commerce spokesman told me that they would have liked Clermont to have become a participant in Florida's highly successful Main Street Program. Officials from Leesburg and Eustis talked to Clermont business leaders about how the program had aided their own towns. But to have joined Main Street would have required an annual town investment of $40,000 for a full-time program director, and Clermont, with a population of under 8,000, is too small to devote the necessary funds.

However, many chamber members feel that Clermont may not need such a program, for they are confident that the conversion of the former Orange Belt Line to a biking and hiking trail linking up with Winter Garden will immeasurably aid Clermont. That is yet to be seen.

A brief tour of Clermont will show its past and its problems, while hinting at its future. Begin by turning north from SR 50 at the "To Downtown" sign on Eighth Street. Eighth Street makes a graceful arch around Center Lake—which in most other states would be called a pond—past the First Methodist Church buildings and a modern hospital to Montrose Street. Here, on the northeast corner, is the two-story brick building where the Roe cousins ran the First State Bank, early Clermont's most important institution.

From Eighth Street stroll east along Montrose, noting the elm plantings and the renovated buildings. Despite the fact that the downtown no longer attracts nationally prestigious companies, nearly all the stores have quality tenants. Note also the benches along the sidewalk. Their installation occasioned some controversy topped by a witty poem that ended thus:

Should on these seats someone get hurt
Or rip his trousers down,
The thing he'll do is promptly sue
Our friendly little town.

In one block you'll come to Seventh Street. On the northwest corner is the former home of the First National Bank, archrival of the First State Bank during the 1920s. With the Great Depression in the late twenties both institutions fell under such stress that they were forced to merge as the Citizens Bank. Even so, their total cash on hand was less than $2,000. Kitty corner from the old First National building is the Jenkins Auditorium. Quiet now except for special events, this was once an active Publix supermarket. The chain's departure was a traumatic event from which the business section has never fully recovered. The chamber of commerce occupies part of the building.

Two blocks east at 915 Montrose Street is the Mulberry Inn. Built around 1890 by a town founder and sawmill owner, Archibald Gano, the two-story dwelling was owned by C.O. Roe between 1900 and 1910. The home is now a highly touted bed-and-breakfast, with rates ranging from $60 to $85. From the inn it is only two blocks north on West Avenue to the 1924 railroad depot—transformed into a small restaurant with refurbished booths in the old waiting room, from which there is a pleasant view of Lake Minneola. Outdoor dining is also available. The cooking is done in a converted caboose.

Now go east along Lake Minneola following the old Orange Belt railroad bed. The city pier is at the foot of Eighth Street, and from there a beautiful promenade extends east along the shore for a block to the bicycle path that will soon be linking up with the exten-

This former railroad station in Clermont is now a restaurant. The old railroad bed and Lake Minneola are in the distance.

sive West Orange Trail at Oakland. Clermont is pinning many of the hopes for revival of its downtown on trail patrons. Lake Minneola Drive ends at Clermont's vaunted beach, claimed to be the longest sandy freshwater bathing area in Florida. It is open to the public for just $2 per car for the day. In the original 1884 town plat, this land was reserved for an orange grove.

The town was fortunate to have its beach, with its imported sand, in place prior to conservationists' demonstrating that the conversion of shorelines to beaches is harmful to lakes, since shore plants are important in filtering out pollution before it drains into the water. In addition, the native vegetation provides food for birds and fish, as well as offering shelter for their young. It is now a violation of Florida law to build sand beaches without permits, which are about as easy to obtain as suntans at night.

Now take Twelfth Street, which is also SR 561, south across SR 50. After a few blocks SR 561 turns sharply to the right. But stay on Twelfth Street until it ends at Lake Minnehaha, where there is a block-long park overspread by the muscular limbs of some of the largest live oaks hereabouts. Lake Minnehaha is lined by medium-size cypress, the larger ones having fallen to pioneer axes.

From the park follow Lakeshore Drive eastward. The homes scattered about do not obscure the lake nor disturb the shady tranquility of the scene. Soon you'll come to Lake Winona on your left. Watch for the short canal between the two lakes. Small steam-powered boats used to haul cypress and pine logs through this canal to a large sawmill on the far side of Winona.

The names Winona and Minnehaha come from Henry Wadsworth Longfellow's *Song of Hiawatha*, and were selected by Mrs. Tom Hooks, who was Clermont's first schoolteacher. The Hooks family was one of Clermont's very earliest. Although Herring Hooks gets the credit for naming what is still known as Hooks Point, just past the Winona bridge on Lake Minnehaha, certainly his wife, Mary, deserves her own recognition for bearing ten children. Long before the Hooks, Indians of unknown tribes built lodges on the point, leaving only a few scattered implements to mark their passage.

Beyond Hooks Point, Lakeshore Drive gradually turns south, still hugging the lake. Private piers and boat houses jut into the water. Reeds often green the shoreline. On the left the land rises rather steeply to where homes overlook the water.

Lost Amid the Cypress: Lake Susan

Soon you come to the bridge over the Palatlakaha Creek, just beyond which is a short road leading to the Lake Susan Lodge and Marina, begun as a fishing camp in the 1940s. There is still a feeling of isolation here, for the single-story, rustic building is almost lost amid the great cypress trees that are long-term tenants of the lake. The lodge is anything but fancy, yet it serves meals and offers a verandah with a captivating view of the lake. It also has cabins ranging from $50 to $70 per night.

For a closer involvement with this charming water system, you can take a $10 cruise leaving the lodge from an outfit with the challenging name of River Rat. (Cruises leave Fridays, Saturdays, and Sundays. Call for times: 352-394-3964. Or you can do without the rat and rent a motor boat at $35 per half day or a canoe at just $5 for an hour or $15 for a half day.

Lake Susan, valued as a wonderful bass habitat, is part of the Clermont chain of fifteen lakes designated as an "Outstanding Florida Waterway" where further building is restricted. The chain includes Lakes Minnehaha, Minneola, and Louisa, which we shall drive to shortly. There is also a small motel here, with a small swimming pool. Rates are small too.

Scenic boat tours leave from the Lake Susan Lodge near Clermont.

Crescent Lake: Hattie's World

From Lake Susan Lodge, Lakeshore Drive leaves the cypress lowlands to ascend low sand hills, the transition being quite abrupt. Suburban homes are springing up everywhere, but they are tastefully done and do not overly intrude on the scenery. Most of the land had been devoted to orange groves before the freeze of 1989, and in places you still chance upon fields with tall irrigation pipes.

Clermont's real estate market is booming, as the graceful hills offer ideal building sites. The forecast is that Clermont's population will double within the next five years.

As the road climbs, Crescent Lake appears on the right. Then comes Log House Road, where you should turn west. Log House Road commemorates a most unusual lady, Hattie Daggett, who once made her home on Crescent Lake.

Hattie arrived in Clermont via the Orange Belt Railroad in 1888. An independent woman of twenty-three, Hattie hadn't meant to settle here, only find out if the climate was suitable for her parents. But she fell in love with the surrounding land, calling it Monte Vista, or "hilltop view." It was covered with huge pines, whose lofty green tops provided coolness and shade. It was almost like a park, and she impulsively purchased twenty acres. Others loved it too, and eventually seventeen pioneer families built their pine cabins in the vicinity.

Most of the orange groves that once dotted the rolling land south of Clermont have given way to suburban developments.

With the money Hattie earned during the summers as a nurse in Philadelphia, she had the land prepared for tomato culture. Then, knowing she needed access to the Orange Belt in Clermont, she determined to build a canal between Crescent Lake and Lake Minnehaha. This was no easy task and Hattie took an active role in seeing that the work got done. She even recruited the laborers from the Sanford docks. During the digging, she supervised the use of dynamite to blow out the stubborn cypress stumps. When it was through, she had a waterway 6,600 feet long and thirty feet wide. Then to haul her produce and that of her neighbors, she purchased a steam launch, which, with typical bravado, she christened the *Hattie M*—the M reflecting her marriage to Robert Millholland, a handsome widower from nearby Oakland.

Although Hattie called the home she built here the Log House, it was three-stories high and easily the most imposing building for miles around. She made it headquarters for her Monte Vista Land and Improvement Company, through which she began marketing properties around Crescent Lake. To add to her income, Hattie and Robert turned the Log House into a hunting lodge during part of the season.

Hattie remained an active force in Clermont for her entire life. It wasn't until 1945, at the age of eighty, that she finally sold her holdings and retired. Although the Log House was torn down in 1959, the road is itself a tribute to this remarkable woman.

The road through Cypress Cove on the outskirts of Clermont offers one of the most memorable short drives in all of Florida.

Florida's Most Scenic Mile

Log House Road is only a mile or so long, skirting Sawmill Lake, whose name alone tells where the pine trees went, before ending at CR 561. For a brief side trip to see one of Florida's most scenic miles, take CR 561 north three miles to Cypress Cove. Here the road weaves through a swampy wilderness where towering cypress stand like pensive titans in the heavy silence. Long strands of Spanish moss sway rhythmically in the slightest breeze. On the right is the unruffled expanse of Lake Minnehaha. On the left is the primitively beautiful Lake Palatlakaha—a word that has a strange, almost musical, quality, once you learn how to work your way through it. Some historians believe the word means "the big swamp," but the only ones who could have told us for certain are Indians long dead.

Now head back south on CR 561 past Log House Road and Sawmill Lake. There are still some orange groves around, yet the smattering of new homes foretells the area's future. You will soon enter a less populated area, however, and as the road descends to Lake Glona, the vegetation changes to that of a hammock, with thick trees and a dank, jungle smell. A few older homes are here and there, but the lake's inhabitants are mostly cypress trees—probably not much different from when James Gloner and his wife (whom historians, as is too often the case, have carelessly left nameless) settled here around 1873. They grew oranges in open space they scraped out from between the trees, then had to haul their fruit by pony cart over the crude Indian trail that led to Clermont by way of Lake Susan and the cumbersome Palatlakaha ford.

As the road ascends from Lake Glona to reveal Lake Nellie on the left, watch carefully for Lake Nellie Road and the sign pointing to Lake Louisa State Park, which is two miles due east.

Lovely Lake Louisa State Park

Lake Louisa is the southernmost body of water on the Clermont chain. The admission is only $2 per car—quite a buy for a park in a setting as beautiful as this. The path from the parking lot to the lake is by way of an elevated walk across a narrow dell overhung with cypress and magnolia. Thick growths of ferns carpet the forest floor.

The beach is in a beautiful setting of live oaks and cypress. Don't be disturbed that the water has an unusual tea color. It is not harmful. So, if you have a bathing suit, you can use the changing rooms and enjoy a swim.

In the early 1900s the lake seemed to be headed for industrial use when the Hammond sawmill was erected on its shore. Then sawdust coated the water as the squealing blades turned grand cypress into roof shingles and other lumber products. Louise Hammond raised a family here, and it was probably for her that the lake was named. Later, plans were made to construct a golf course along part of the shore and convert the rest into ranches and citrus groves. But the state bought the park area in 1973 and opened it to the public four years later.

The Great Green Swamp: It's Not What You'd Expect

Return to CR 561. Head south into the Green Swamp. This is not a swamp as you might picture it, with stagnant water and big-eyed alligators watching for suitable humans to eat. Indeed, the land seems dry, and there are almost imperceptible rises where farms have been established. In places suburban-style homes have even been constructed. But it is classified as a swamp, nonetheless, due to liquid filtering down into the Florida aquifer where most of the state gets it drinking water.

Most people do not realize the importance of the Green Swamp. I remember when a newcomer to Florida asked me where we got our drinking water. I replied out of the Green Swamp. To say she was incredulous was an understatement. But I think she'll remember the Green Swamp.

Floridians have grown so accustomed to alligators that swimmers at Lake Louisa State Park enjoy the water despite the warning sign.

The Green Swamp is a vast lowland that extends for thirty miles between SR 50 on the north and Interstate 4 on the south and twenty-seven miles between Lake Louisa on the east and US 301 on the west. Although standing water is rare, the soil is almost always wet, as you can tell by the prevalent stands of cypress. These stands are often in the distance, for the road has been built along the low, dry ridges, which often support orange groves and tree sapling farms. But the damp cypress environment is always in the background, and in it are are wood storks, white ibises, great egrets, and more than 230 other animal species, including thirty that are endangered.

The fact that developers are inserting private homes onto the swamp's relatively dry ridges concerns environmentalists greatly. They thought they had the problem solved when the region was officially proclaimed an "area of critical state concern." Nonetheless a recent editorial in the *Orlando Sentinel* complained that the commissioners of Lake County, in which much of the swamp is located, continue to be far too lenient in allowing the encroachment of builders.

In four miles turn north on SR 33, which is the only route across the Green Swamp. Although the state road is busier than the byway you have been on, it is still only a two-lane, secondary affair. At first it traverses a flat region where cypress stands approach the pavement. But as it approaches Groveland, eleven miles north, the land gradually becomes drier, and farms and buildings appear.

*Cypress, marsh grass, and wetland shrubs, not murky water,
predominate in the vast Green Swamp.*

The Town With an Edge: Groveland

Groveland is popular with retirees, and it is easy to see why, for it retains a small-town atmosphere while being astride SR 50, an active road that connects with Clermont, and Orlando's sprawl not too far beyond. On the south side of town is a picnic pavilion beside a small lake named David after an early hunter who killed a bear on its shore. Nearby is the public library and the Edge Memorial Methodist Church.

The Edge family, for whom the church is named, was a dominant factor in Groveland's early development. E. E. Edge initiated the town's prosperity when he bought out the Taylor brothers' turpentine mill, which stood on SR 50 close to the old Orange Belt Railroad, then part of the Atlantic Coast Line. In 1923 his son, L. Day Edge, constructed a mercantile store that attracted patrons from all over due to its vast stock of goods—everything from darning needles to tractors. With his wealth and energy, Edge became what historian Emmett Peter calls "a towering figure in Florida as well as Groveland."

L. Day Edge is long gone, but his two-story brick building remains beside SR 50 westbound. Although it is not the proud structure it once was, Edge's name is still emblazoned prominently above the main entry.

The Land of Trembling Earth

 Now drive west on SR 50. In a few miles you'll pass through the hamlet of Mascotte, named for a sailing ship that carried

A few riders brave the desolation of the Van Fleet Trail through the Green Swamp.

passengers between Boston and St. Petersburg, where they took the train to their new homes. But the town lacked a certain "edge" (pardon the pun) and eventually lost out to its neighbor, Groveland.

Beyond Mascotte the gently rolling land is devoted mainly to cattle, although large portions have been left to deciduous trees. Evidently the land is not particularly productive, however, for the farm houses are small and many are run-down. In about five miles you'll reach the state trail named for General James A. Van Fleet, the American commander who helped saved South Korea from the Chinese Communist invasion in 1951. Van Fleet later retired a hero to Florida.

A short drive leads to the trailhead (admission is free). The trail itself occupies the bed of the old Seaboard Coast Line and, for this reason, runs straight as a freight train south for thirty miles through the wild heart of the Green Swamp. "It can be a lonely place," an employee at the trail's Clermont headquarters told me, "with access roads only every five or ten miles. It can also be weird, for sometimes you feel the ground shake from the layers of spongy peat beneath you. Be off of it by sundown because of the mosquitoes. Take your own water and food. And I'd advise you not to get sick." A sign on location also advises cyclers to wear fluorescent clothing, for trigger-quick hunters frequent the nearby land. Small wonder, therefore, that the Van Fleet Trail is not among Florida's most popular.

Timber! Tarrytown

From Van Fleet SR 50 passes through a largely forested and mostly uninhabited countryside. Therefore it is something of a surprise when Tarrytown suddenly emerges at the SR 471 crossroads. The interesting aspect of Tarrytown is its impressive lumber operation. From SR 50 you can see large piles of tree trunks stripped of their bark, glimmering with an almost skeletal luminescence. Behind them is the long, low mill.

I drove to the installation's entrance off SR 471, and after passing the "No Visitors" sign, I stopped at the weigh station. A large truck was there with thirty-foot pine logs trailing from the flatbed. Once such logs were delivered by the railroad, and, although it is gone now, its right-of-way can easily be seen from SR 471 a little south of the mill's entry.

From an employee at the weigh station I learned the following facts: The mill is owned by the Robbins Manufacturing Company of Tampa and was started almost sixty years ago. The company is not

Timber from nearby forests is converted into utility poles at the Tarrytown mill.

involved with felling the trees, but buys the cut timber from logging companies, which harvest them from private tracts, as well as from government forests, such as the Ocala and the Withlacoochee. After the Tarrytown facility strips the bark, the trunks are sent to Tampa, where they are weather-treated and turned into utility poles. The reason for the no visitors policy is that heavy equipment scurrying around the grounds poses a danger for private cars.

Few persons realize the extent of lumbering in Florida. In just the four counties between Clermont and Dade City almost half the land is forested and the value of the annual timber harvest comes to more than ten million dollars. There are about eighty active sawmills in the state, fed by thirty logging companies. However, the public is not aware of most of the lumbering, for it is done in the backwoods away from disapproving eyes.

Lightning Alley: The Withlacoochee State Forest

From Tarrytown the land flattens as it approaches the wetlands of the Withlacoochee River, which has its headwaters in the Green Swamp. The transition is quick: one moment there are broad pastures, then, within a few hundred feet, it all changes to a wetland where trees predominate. The road-ribbon seems the only lifeline to civilization.

When Hernando de Soto and his would-be conquistadors encountered the Withlacoochee swamp slightly farther north in 1539, they were dismayed, for none of them had ever seen anything like it. Only the lust for gold enabled them to slosh their way through the muck. One can only surmise what de Soto's comments would have been to the World Wildlife Fund, which more than three centuries later named the Withlacoochee State Forest one of the "Top Ten Coolest Places You've Never Seen."

During the Second Seminole War of the 1830s and 1840s this was the lair of Osceola. The U.S. Army did not care to hunt Indians in this hostile wilderness, and could the Seminoles have remained here, they would probably still be undefeated. But even they could not remain long in this forbidding place. Ultimately all but a small number would be captured and shipped off beyond the Mississippi.

Driving through this area can be somewhat disconcerting, particularly toward evening as the trees throw grotesque shadows across the road. And in the summer it can get downright scary when the afternoon thunderclouds roll in and the air booms and bolts of lightning stab earthward. SR 50 follows what is known as the nation's Lightning Corridor between the Gulf of Mexico and the Atlantic. On a day of heavy storms it is estimated that the corridor can sustain nearly 100,000 cloud-to-ground strikes. Although the vast majority are harmless, in 1996, an average year, twelve persons were killed and 102 injured.

At last the road goes over the Little Withlacoochee River and, four miles beyond, reaches dry ground at the junction with CR 575. Turn south on CR 575, which is a narrow, nicely paved byway. It weaves through trees, including moderate-size live oaks dripping with Spanish moss, then past neat little farms with retaining ponds surrounded by pastureland. Shortly it crosses a small river, which, although it is unmarked, is actually the main branch of the Withlacoochee. It seems too insignificant that a tributary could have created the swamp through which you have just passed, and perhaps for that reason it received its awkward Indian name, which means the "big little river." During the Second Seminole War an army fort stood briefly beside the river about a quarter mile west of the bridge. Later the river bank was lined with orange groves, but a severe freeze in 1898 wiped them out.

At the Withlacoochee bridge is an RV park and canoe rental. For $22 two persons can get driven eight miles up the river, then enjoy a four-hour paddle downstream. (Each extra boat passenger adds $10 to the fee.)

Beyond the bridge CR 575 passes a smattering of mobile homes. Then, after a sharp turn, it crosses some railroad tracks and enters what once was downtown Lacoochee, but now is merely a cluster of decrepit buildings along with a small, but still-active U.S. post office.

The Shell of an Era Past: Lacoochee

Lacoochee is an undignified name for a town. But, silly as the name might sound, the town was once respected throughout the state as the site of the enormous Cummer cypress mill and lumber yard. Cummer, attracted by the great cypress stand in the Withlacoochee wetlands, constructed the mill in 1922. Soon the blades were humming and sawdust flying as monster logs were fashioned into high stacks of lumber that occupied many acres around the plant. From here freight trains hauled the wood to northern markets. Cummer was one of Florida's major employers, and the town of Lacoochee thrived with the company.

Soon where towering cypress once stood was only weedy, rancid water. So Cummer had to reach out for trees from hundreds of miles away. Yet year by year the harvest grew smaller and the expense of transportation greater. The stacks of lumber no longer were mountainous and the work force no longer numbered in the thousands. At last, after four decades in operation, the plant closed. Then Cummer disposed of the equipment, shuttered the company store, and sold the workers' quarters. The era was over. Florida's once magnificent virgin

"Downtown" Lacoochee was left to decay when the Cummer sawmill closed.

cypress had been almost completely consumed.

The demise of the mill meant the virtual end of Lacoochee. The downtown died and eventually all that remained was the post office and, across the road, the railroad station. Then the station was torn down.

Although the Cummer mill is closed and dismantled, the huge shell remains. To see it, cross the tracks on Bower Road, which is immediately beyond the post office. Then drive two blocks to Coit Road, and turn left along the 100-acre former Cummer grounds enclosed by a cyclone fence. The plant is in the distance, its exterior stained with rust. You can see directly into the cavernous, gloomy interior. The company water tower still rises beside the main building, just as if there were some reason for its continued existence. Near the tower, but gone now, was the company office, a hotel for guests, a commissary for the workers, and a medical center. The multiacre lot, once stacked high with cypress boards, is barren except for weeds. The whine of saws, the chug of trains, and the shouts of workers no longer ring through the air. All is quiet except for the wind rustling through the thick weeds.

The plant has been on the market for many years. Scuttlebutt had it sold several times. The latest rumor is that a feed company is the new owner. But that is still in question at this time.

There is an old cemetery across from the plant. The inscriptions on the weather-worn tombstones seem quite appropriate. "Sweet Be Thy

The graveyard in Lacoochee has some poignant inscriptions.

Sleep" reads the marker of J. F. Trowell, who died in 1933 at the age of seventy-three. "When the toil is over, then comes rest and peace." It could be the plant's own epitaph.

A Storybook Village: Trilby

Leaving Lacoochee on CR 575, continue a mile and a half to Trilby. This village too dwells in another time. It received its name from a novel by George DuMaurier that was popular at the end of the nineteenth century. The story's setting was Paris and the plot concerned an Irish lass, Trilby, who fell under the hypnotic influence of the evil Svengali. The purpose of naming the Florida town after the novel must have been either from whimsy or solely to gain national attention, for the book had nothing to do with America or railroads or small towns. Originally some of Trilby's streets were called after characters in the story, but, as the novel was forgotten, they were changed.

Although Trilby originated as a stop on Henry Plant's north-south railroad, the completion of Peter Demens' east-west Orange Belt Line a year later put it squarely at the cross-roads, and soon Trilby's railroad yards became the third largest in the entire state. During the

Trilby's "Little Brown Church of the South" recalls the days when this now-quiet, backwater village was an active railroad stop.

peak of rail travel in World War II it was not uncommon for more than fifty trains to stop at Trilby over a twenty-four-hour period.

But those glory days are long past. Standing in front of the picturesque little Methodist church and looking west down CR 575, it is difficult to imagine that the deserted land was formerly a bustling business community facing the Plant line (later Atlantic Coast) tracks. Next to where the church now stands was the jail, and beside it was the Trilby State Bank, subject to at least one daring robbery—its proximity to the calaboose notwithstanding. South along the tracks was the Masonic building, hub of the community's social activities, and farther on the two-story Trilby Hotel.

Today all those buildings are gone, lost to a devastating fire that raged out of control when the Model T fire truck scampering down from nearby Dade City lost its hoses during the bumpy trip. It was a catastrophe from which the little town would never recover. Some people remained, but most moved away.

So it all ended, recalled Charlotte Tyer in 1976 when she was in her seventies. Gone were the festive peanut boils, the taffy pulls, the fish fries under the oak trees in Peterson Park, the get-togethers at Tom Blitch's soda fountain. "It's sad, somehow, to see things change so," Mrs. Tyer lamented. "Things that seemed so important vanished, along with the people that lived with them."

But Trilby did not quite die, for the Methodist church, with a congregation of barely eight, remained. Built in 1898 and originally standing near the railroad tracks, it was put on rollers a few years after the fire and hauled by mules to its present location. From there, amid the desolation, it called out to the countryside. New members came, but they were so few in the 1930s that much of the building was rented as a children's clinic and dry goods warehouse. In the 1970s the congregation was augmented by worshipers from the Lacoochee Methodist Church, which had crumbled with that community. Yet today the "Little Brown Church of the South," as it calls itself, has been resurrected. The congregation stands at around three hundred, and visitors flock to see the picturesque building that wouldn't give up. It is open Sundays through Fridays from 9 A.M. to 5 P.M., and Saturday too, "if the pastor happens to be there."

As for Trilby itself, perhaps a new settlement may even arise where the former once stood, for the old railroad bed has been converted into the forty-six-mile Withlacoochee State Trail, whose lower terminus is just a half mile south.

Happenings at the Courthouse Square: Dade City

Now head south for Dade City, the seat of Pasco County, on US 301, a throbbing highway that makes one appreciate quiet country roads. The northern approach to Dade is dominated by the huge Lykes Pasco citrus plant. Lykes' main brand locally is Florida Gold orange juice, but it is also the exclusive manufacturer and marketer of Sunkist juices in North America. Another Lykes brand, Old South, is popular in Canada. The saga of the Lykes family is a Florida phenomenon. Shortly after the Civil War Howell Lykes migrated to the frontier community of Pierceville, just north of what would become Brooksville. He and his seven sons grew citrus, then turned to cattle, and eventually their many business interests included forestry, fertilizer, trucking, and even personal insurance. A separate branch of the family ran a major steamship line.

Today, with its headquarters in Tampa, Lykes is still a tight family corporation. As such, it does not disclose its financial condition, nor much else. Neither does it care to offer any visitor facilities at the Dade City plant. Indeed, the company official who gave me the information above politely refused to divulge any hard statistics, aside from pleasantly boasting that Lykes employs more than 3,000 persons, with 1,300 of them at Dade City. Since Dade City itself has a population of only around 6,000, that makes Lykes far and away the region's dominant employer. It was frustrating not to be able to learn more about the company, since it is unusual that a company so involved with retail sales does not provide some sort of public facilities in its major plant.

Immediately south of Lykes on Pioneer Museum Road is the impressive Pioneer Florida Museum, open Tuesday through Sunday between 1 and 5 P.M. Admission is $5 for adults and $2 for kids eighteen and under. Children five and under are free. The museum, with its nine buildings, occupies twenty acres. A highlight is a steam locomotive once used by the Cummer Cypress Co. Behind the locomotive is a flat-bed car with a few massive cypress logs representing the thousands it carried for destruction to the Lacoochee sawmill. Before the locomotive was fenced in, rambunctious town kids sometimes cavorted around it at night. One morning startled caretakers even found a fire roaring in the train's belly and smoke rising from its stack.

Beside the locomotive is the old Trilby railroad depot dating back to 1896. Nearby is the one-room Lacoochee school house, built in the

1930s. The interior is complete with desks for students of various ages, an upright piano for class songs, the obligatory portrait of George Washington, and even a realistic teacher-manikin holding a switch that meant business.

The museum's earliest displays were housed in a dilapidated school on the fairgrounds, then in a patched-up auditorium building. When the current museum opened in 1975, there was a grand celebration, complete with a barbecue dinner and such crowd-titillating contests as tobacco-spitting and greased-pig chasing. Although tobacco-spitting is now a bygone pleasure, the museum is filled with many fascinating exhibits of early life in Pasco County and vicinity.

The Pioneer Museum helps recall a bygone era, but Florida existed long before the pioneers. For countless centuries Timucuan clans raised their families here, tended their scattered corn fields, played their games, fought their battles, and honored their earth and sky spirits. A trail ran south to Tampa Bay, where clams were dug, and north to hunting grounds around Ocala. This was an important location, for it was here that their trail skirted the Withlacoochee swamp. De Soto marched over this ground in his futile hunt for gold. So too did Major Francis Dade and his hundred-odd troopers in 1835 on their way from Tampa Bay to reinforce the Fort King garrison at modern Ocala. Dade and his soldiers, ambushed by Seminoles twenty miles north, were virtually wiped out—and Dade City was later named in

The Pioneer Florida Museum in Dade City has many excellent exhibits.

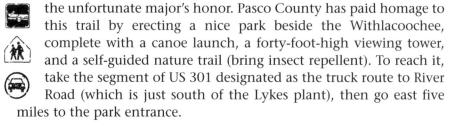

the unfortunate major's honor. Pasco County has paid homage to this trail by erecting a nice park beside the Withlacoochee, complete with a canoe launch, a forty-foot-high viewing tower, and a self-guided nature trail (bring insect repellent). To reach it, take the segment of US 301 designated as the truck route to River Road (which is just south of the Lykes plant), then go east five miles to the park entrance.

Continuing south, the truck route reaches Meridian Avenue, Dade City's main cross street. On the left is the recently renovated railroad depot. It was one of the most active buildings in early Dade City, but the advent of the automobile eventually caused most passenger service to cease. You can still catch an Amtrak there, however, if you care to board before dawn or around midnight. Otherwise, the tracks belong to CSX freights.

From the old depot drive west on Meridian Avenue. During the 1920s, when electricity was just coming into vogue, the town installed streetlights down Meridian to just beyond courthouse square. Everyone liked the idea, but the expense was more than the little town could bear, so they illuminated just two blocks from the depot half

Water and cypress form a colorful pallet at the canoe launch in Withlacoochee River Park, just outside of Dade City.

way to the square. Short as it was, it created a most favorable impression, and "Dade City," remembered longtime resident Thelma Touchton, "became known as one of the prettiest towns in central Florida."

On Meridian is the modern Hugh Embry Library, descended from the modest book collection started by an unfortunate college lad who read everything in town as he wasted away and died. Just beyond is the 1915 city hall, an attractive, two-story building that is now a coffee house.

Meridian Avenue continues to Business 301, the center of Dade City, where the Pasco County Courthouse stands on a spacious lot. When Pasco attempted to break off from Hernando County in 1887, the state legislature, heeding the protests of Hernando's delegate, refused to consider it. But after Dade City's boosters announced they would name their new county after Samuel Pasco, the powerful speaker of the house, behold, their request was promptly granted. Yet despite the honor, there is no indication that Sam Pasco ever bothered to visit the then remote county that had immortalized him.

For nearly a hundred years the Pasco County Courthouse has highlighted the Dade City town square.

Today the 1909 courthouse has been largely replaced by a newer, far larger county building several blocks east. But memories linger about the square and the old building, which now houses some county administration offices. During the early part of the twentieth century courthouse square was the town's focal point, especially on Saturdays when the farmers and their families, on horseback or jammed aboard work wagons, flooded into town; Dade City was about the only excitement this side of Tampa, which, being more than thirty miles south, might as well have been in the land of Oz.

"Everyone came to town on Saturday night to walk around the block [where they would] meet friends, gossip, and shop," recalled Lawrence Puckett, former Dade City mayor. There weren't any good restaurants, so ladies seeking funds for the Embry library made goodly sums selling their home cookin' in the square. The square was also a natural place for concerts. After John Philip Sousa visited the town in the 1920s, the citizens decided to build a bandstand so he would return with his musicians. The brick structure, which still stands, was put up, but Mr. Sousa never came back.

Folks in the 1920s and 1930s would linger around the square until dusk, then hurry to do their last-minute shopping. Griffin's Drug Store on Meridian Avenue was among the most popular stops. Here, in a building with the name still prominently displayed on the front, cranky old Hank Griffin would lounge in a rocking chair and yell at patrons to help themselves and leave the money on the counter, for he trusted them, and, besides, he preferred not to interrupt his rocking. The Pasco Telephone Company shared Griffin's building, although the clanging little devices were regarded more as toys than necessities, there being only 135 subscribers, most of whom were neighbors anyway.

Another destination was the Bank of Pasco County at the northeast corner of Meridian and Seventh (Business US 301). During the 1920s it proudly called itself "Old Reliable," emphasizing its financial stability. But when the Great Depression came, Old Reliable shuttered its doors with the rest of the nation's banks. Nevertheless, it didn't go under, and after fifteen long years, eventually paid off its depositors—or their heirs. Although Old Reliable's building was later replaced, the new structure is a faithful recreation of the original.

The only attraction competing with courthouse square was the three-story Edwinola Hotel, its name being an amalgamation of Edwin and Lola (Gasque), the owners. The Seaboard Line once had a station immediately south of the Edwinola—a great convenience for the patrons. The Edwinola (now a comfortable retirement home) was locally famous for its long porch. Here, in the Roaring Twenties, Dade City's fashionable younger set courted during jazz band shindigs. Thelma Touchton remembered the dancers: the girls, with names like Edna, Daisy May, Fountain, Annabelle, and the boys, such as Darryl, Frank, and Woots. Did they find their mates at these affairs? Did they live happy lives? I hope so.

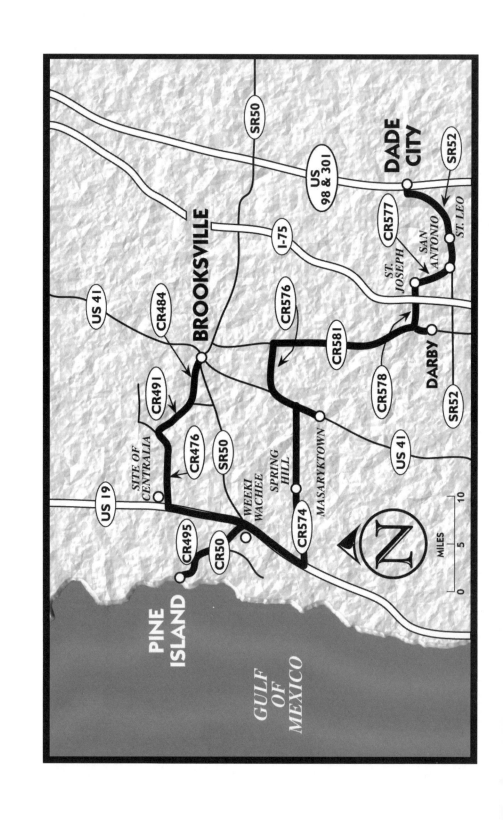

Through Pastures
and Yesterdays
Dade City to Brooksville • 81 Backroad Miles

The Song of the Road: Where the Byways Lead

The fourth exploration travels mainly through the rolling countryside of the Brooksville Ridge, a series of former dunes created by waves and winds during the Ice Age. Your first stop allows you to tour the spacious campus of St. Leo University and visit its beautiful abbey church. Next it's on to nearby San Antonio, a cozy village that once dreamed of becoming the vibrant heart of a Catholic community numbering in the millions.

Then you'll drive through some of the most appealing pasture country anywhere, ending up at Masaryktown, begun by Slovaks in the 1920s. Perhaps you'll want to stop for a meal at the old Slovakian restaurant, built by the pioneers, but now serving Cuban food.

Next, the route will take you through Spring Hill, where you'll see the successful development of the Mackle Brothers—and hear the sad story of their demise. From there you can pause at the well-known Weeki Wachee Spring to enjoy the mermaid underwater show or a boat ride through the wild marshes that extend to the Gulf of Mexico. For a swim in the gulf, you can take a short side-trip through this same exotic reed-land to Pine Island, where there is a fine county park that offers changing rooms and a sand beach.

Finally you'll travel through more of the fertile ridge country to Brooksville, the bustling administrative center of Hernando County. The modernized 1913 county courthouse is a pleasure to visit, as is the town square and the local museum.

Off to Saint Leo

Heading west from Dade City on Meridian Avenue, which is also SR 52, you'll pass comfortable residences sheltered by cool shade trees. Once out of town, SR 52 ascends the low hills that are the southern terminus of the Brooksville Ridge, which fronted the Gulf of Mexico when it was higher during the Ice Age. The highway is busy, for it connects with Interstate 75 ten miles west.

In a Reflective Mood: St. Leo University

Five miles west of Dade City you'll come to St. Leo Abbey and University. The entrance to St. Leo is marked by a pair of large Romanesque pillars. Immediately on the left is the Administration Building, where you can pick up a visitor's guide with a good map of the grounds. St. Leo has around a thousand students, allowing both undergraduates and faculty to get to know each other well. It offers its male and female students thirty majors as well as a thorough grounding in Benedictine teachings. "The campus is tranquil and beautiful," remarked one student in a university brochure. "It gives you a sense of community, and of peace."

The monks who founded the abbey on this hilltop site in 1889 must have experienced the same feeling. Although their numbers were few, only twenty-four by 1902, their ardor was great, and two years later they began the abbey building, which took sixteen years to complete. Initially the abbey was used both by the monks and the

The church at St. Leo College is an inspiration to students.

students, who did not total much more than a hundred until the late 1920s, when work began on their own dormitory called St. Edward's Hall. St. Edward's (which is the first major building west of Administration) brought the abbey considerable financial stress, for enrollment income plummeted during the Great Depression, causing difficulty in meeting the mortgage payments.

Conditions improved in the late 1940s and construction started on the abbey church, immediately northwest of St. Edward's Hall. Even then the hard-strapped monks had to barter oranges from their groves for the sandstone that formed the building's trim and beautiful entrance archway. But when it was finally completed, the church, with its eight-story tower, became the symbol not only of St. Leo's fortitude, but, in a way, of mankind's persistence in the face of adversity.

The tower dominates the campus, both from its physical presence and its beautiful chimes that sound every fifteen minutes. "When the tower was built," a monk told me, "it had only one bell, which was swung manually by a rope. But about twenty years ago the tower sustained a lightning strike that so damaged it that we were warned against the stress the bell would cause when it was swung. Therefore it was replaced by the digital recordings of Italian bells that you hear today."

The abbey church, open seven days a week, lends a medieval air to St. Leo. You don't have to be Catholic to feel a sense of history mixed, perhaps, with a hint of mysticism. Somehow the quietly religious aura about this place carries us back to the twelfth century when there was only one Christian church and everyone believed that the words of the Bible, as interpreted by the church leaders, were immutable and eternal. There was certitude of mind and strength of conviction.

Currently thirty-five or so monks reside in the old abbey beside the church. They live fairly isolated from general society, spending their time praying, tending to citrus harvests, or doing other projects, for work and prayer are central to the Benedictines' beliefs. Although they originally served as teachers when St. Leo was a prep school, they have

Chimes ring out from this church tower at St. Leo College at regular intervals.

not taught since it became a college more than three decades ago (it only recently graduated into a university.) Neither do the monks administer the school—that is the job of a lay council. Yet Benedictine principles still permeate St. Leo. These codes of righteous behavior are appealing to young people: almost half the students are non-Catholics who attend, not for religion, but to learn how to lead morally rewarding lives.

Where the Angelus Still Rings: San Antonio

Now return to SR 52 and head west. You'll quickly pass Holy Name Monastery, where about thirty Benedictine sisters reside. These nuns, who wear modern clothing, spend much of their time teaching. They reside in modern tan-and-turquoise dormitories. I had expected something a bit more timeworn, given the fact that the Benedictine order is the oldest in the West.

When the highway makes a sharp left turn about a mile from St. Leo, stay on the small road that leads a quarter mile to the hamlet of San Antonio. Drive left around the central park to the two-story brick school, bordered on the west by the village church. This is a good place to stop and read the story of the little town.

Today San Antonio is quiet, except for children playing in the park during school recess, and it is difficult to imagine that when the town was founded in 1881, plans were made for a population larger than the city of Chicago. Judge Edmund Dunne, the founder, was a dynamo of a man who had risen to Chief Justice of Arizona before being chosen by Hamilton Disston to help him build a real estate empire in Florida. The state, being almost bankrupt, wanted a buyer for great chunks of its uninhabited territory; Judge Dunne not only handled the delicate and complicated negotiations for what resulted in Disston's purchase of about 16 percent of peninsular Florida, but personally tramped over much of this territory in order to inform Disston as to the land's physical characteristics. The purchase was perhaps the largest ever in American history by a private individual, and Dunne's commission included control of 100,000 choice acres from just west of Dade City all the way to the Gulf of Mexico.

Dunne ardently desired to create a sanctuary where Catholic families could live away from the distractions of secular society. He chose a site for the capital of his religious province on the rounded summit of a low hill free from malaria. As for the name, he was already beholden to St. Anthony, who had guided him to safety when he had been lost in a Western desert. Almost immediately Dunne began constructing a church devoted to his patron saint. It was a rough wooden structure where the first worshipers sat on stumps. But it was enough to hold the little community together, particularly when its bell sounded the Angelus at dawn, noon, and eventide, everyone pausing in prayer and in reaffirmation of their reason for settling in San Antonio.

While the church was going up, work was also started on the school. When Benedictine nuns from the priory at St. Leo on the neighboring hill took over the school administration, it seemed as if Dunne's dreams for a Catholic colony were being fulfilled. Soon citrus groves brightened the landscape where only pines had grown. Sand roads began radiating out to other Catholic colonies nearby. In 1888 the Orange Belt Railroad established a station on the northern outskirts.

But the great freeze of 1895 brought a disaster that Dunne had never anticipated. Around San Antonio dead citrus trees stood like corpses on a battlefield where evil had won. Most of San Antonio's inhabitants moved out. Eventually Dunne's spirit too was broken, not only by the freeze, but by the fact that his sanctuary had never attracted more than a few hundred devotees. So, with great sorrow, he gave up his dream and relocated to Baltimore.

Although in today's San Antonio the idea of a self-contained Catholic colony no longer has primacy, the idealism is still there. The present church dates back to the village's revival in 1911. The brick grade school beside it was built eleven years later and has become a magnet for young Catholics from miles around. During school days the park is alive with laughing children. And the Angelus still sounds at noon, when all activity suddenly stops for silent thoughts and prayers.

Across the park on Pennsylvania Avenue is the

This quiet village square in San Antonio was actually designed to be a thriving city hub.

village hall, a one-story building of field stone. As you drive west along Pennsylvania Avenue, you'll see a few old commercial buildings. At Curley Street turn north, and at the corner of Michigan you'll come to a two-story frame structure that was once the St. Charles Hotel, catering mostly to visitors arriving on the Atlantic Coast Line.

The half-century-old train depot has been restored and is on Railroad Avenue a few blocks north of the former hotel. Although the rails have long since been dug up, the station is in wonderful shape and you can stand on the platform and almost hear the wail of a locomotive coming down the imaginary tracks. Many times the train would arrive at night: "There was no electricity then," recalled Theresa Schrader, "and darkness surrounded the small depot. I remember looking out the window, waiting to get off, and seeing white sand glistening in the moonlight like snow." Charlie Barthle, proprietor of the hotel, was usually there with a lantern, and guided grateful travelers to their lodgings.

Here we say adieu to the old Orange Belt Railroad, built between 1886 and 1888 of hopes, dreams, and little else by Russian nobleman-turned-refugee, Peter Demens. If you took our earlier explorations, you'll recall we picked up Demens in Longwood where he took over the line, then hardly more than a few miles long, in place of cash payment for a debt. Then he struggled to build it across a virtual wilderness, running into such severe financial difficulties along the way that he was almost lynched by unpaid workers in Oakland. From there we traced his line through Clermont and Trilby until we encountered it again here in San Antonio. The rickety narrow-gauge tracks originally ran on westward to the gulf, then stumbled down the coast past Dunedin and on to St. Petersburg. It never won any prizes as a railroad, not with rails so shaky that sometimes the locomotives actually fell off, even though they rarely went faster than a long-legged farmer could walk.

Although the last train chugged off to oblivion in 1978, the railroad bed remains, and in several places, such as we have seen in Winter Garden, has been converted into a popular hiking and biking trail. In a way, the hard-luck Russian, whom you can only admire, still lives.

From San Antonio continue on Curley Street, also designated CR 577, three miles north through a succession of orange groves. This quiet byway is a pleasure to follow as it leads over gentle hills past groves and pastures to St. Joseph. Although the hamlet is not much more than a few buildings, in 1883 its German-speaking founders thought it would become part of a vast Catholic community based around San Antonio.

At St. Joseph turn west on CR 578. The road is narrow and you may feel that you're leaving civilization—that is, until you pass over Interstate 75 with its too-familiar rasp of engines and odor of carbon monoxide. There is no entry or exit here, so within a minute or two you'll will be back in yesterday.

Many yesterdays, however, are more pleasant when viewed from a distance than they were in actuality. Picture the area as it was during frontier times: pine trees grow thick and tall, creating shadows that flicker when the wind blows. Needles cover the forest floor, muffling all sound. Birds flutter darkly among the matted upper branches, and once in a while their calls shatter the stillness.

Imagine you are farmer Robert Bradley or his wife (whom history has left nameless) and you have labored hard to carve your plot out of the pine lands. At last you have a cabin and a field that is producing more than mosquitoes. Nonetheless you are gravely worried, for the Indians have taken to the warpath for what has become the Third Seminole War. You tell yourself you have nothing to fear, since the tribe has been reduced to a few hundred half-starving, pitiful folk concentrated around Ft. Myers far to the south. Yet you and your family are dangerously isolated and vulnerable out here. A dozen painted warriors could be scowling behind the pine trunks and you'd never know until they struck. Could the bird calls really be Seminole signals?

The Bradleys' fears were well founded, for in the spring of 1856, a war party found two of the Bradley children unprotected and killed them. The fact that this would be the last such attack east of the Mississippi River was of no consolation to the grieving family. A polished stone marker at the tiny crossroads of Darby, a mile south of CR 578 via CR 581, commemorates this bloody event.

From Darby turn back north on CR 581, which meanders through a pleasant countryside of low hills interspersed with forests and pastures. Predominantly cattle country, you'll come upon some horse farms too. There is little traffic, so you can pull over to the side of the road and enjoy the bucolic scene whenever you get the hankering. In a half-dozen miles you'll pass into Hernando County and in another mile reach CR 576 (Ayers Road), where there is a traffic light, though for what purpose is a mystery. The five-mile drive west on CR 576 is much the same as on its two chums, except there are more trees and fewer pastures. The road ends at US 41, which you should take a half mile south to Masaryktown.

Goodbye, Old Masaryktown

You may think Masaryktown is a strange name for a settlement and so too are the names of the streets that cross US 41 as you drive into town from the north: Hviezdoslav, Palacky, Hodza, Wilson. Wilson? Ah, you see, there must be a story here. And so there is

Thomas Masaryk was a Czech professor in Prague in the early part of the twentieth century. As the First World War broke out, Masaryk fled to the West, where he and Milan Stefanik, a distinguished Slovak scientist and, later, wartime aviator, began agitating for the independence of the Czech and Slovak peoples from the Austro-Hungarian Empire.

Masaryk, with his American wife, was very popular in the United States, and most importantly with President Woodrow Wilson. When the war ended in 1918 with an Allied victory over Germany and Austria-Hungry, Wilson was instrumental in founding the new country of Czechoslovakia, with Masaryk the first president.

The formation of Czechoslovakia overjoyed Slovak expatriates in the United States. And so, when a small group of them decided to set up a colony in Florida, it was natural that they would name their

Horses and cattle graze peacefully in the many pastures east of Masaryktown.

settlement Masaryktown (pronounced Ma SAR ek town) in honor of the president of the new country.

The first contingent of 135 settlers came in 1925. They laid out the streets, naming them after their heroes: Stefanik, who died just a year after Slovakia became free; Hviezdoslav, nationalistic Slovak poet; and Hodza, a Slovak patriot who would become premier a decade later. Other streets they called after their favorite American presidents: Wilson (of course), Lincoln, and Roosevelt.

Among the settlers were John and Anna Cimbora, who erected a small hotel that quickly became the colony's focal point. Here newcomers could stay while their homes were going up. When the hotel did not have enough rooms, families simply slept in tents around it. The work of clearing eight hundred acres of pines and underbrush was difficult, particularly in the subtropical heat. And once this had been accomplished, the land had to be plowed and citrus seedlings planted. But this was an inspired group, and everyone agreed it was worth it—not only for themselves, but for their unborn children.

The saplings grew well, and despite the Slovaks' strained finances, happiness and confidence reigned among them. But during the winter of 1926–27 an unexpected freeze strangled the trees. The Slovaks were used to hardships and they replanted that spring. Yet the following winter another freeze again killed the trees. With that, a majority of the pioneers, almost destitute, reluctantly left the settlement. Nonetheless, some stayed, among them the Cimboras, who managed to scrimp by with their hotel/restaurant on US 41. Others turned to truck farming. But it was tough going, for soon the Great Depression was on them, although they were better off than their relatives in Europe.

The inhabitants of Masaryktown could only watch with alarm as the tragedy of Czechoslovakia unfolded. Premier Hodza resigned in despair as Britain and France buckled before Adolph Hitler's territorial demands in 1938. The ruthless Nazi legions then invaded Czechoslovakia, destroying the Czech portion of the fledgling country and setting up Slovakia as a puppet state under German domination. Next came the horrors of the Second World War with incessant Allied bombings and eventual pillage by invading Soviet troops.

The war's thunder reverberated in Masaryktown, where every able-bodied young man left for military service. Although Hitler was defeated, their Czechoslovakian homeland merely exchanged one harsh master for another when the Communists took over. In protest Foreign Minister Jan Masaryk, son of the nation's founder, committed suicide.

But no matter what depressing events happened in Slovakia, life in Masaryktown unfolded in its own way. One settler arriving in the 1940s was Violet Cimbora, who offered me her vivid memories of those days:

Milan Cimbora [son of the hotel owners] and I got married just after World War II. We bought our land by paying the delinquent taxes owed by people who had not made a go of it. We built a twenty-foot by thirty-foot shack on the land. The house cost eight hundred dollars and we lived in it for seven years. We raised three beautiful little girls there. Those were wonderful times. We danced at the hotel. Some of the men played accordions and there was a piano. We did the beseda, that's like your square dance. On festival days we wore our costumes. They were beautiful things and very expensive. There's one on display in our museum. I bought that myself in Slovakia. I have two others that I am willing to my daughters when I go.

Masaryktown began to prosper. The wealth came in the form of squawking chickens. Almost everyone in town raised them. Milan and Violet Cimbora turned five acres behind their home into a poultry farm. "We put our money into our coops, a brooder house, and the care of our chickens," she recalled. "We had up to ten thousand. But you were a little guy if you didn't have ten times that number. So we got out of chicken raising in 1966."

The poultry business continued to grow, however. The Hernando Egg Producers Cooperative was organized by six Masaryktown people, including Milan Cimbora, who served as vice-president for a number of years. The cooperative constructed a large storehouse and a feed mill and quickly became an important force in Florida agriculture. Florida's great Publix supermarket chain relied on Masaryktown for most of its egg supply as the village became the undisputed egg capital of Florida.

There was a downside, though. The prosperity was not spread evenly, for the big producers tended to squeeze out the small farmers. Concurrently, the village's population stagnated at around 1,000. "Nobody wanted to move to a town where there was nothing but chickens," admitted Violet Cimbora, who was mayor for several years in the 1960s. Chickens were everywhere. Their feathers floated on the breeze, their jabber formed a constant undertone, their odor penetrated the most perfumed bedroom. By 1970, when the business climaxed, there were two thousand chickens for each man, woman, child, and family pet in town.

Masaryktown is no longer the egg capital of Florida; raising chickens was a difficult business, and as the older generation died out, the children no longer felt cackles in their blood. The children adopted American habits, and slowly the village began to lose its Slovakian identity. Then non-Slovak retirees from other parts of the country began moving in.

Today only around 300 of the village's approximately 1,200 citizens are of Slovakian descent. Rather than eggs and drumsticks, Masaryktown is now known for the popular bingo games held each Wednesday and Saturday evening after six in the Community Center at Hodza and Lincoln. Although there is a small museum in the Center where Violet Cimbora's colorful Slovak costume hangs on a mannequin, about the only time the museum is open is when it is used as a smoking room during the bingo games. As for the old hotel/restaurant, once the linchpin of Slovakian life, the building still stands at the corner of US 41 and Wilson. But it is now owned by an outsider who specializes in Cuban food. No longer painted its traditional white, instead it is a brilliant commercial yellow. The new owner did a yeoman-like job modernizing the aged structure, which he purchased for just $40,000 at a public auction. He has tried to keep at least a little of the Slovak tradition alive, for there is a Slovak doll over the original fireplace and a large photograph of what must have been most of the Slovak community posing in front of the building many decades ago.

Milan Cimbora even attended the dedication ceremony in 1998—and his name is on a plaque beside the fireplace. But these are superficial things. The essence of the place is gone.

So what are Violet Cimbora's thoughts as the era closes? "We expected that the community would keep the Slovak heritage alive," she mused. "When we came here, everyone spoke Slovak. But now no one speaks it. Of my own daughters only the oldest

The For Sale sign beside Masaryktown's hotel and restaurant indicates the passing of the pioneer Slovak generation.

even understands it. The children nowadays go to school in Brooksville, and no one there teaches Slovak traditions." She sighed. "I guess it will all go down the drain when the old timers die. Nobody will remember Slovakia. I guess that's progress."

She paused. "I don't feel anything about that fact. No one seems to care. There are only three of the original settlers alive. When they go it's over."

Now it's time to leave Masaryktown. Driving north on US 41 you'll pass the streets that once held such meaning: Hodza, Palacky, Hviezdoslav. Almost no one hereabouts seems to know who the men with the funny names were. Goodbye, Old Masaryktown.

"We're the Brew!": Spring Hill

From Masaryktown US 41 goes back north past Ayers Road where once a sawmill on the southeast corner fashioned lumber for the Slovakian pioneers. You'll skirt the Hernando County Airport before reaching CR 574, also known as Spring Hill Drive. Turning west on CR 574, you'll pass the entrance to what will be a major interchange for the Suncoast Parkway, linking central Hernando County with Metropolitan Tampa/St. Petersburg. This is bound to have a profound effect on the still largely forested land hereabouts, as well as on peaceful little Masaryktown.

Soon the four-lane boulevard begins curving through the community of Spring Hill. Ordinarily I would not bother with a road through such a populated area, but Spring Hill involves the once mighty Deltona Corporation, with which I had my own personal experience.

Deltona was owned by the three Mackle brothers: Elliott, the eldest, had an uncanny ability to pick out good land for development; Robert was an acute businessman and ran the day-to-day operations of the company; and Frank, the youngest, was a master at public relations and corporate planning. He dreamed the dreams. The Mackles had land development in their blood, for their father, Frank Senior, the company's English-born founder, had set the company on track back in the 1920s. After his death, the brothers took over, doing major projects during World War II, including the construction of the gigantic naval base at Key West, for which the company won the coveted Army-Navy "E" for excellence.

The Mackles' Spring Hill development opened to the public in 1967. A prominent writer called it at the time "the greatest single real estate development in the history of Hernando County." Sales of homes soared right from the beginning, thanks in part to the reasonable prices aided by the aggressive efforts of over six hundred salespeople. Spring Hill, when added to the profits from another up-from-scratch community, Deltona, eighty miles east, filled the Mackles' coffers and encouraged them to commence a third large real estate venture, at Marco Island on the gulf coast near the town of Naples.

Marco Island was a swampy place that could be made habitable only by a massive dredge-and-fill operation involving the destruction of thousands of mangrove trees, a perfectly normal procedure that had long been used by developers up and down the coast. But suddenly the environmental movement emerged, and when the Clean Water Act became law in 1972, the Mackles were in trouble. Through no fault of their own, they were suddenly unable to continue to develop Marco. The problem was that they had sold lots that were still unimproved, guaranteeing that they would be fully developed by the time the contracts matured.

The Mackles had plenty of land that they offered to trade in return for permission to develop the land already contracted for. Under present-day mitigation policies, this is an accepted practice. But not in the 1970s. When the purchasers learned that the Mackles would not be able to make good on their contracts, they demanded refunds. To accommodate them the Mackles were forced to sell almost everything they owned, including several shopping centers in Spring Hill.

Having owned property in Marco, I was familiar with the Mackles, and, in preparation for a book I was doing, interviewed Frank Mackle in 1991. At this time he was no longer the ebullient, confident man from his Spring Hill days. Now he was old, and his back was bent from a fall he had taken in the hospital where he had gone after a heart attack. Both his brothers had long since died, and he had been forced to resign from his almost bankrupt company. But the fires still burned, and he was bitter toward the forces that had crippled the company that his father, his brothers, and he had worked so diligently to erect and to run in an honorable manner.

"One thing people have always said about Florida developers," he told me, "was that they wanted to sell you worthless land under water. But in my case I wanted to sell a good piece of land that was developed. But they wouldn't let me!"

Mackle and I sat for a while in his Florida office while he paged through the scrapbooks he had kept during his long and mainly successful career. A large portrait of his father watched us from an opposite wall. After reminiscing, he walked with me to the door. His eyes were misty. "I tried the best I could," he said softly. "I gave it a damned good shot. But they beat me." A couple of years later he was dead.

There is nothing much to see in Spring Hill, except a lot of homes. Those that are small, with just single-car garages, were built by the Mackle brothers back in the sixties and seventies. Shopping centers pop up along the road, most also built by the Mackles. There is no town hall, for Spring Hill is not a town, being run by the county commissioners in Brooksville. Yet Spring Hill has a population approaching 80,000, which makes it ten times the size of Brooksville. "They're just the suds; we're the brew," was how a waiter in Spring Hill described the relationship.

Spring Hill Drive ends at US 19, where the Mackles had a park and a fountain to call attention to their development when they dreamed of a community maxing out at 6,000. The fountain is still there, but has been moved to a rather inconspicuous part of the intersection. Turn on US 19 to Weeki Wachee Spring, six miles north.

Weeki Wachee Wonderland

The Seminoles named the bubbling pond "weeki wachee," which meant little spring. The clear, cool water refreshed them when the days were hot. The runoff formed a river which led to the bayou with abundant fish. When roads began to be built in the 1920s, the "little spring" attracted a smattering of tourists, who could park directly beside the pond and, after forking over a small fee, jump right in. Weeki Wachee remained a minor attraction until after World War II, when it was purchased by the city of St. Petersburg, which regarded it as a future source of drinking water. To make it pay until that day came, the city leased it to an ex-Navy frogman, Newton Perry. It was Perry who decided the crystal waters were ideal for underwater mermaid shows and he presented the first in 1947. The attraction took off, particularly when the American Broadcasting Company became owner in 1959. Now Weeki Wachee belongs to a company called Florida Leisure.

Weeki Wachee is a glitzy commercial enterprise, and its prices are steep: $16.95 for persons over ten and $12.95 for kids as young as three. Yet it does have its appeal. The view of the spring from the glassed-in auditorium is pleasant even when interrupted by "mermaids" and other costumed swimmers cavorting as characters in skits that are amusing to kiddies—and to us adults with kiddie quirks.

The spring is not small, despite what the Seminoles led us to believe. Indeed, it is one of Florida's major effluences, sending forth almost 170 million gallons of pure, fresh water daily from a gaping circular cavern in the underlying limestone. This cavern is actually the mouth of a dark underground river of which only around four hundred feet have been explored by cave divers with flashlights and courage. The water comes from surface liquid in and around the Green Swamp east of Dade City. This water has filtered into the underlying limestone but cannot penetrate the impermeable rocks below, which were laid when dinosaurs roamed. So it simply follows the tilt of the limestone toward the west in a wide tunnel until it reaches the surface at Weeki Wachee.

Electric boats take visitors on thirty-minute glides along the Weeki Wachee River's wilderness banks. These are excellent trips where the quiet vessels hardly make ripples or enough noise to disturb the great numbers of birds feeding in the vast marshlands.

For persons who want to swim in the spring, you can enjoy the adjoining beach at Buccaneer Bay Water Park from early April to early September. But here again you'll encounter eye-popping prices: **PAY TOLL AHEAD** $12.95 for persons over ten and $9.95 for kids three and over. While you're there you can also see an exotic bird show, a birds of prey demonstration, a petting zoo, and an injured pelican rehab facility. If you still have any money left, you can rent a tube to float along what management calls the "Lazy River." Then, if it's late in the day and you're tuckered out from all this activity, across US 19 is a Holiday Inn built around one of the largest and prettiest motel courtyards in these parts (reservations: 800-465-4329).

The Exotic Salt Marsh World

Perhaps, in place of the gold-plated swirl of Weeki Watchee, you'd settle for just a swim in the Gulf of Mexico and a drive through one of the world's most extensive black needle rush ecosystems. If so take CR 50 (Cortez Boulevard) five miles west from Weeki Wachee to CR 495 (Pine Island Drive), then right two more miles to Pine Island. This is certainly one of the most exotic road segments in all Florida. The rushes present an almost limitless expanse of olive gray broken only by distant hammock upsets of green and, to the east, the dark outline of forested dunes that mark the ancient Pleistocene shoreline. The entire aspect is so out of the ordinary that you may decide to stop on the road shoulder to savor it. If you do, you'll find that the black needle rushes to be within arm's grasp, so why not examine them more closely. The plant I inspected had just three spikes, which I called Yesterday, Today, and Tomorrow. Yesterday was about two feet high, broken off at the top, and entirely dead. It had obviously given its all for the plant. Today was three feet high, gray at the top but green farther down. The tip was still sharp as a needle, for Today was obviously in the prime of spike-hood. Tomorrow was a little guy only a foot high. It was bright green and apparently eager to gain the full stature of Today. The future beckoned the shoot, its head pointed toward the sky and its roots grounded firmly in the muck. Although the black needle rushes seemed dead to all who see only Yesterdays and the tip of Todays, they are full of green Tomorrows down below.

While you are examining the rushes, why not peek at the floor of the marsh itself. What is "muck" to our species is "home, sweet home" to others. Although we cannot see the microscopic algae and diatoms, we know they are there in the countless millions, for the soil is squirming with snails having jolly feasts. Oysters and clams also enjoy dining on the microscopic critters. Possibly the most active citizens of salt marsh country are the fiddler crabs. The muck is literally honeycombed with their burrows, some going down almost three feet, thereby giving the animal access to water at low tide as well as providing vital aeration of the soil. Other animals also love this murky water-world.

The little road leading to Pine Island goes through an extensive salt marsh.

Lumbering terrapins often roam the marsh bottom by day, then bury themselves in a snug mud blanket as night falls.

Above the waterline, the marsh supports an entirely different group of animals. Raccoons, which live on the higher land, come into the marsh to search out the eggs of the terrapins, wrens, and sparrows that nest in the hammocks or in the low bushes along the creeks and bayous.

Now it's back on the

road, which soon makes a sharp turn as it crosses over a little
bridge to Pine Island. Pine Island is small and the few homes are
on stilts because its low coastline is exposed to hurricane mischief.
CR 595 ends at the Alfred McKethan County Park, where, after an
entry fee of only $2 per car, you can use their changing rooms
and enjoy a swim in the gulf. The beach is made from imported
sand. Public swimming dates from 1925, when L. B. Sanders, the
island's owner, agreed to donate the land if the county would build a
road from Bayport. The park charges a small admission fee, but it
affords about the only public gulf swimming for miles. Don't get your
hopes up for Daytona-type crashing surf, for the Nature Coast is what
geographers call an area of "zero wave energy," so you'll be lucky to
feel a good lapping. It is otherwise, of course, when a wayward hurricane sometimes comes calling between midsummer and midautumn.

Early settlers found the calm, brackish lagoons of this coast ideal
for making salt, which, during the Civil War, was so important to the
Confederacy that salt-makers were excused from serving in the army.

"Look Upon My Works, Ye Mighty, and Despair!": Centralia

Back at Weeki Wachee go north on US 19 through sand and
pines. Most of the area on the west side is part of the large
Chassahowitzka Swamp. Originally this wetland was shaded by
massive cypress, but they were transformed into planks during the
early 1900s. The swamp is the steamy abode of alligators, spiders,
mosquitoes, and black bears. Why the endangered bears would want
to call such a locale home is a mystery. And perhaps they don't find it
that much fun, for they habitually wander across the highway in sufficient numbers to represent a hazard to motorists as well as to themselves. Road signs alert drivers to watch for the furry pedestrians.

In a half-dozen miles you'll reach CR 476, also called Centralia
Road. Although the intersection is completely devoid of buildings, in 1910 the large Tidewater Cypress Company sawmill stood
here. The mill could cut 100,000 board-feet a day—enough to lay
planks end to end for twenty miles. Tidewater employed 1,500
workers, most of whom lived with their wives and children in
Centralia, the company town beside the plant. To clothe and feed
these numbers, locomotives freighted in such necessities as flour,
sugar, grits, and beans hundreds of barrels at a time. These and other
supplies were sold to employees from the company commissary, a
huge building where goods were stacked so high that the clerks

needed extension ladders to reach the top. The great commissary attracted patrons from miles around, many of whom stayed after making their purchases to enjoy a meal at the popular restaurant or a silent film at Centralia's movie theater.

But after only six years the timber began running out. Then the town began to die, and within a decade it was a deserted shell—so rapidly did the cycle turn on the timber frontier.

Today Centralia has utterly vanished. The only reminder of the operation is a solitary road sign beside a semi-treeless expanse on the northeast corner of US 19 and CR 476. I was reminded of a poem by Percy Shelley describing how a traveler came upon an inscription in the desert:

My name is Ozymandias, king of kings:
Look on my works, ye Mighty, and despair!
Nothing beside remains. Round the decay
Of that colossal wreck, boundless and bare
The lone and level sands stretch far away.

A Lesson in Florida Real Estate

Once I had my own experience near this corner. In 1972 my wife and I bought property on Peregrine Falcon Avenue, which ran parallel to Centralia Road, a half block south. This was part of the Royal Highlands development, which its salespeople claimed would be the next Spring Hill as soon as US 19 was four laned. Scores of little sand roads ran here and there with cute names like Piping Plover, Indigo Bunting, and Purple Sandpiper. Buy now, they urged, and you'll even get a quality camera as a free gift! We bought and received the camera, which took pretty good photos until it died a few months later.

The federal highway was four laned, just as the company had promised—although, of course, they had nothing to do with that. Then we waited for Peregrine Falcon to help fly our son through college. But the falcon just laid an egg, and Jeff had to make it without that bird's help. About the only one interested in the property was the anonymous person who used it as a dump for his broken barbecue and worn-out mattress. It was bad being taken by the company, but somehow it was even worse when Hernando County began taxing me for fire protection—as if this pile of sand could burn!

Peregrine Falcon and I ended our association twenty years after we made our acquaintance. The purchaser paid the back fire taxes plus the realtor's fee. I was left with a thousand dollars to use for my pleasure and to haul off the mattress and grill.

The Other Spring Hill

Moving east on CR 476 from the likes of Ozymandias and Peregrine Falcon, you'll ascend a low sand scarp that was once the gulf shoreline. In about five miles you'll come to CR 491, where you should turn south. The road is narrow but paved, and cattle graze in wide, hilly pastures that were originally dense. You have now entered the Brooksville Ridge. Although now the ridge is low and rounded, it formed as lofty dunes when the ocean stood 175 feet higher. Most of Florida was beneath the sea then, and a view from the crest of one of these hills would reveal nothing but water and the spires of cumulus clouds forming over another dune ridge thirty miles east.

In a moment you'll reach CR 484, also called Fort Dade Avenue. This intersection was the site of the original Spring Hill, from which the Mackles undoubtedly took the name for their development. This particular junction is of interest, not only from its pastoral aspect, but because it was the springboard for one of Florida's economic powerhouses: the Lykes Brothers, one of whose mammoth plants you saw on an earlier exploration near Dade City.

The Lykes family settled here in 1851. Howell Lykes was only ten years old when the Third Seminole War broke out and the area was terrorized by the news that Indians had killed two children at Darby, eighteen miles to the south. The Spring Hill school was closed, and fear gripped the families, who felt quite vulnerable in their isolated farm cabins. But the war quickly ended, as the few Indians were quickly defeated. Then the Lykes family turned to ranching, and eventually Howell's seven sturdy sons got into businesses including not only cattle but also citrus and shipping.

This road, cut through the Brooksville Ridge, reveals its dune origin.

Lykes Brothers is a strange business organization: It seems to shun publicity. Even family history is something it apparently does not care to divulge. It took some prodding of a company spokesperson for me just to learn that the original homestead burned down and was rebuilt in the 1940s, at which time it was used by Lykes Real Estate. Although the family is currently collecting historical artifacts, there are no plans to allow public viewing.

 Now take CR 484 east four miles into Brooksville, seat of Hernando County.

The Lonesome Statue at Brooksville

When Hernando County was created in 1843, it reached from the environs of Tampa north to the mouth of the Withlacoochee River—sixty virtually trackless miles. Since there were no towns of any size, the county legislators met in one tiny settlement after the next for the first thirteen years, until a couple of good-hearted persons donated land for a permanent county seat. The site was on a low hill, which, although it afforded a pretty view and was in the approximate middle of the county, had little else to offer. Few persons lived there, and no good roads connected it to the outside world. But a surveyor dutifully laid out the phantom town's boundaries, and soon a crude wooden courthouse rose in the deserted square.

Now, what to call this collection of surveyor's stakes? The solution was provided in 1856 by an incident in the nation's capital. It seems

The road along the gentle ridge north of Brooksville is often shaded by live oaks.

that one Preston Brooks, a hothead from South Carolina, was incensed when Senator Charles Sumner from Massachusetts referred to his uncle, also a senator and a spokesman for slave interests, in a derogatory manner. To satisfy Southern honor, Brooks beat Sumner senseless with a cane on the floor of the United States Senate. Brooks' action was cheered throughout Dixie, and a few years later the citizens of Hernando County decided to name their county seat Brooksville. What they chose to ignore was that Brooks was hardly of heroic fiber, for he had attacked Sumner without warning while he was bending over some papers. Later it also came out that Brooks used a cane specifically because he was a publicity agent for a walking stick manufacturer.

The Brooks attack riled the North and was another of the events leading to the outbreak of the Civil War five years later. During that conflict Brooksville served as a stopover for herdsman driving cattle up from south Florida to help feed the Confederate armies. Lincoln's strategy called for disrupting this flow, and for that purpose early in July 1864, four Union ships carrying around 240 men occupied Bayport on the gulf. From there the troops, composed mainly of free blacks and runaway slaves, marched inland, destroying crops as they headed for Brooksville along a route now followed by SR 50. Meanwhile news of the foray had traveled inland and about sixty Confederate militia mustered on the courthouse grounds.

The Union force, halting before Brooksville, divided into two groups. As one prepared to attack, the other began an encircling movement. The defenders, seeing the superior numbers and fearing that their rear might soon be exposed, fired a few shots, then scrambled off into the woods. The raid was a limited Union success, for the soldiers were able to herd off barely a dozen cattle before withdrawing. Yet the Brooksville raid eventually became a Southern victory, for its reenactment every January now brings the small town significant profits.

After the momentary excitement of the Civil War, Brooksville settled back into isolation, its only communication with the rest of the United States via a stage coach road that wandered thirty miles north through Floral City and across the Withlacoochee swamp to the rail head at Wildwood. Of course, Brooksville citizens tried desperately to lure a railroad to their settlement. But the town was ignored, being too far from established trade routes. Although in 1885 a wheezing locomotive pulled up to the new wooden station near the foot of South Main Street, the line was nothing more than a dead-end appendage to the mainline running through Inverness, Trilby, and Dade City to Tampa.

The fact that Inverness and Dade City were on the main route rankled Brooksville, particularly after 1887 when each of those towns broke away from Hernando to form a county of its own. Their reasons for doing so were the same: Brooksville was simply too difficult to reach. After all, it was fully twenty-one miles from Inverness to Brooksville and even more than that from Dade City—and who could be expected to go THAT far on county business?

In the 1880s Brooksville went on a self-promotional jag. One booklet boasted that it "is the most beautifully located town in all Florida. . . . Standing on the public square and gazing in any direction you please, a fine view is spread out before you. . . . Range after range of hills appear until they are lost in the distance. The air, fresh from the Mexican Gulf, tinctured with salt from the sea and redolent with the resinous exhalations from the pine forests over which it sweeps possesses a mystic power."

"Mystic power" or not, the town was really not much. Despite the railroad, it still suffered from isolation. With a population of barely 500, Brooksville was just a primitive, often violent, wilderness village. Fighting on the streets was common, and one of the first town ordinances decreed that all those who wanted to bite and eye-gouge had to commit such indulgences outside the town limits. Since there were no public restrooms and since the outhouses behind the saloons were overly pungent, one town ordinance warned of arrest for anyone "voiding his urine" on the streets. Another prohibited rambunctious citizens from racing their horses helter-skelter through the town.

There must have been a lot of grumbling about these restrictions, for what else was there to do when a person was through working at one of the sawmills except fight, race horses, or get drunk at one of the saloons that ringed the courthouse? But humans are blessed with inventive minds and eventually a new kind of entertainment was discovered. Nothing can really beat the thrill of a wooden building being consumed by a roaring fire. Especially at night. Thus was born the mysterious Brooksville firebug.

One of the first buildings to be torched was the courthouse, which, since the town had no fire department, went up in a beautiful blaze. Then a house here and a house there burned, although faulty fireplaces and overturned oil lamps competed with the firebug for credit in some of these events.

Brooksville officials took steps to combat the fires. Volunteer fire companies were formed and were trained to listen for the alarm, which was the pounding of a circular saw with a mallet. The saw, hung on a post in front of the new brick courthouse, could be heard all over town—if the air was quiet. But this did not prevent a fire of mysterious origin from destroying nearly nine blocks of town in 1899. The continuing scourge finally forced the town to purchase a couple of one-cylinder chemical engines in 1909. Then, three years later, Brooksville loosened the purse strings a little more and actually established an honest-to-goodness fire department. The presence of engines and real firemen apparently inspired the firebug to greater activity. In 1914 he set a blaze that ate up the entire block of Broad Street opposite the courthouse.

But the best was to come, at least in the firebug's smoky mind. The pride of Brooksville was the Varnada Hotel, a half-block-long, three-story structure with an entry distinguished by four tall Corinthian columns capped by a classical pediment. The Varnada made a magnificent fire, so magnificent, in fact, that Brooksville's mayor, believing the courthouse directly across Jefferson Street, as well as the entire business section, to be in danger, wired Tampa for help. Firemen there loaded equipment onto the next train and hurried to Brooksville. But, to the townsfolk's extreme embarrassment, Brooksville had no public water system to connect with Tampa's hoses. So the visiting firemen could only join the throng watching the show. The firebug, who was certainly in the crowd, must have been suitably amused.

The arsonist was never caught and to this day no one knows who he was. But he either reformed or died in 1925, for in that epic year the rash of unexplained fires ended.

Another historic event happened in 1925: Brooksville, with a population of nearly 2,000, decided it was large enough, as well as sufficiently prosperous, to replace its gas streetlamps with electric lights. Florida Power agreed to construct a power line down from its dam on the Withlacoochee near Dunnellon. On the evening of January 30th the following year, nearly the entire town assembled at the courthouse square to hear speeches by the mayor and company officials and to see little Charlie Price ceremoniously pull the switch that flooded the city with light. The crowd first gasped in wonder, then let out a great roar of approval. Brooksville had finally entered the twentieth century.

Unfortunately the twentieth century was more complicated than it first seemed, for within weeks the bust of 1926 hit the state. Brooksville was devastated and quickly learned that the electric bill was more than the strapped little town could pay. So, horror of horrors, the lights were ignominiously turned off. They remained off for many years, except for a few lonely bulbs around the courthouse—after all there was a matter of civic pride.

Today the lights are definitely on at Brooksville, and the entire town of 8,000 is bustling. The 1913 courthouse has been remodeled and is still used by county agencies. Attached is a new county building, sparkling with glass and boasting a spacious lobby and sleek architectural lines that are surprisingly harmonic with the older structure.

Although the courthouse square hums with activity, it has been kept almost as it was in the early twentieth century. Across Broad Street is the J. A. Jennings Building—the 1915 date on the facade indicating that it was constructed the year after the entire block had been burned by the firebug. It was handsome Jim Jennings, who, as an indefatigable town booster, was in charge of locating a site for the first public toilet. Did he find one? Public records are strangely silent on this vital fact.

Kitty-corner from Jennings' building is the former First National Bank, with its Greek columns making it look as strong and permanent as Plato's Acropolis. In the early years the bank's president was Raymond Robins, who, though confined to a wheelchair, was an effective official. Yet he could not keep the First National from going under during the Depression, costing many depositors, including Robins himself, much of their life savings. Down Main Street is a building with "McCrory" on the front. Once, a town knew it had arrived if the mighty McCrory chain built an establishment there. Now McCrory is in bankruptcy and virtually forgotten.

When this former bank closed during the Great Depression, it was a catastrophe of major proportions in Brooksville.

The Varnada Hotel was on Jefferson Street across from the courthouse. It was the pride of L. B. Varn, idealistic tycoon of the turpentine industry. Varn, with his brothers and kinsmen, was a power in local affairs and wished to crown his career with the fine hotel. Yet with all his power, he had to watch helplessly as his monument vanished in one horrible night at the whim of the demented firebug. Varn's pride is now a parking lot.

The old railroad depot, in the process of being renovated, can be reached by taking Main Street five blocks south from the courthouse square to Russell Street, then going east. The wide area around it was once filled with commercial buildings, including a large citrus packing house—that is until the firebug turned it into a pile of cinders and stewed oranges. More of the town's past is on display in the Heritage Museum at Jefferson and Saxon Streets. Admission is only $1 and the museum is open Tuesday through Saturday between 10 A.M. and 3:00 P.M.

Museum or not, the most symbolic monument in town is on the southwest corner of courthouse square where the statue of a young Confederate soldier stands guard. Old-time Floridians insist he was not defending slavery, for few Southerners actually owned slaves, but a way of life that differed markedly from that of the money-grubbing North. He fought to protect his wife and his children. He fought to preserve his right to live as his parents had taught him. He fought to defend the chivalric idealism and genteel spirit of the Old South. Yet today he stands a lonely vigil, his cause misunderstood even by the seed of his compatriots who hardly pause as they hustle to the courthouse on business.

A Confederate statue stands guard before Brooksville's county courthouse.

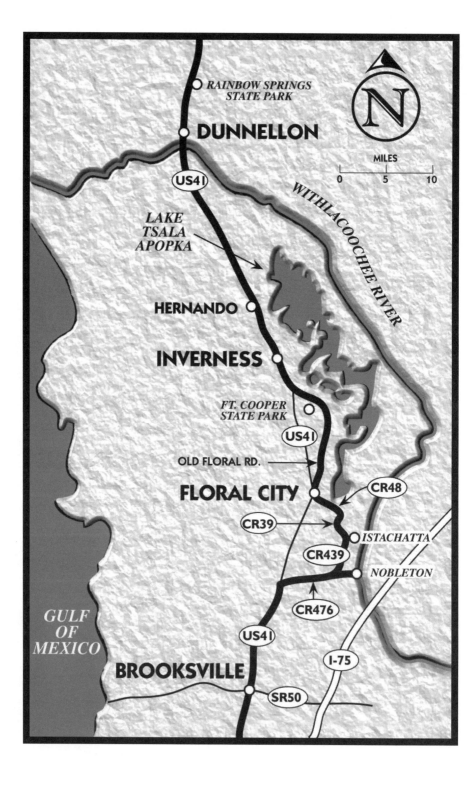

Rails, Trails, and Old Miners' Tales
Brooksville to Dunnellon • 47 Backroad Miles

The Song of the Road: Where the Byways Lead

The fifth exploration will take you through the small towns and down the quiet byways of the old miners' frontier, an era little known, even to most Floridians. The region is bounded by the Brooksville Ridge on the west and by historically almost impassable swamps and wetlands on the east. During times when the oceans were higher, the high dunes of the ridge separated the gulf from the wide lagoon that formed here. It is believed that the slowly evaporating water from this now-vanished lagoon affected the region's precipitated phosphate in a narrow north-south band some hundred miles long and five to thirty-five miles wide. When this rich lode of phosphate, an essential element in fertilizer, was discovered in the late nineteenth century, it fueled a turbulent mining era during which the men toted pistols and violence was commonplace.

The area also has a unique beauty not found in other portions of the state. You can enjoy it in a rented canoe from Nobleton. You can rent a bike at Inverness and peddle along the forested beauty of the Withlacoochee Trail, a paved path along the bed of a former railroad. The little road running north from Istachatta offers pleasurable vistas at every turn. The magnificent live oak archway at Floral City is an inspiration.

Inverness boasts one of Florida's most charming county courthouses as well as a quaint country inn famous for decades of hospitality. And Dunnellon offers a refreshing swim at beautiful Rainbow Springs State Park to counter-balance its rash of murders and lynchings during the phosphate era.

US 41: It's Not What It Used To Be

The exploration begins at Brooksville, from where you will head north on US 41. This is the route of old State 5, constructed after the creation of the state road department in 1915. When this

117

roadway was completed, it was a momentous event, for it linked Florida's money-starved inland communities with the Midwest's sunshine-starved states. Midstate Floridians felt they were at last part of America's mainstream when the highway received its federal number in 1935.

But US 41 is not what it was in its glory days. Largely superseded by Interstate 75, ten miles east, it has regressed almost into a secondary byway. Yet things may be about to change. Plans for the Suncoast Parkway from Tampa indicate that soon US 41 could be an important access road for the new communities that seem certain to sprout here when good transportation is provided. Although change is coming, for now you can still enjoy the relative tranquility of US 41 over the six miles to CR 476, where you should veer off through the country-side to the hamlet of Nobleton on the Withlacoochee River four miles east.

Canoe Outpost: Nobleton

Nobleton is known primarily as a canoe launching location. The river here is about twenty feet wide in the winter and spring, although during dry summers it sometimes it drops to a level where canoes have to be dragged over the shoals. But don't be misled by the Withlacoochee's small size. It was the big little river to the Indians, and in the early days wagons often required the flat boat at Monroe's Ferry to get across.

In 1925 Harry Nobles, caught in the euphoria of the great real estate boom, built ninety homes on pure speculation here. But the boom quickly became gloom when the good times vanished the following year, and today the village has survived mainly from its association with Nobleton Boat Rental, Inc., a long-time attraction open seven days a week from 8 A.M. to dusk. There are more than 150 canoes for rent. They hold up to four people and cost a minimum of $30, which gives it to you for the day, if you care to use it that long. For this price the operator will take you upstream either to Hog Island for an hour-and-a-half idyllic paddle-drift down the river, or to Silver Lake for a half-day journey—but, of course, you can dawdle much longer, since the boat is yours for the day. For quicker thrills thirty-minute airboat rides for $20 a person are offered. Whether canoeing or airboating, you are likely to see alligators, as well as a goodly assortment of birds and animals.

The Outpost wants to cover everything, so they also have rental

bikes at $12.50 for up to four hours The nearby Withlacoochee
Trail is ideal for cycling.

Since you are going to hear a lot of the Withlacoochee Trail on this exploration, this is the place to describe it. The trail occupies the old right-of-way of what was once a railroad mainline. Master builder Henry Plant built it in the early 1890s. After Plant's death, it became part of the Seaboard Coast Line and then CSX Transportation. In 1989 CSX sold the right-of-way to the state, which converted it into the Withlacoochee Trail. Creating the trail was a major enterprise that involved transforming forty-six miles of abandoned rail bed into an asphalt pathway twelve feet wide. The enterprise was eminently successful, and today the trail offers bikers and hikers unparalleled vistas of rivers, forests, and little towns. Its southern terminus is currently near Trilby, which you may have visited in an earlier exploration. The northern portion ends at this time just south of Dunnellon.

A Relic of Yesterday: Istachatta

From Nobleton take the road back west a mile to CR 439, which, although it is paved and pretty, is too narrow to receive unreserved accolades. In a mile it stumbles into Istachatta, an interesting Indian name the meaning of which no one seems to have the vaguest knowledge Once Istachatta boasted two sawmills, two gristmills, and one general store. The stagecoach stopped here three times a week. Now the tiny settlement consists merely of a post office, a scattering of modest homes, and the ruins of the general store. The Withlacoochee Trail runs past the store, and across the trail are the remains of a resort once known as Big Bass. With its marvelous location beside the Withlacoochee River, it is easy to imagine the boisterous good times that must have occurred here when the bass were jumping and the beer cans popping.

There is not much activity in Istachatta today. I talked to a postal worker who, between yawns, told me that he knows of only about fifty persons in the settlement, most of whom are quietly retired. There are not even village politicians with their petty squabbles to enliven things, for the hamlet is run by the county in far off (or so it seems) Brooksville.

But Istachatta has had its moments. When the railroad was active, there was a large depot near where the post office now stands. It was a story and a half high with a roof suggesting an Alpine chalet. When the trains arrived, the air was rent with whistles and whirling clouds of sooty cinders. Horses snorted as farmers in buckboards met the latest newcomers to this active phosphate mining town.

Now continue north on CR 439, which in a half mile becomes just plain 39 when it crosses into Citrus County. CR 39 is wide enough to qualify as a real road, yet narrow enough to be a backroad.

The Great Wall of Citrus County

The county line was once a point of great local importance. During the 1930s, when cattle fever ticks were discovered on some Hernando animals, Citrus threw up a bristling barbed wire barricade that extended through forests, across creeks, and over hills for twenty-five miles to the Gulf of Mexico—not exactly of Chinese proportions, but pretty good for a rural Florida county.

Now the countryside settles in. The narrow roadway is overlapped by trees, many supporting festoons of moss swaying like the beards of de Soto's grim soldiers, who may have marched over this very ground. But whether or not the Spaniards were here, the raucous railroaders certainly were, for CR 39 closely follows the old railroad that is now the Withlacoochee Trail.

The Pleasures of County Road 39

CR 39 wends here and there, and were it human, you'd say it was lost. The speed limit is 35, although you wouldn't need a sign to induce you go slowly around the many turns. Even utility poles have abandoned the confused roadway as it eases by farms and forests and a hint of Lake Bradley, named after one of the mining companies.

This was phosphate country in the early 1900s and the place where the old railroad (now the Withlacoochee Trail) crossed CR 39 was a tiny mining town called New Hope, an ironic name given the fact that the community has now largely disappeared except for the little Methodist church. Although the picturesque church building dates only from 1940, the congregation's roots go back a hundred years—making it the oldest in Citrus County. Beside the church is a cemetery that seems far too large for such a modest settlement. The earliest legible tombstones date to the 1880s. The markers of the loved ones who were buried before that are nothing but blank stones now.

Floral City: Echoes of a Turbulent Era

CR 39 finally emerges from its six miles of charming confusion at

CR 48, where you should turn west a mile to Floral City. The little town's main attraction is the memorable archway of live oaks and Spanish moss on Orange Avenue (CR 48). This archway is so memorable that you might want to park your car and enjoy a stroll amid the trees. Watch, too, for Aroostook Avenue, which runs three oak-shaded blocks to Lake Tsala Apopka, the town's original steamboat landing, long since fallen into disuse.

The oaks were planted by Jim Baker in 1884 as an attractive entry to the town he was planning. It was Baker who called the site Floral City, a pleasant sounding name designed to entice buyers for the plots he was trying to sell. He also must have had dreams of attracting an institution of higher learning, for he named one street (there were only a dozen or so) College Terrace. Then he opened a general store and waited for the crowds.

But few settlers came, for it was a hard day's journey from that font of civilization, Ocala. First one had to take a buggy to the head of Lake Tsala Apopka, then a steamer across the convoluted bays to the dock Baker had provided at the foot of Aroostook Avenue.

Oddly, within a few short years everything changed. It began with the discovery of phosphate deposits in nearby Dunnellon. Newspapers throughout the nation heralded the discovery, and by 1893 railroad magnate Henry Plant had constructed a line from Dunnellon south through Floral City and on to port facilities at Tampa.

Floral City is justly proud of its live oak archway.

Aided by the rail connection, a horde of phosphate prospectors descended on this part of Florida. They arrived with their usual high-tech tools: a spade to dig out phosphate rocks at the surface and a twenty-foot rod with a slot on the end to grab blindly for buried phosphate deposits. One of these prospectors was a man named Charles Pinkney Savary, or "Pink." Pink was better than most prospectors, for he also carried chemicals with which to test his specimens. Therefore it is not surprising that he soon became a respected chemist for such an important local company as Camp Phosphate. Ultimately Savary located one of Floral City's largest phosphate deposits at Snow's Hill.

Pink was important in another way: He recruited the first black workers to replace the indolent, native white crackers to whom fast movement was a sign of mental deficiency. Black men poured into Floral City, where they lived in a hurriedly erected shanty town west of the tracks. Local historians believe there were nearly 10,000 blacks around Floral City—to a population of barely 400 whites. But this figure seems excessive, since a thoughtful study by Professor Arch Fredric Blakey published by Harvard University put the total phosphate workers in ALL Florida during the boom at around 5,000.

Whatever the exact number, there were more than enough blacks to concern the white folks living comfortably east of the tracks. Town marshals carried pistols at all times, and were particularly alert on weekends when the black men had company scrip in their pockets

Floral City's founder, Jim Baker, lived in this twin-gabled home, the first in these parts to have electricity.

and often whiskey in their bellies. Some blacks also sported pistols, and when a black named Vogt shot Constable Sherrod Newsome, an enraged white mob lynched him at the livery stable. Such actions were not uncommon, and the most unusual aspect of this event was that the victim's name was even reported.

But getting back to Jim Baker. Not only was he now selling his plots for juicy profits, but he was working one of the earliest mines, which was a mile southwest of town in the Pine Lake area. To take advantage of the building spree, he opened a sawmill on the south side of Lake Bradley. With the greenbacks rolling in, Jim built himself the finest house in town, a large two-story structure that still stands at 8375 Orange Avenue. Stained glass windows, a wedding present to his bride, Celeste, highlighted the home. In 1912 the Baker home was one of the first buildings in the area to glow with electric lights when the Camp Phosphate Company ran a power line into town from its dam on the Withlacoochee River, though by that time the Bakers had sold out and the building had become the fancy Commercial Hotel.

During the heyday of rock phosphate mining Floral City's train depot, just north of Orange Avenue, was a hive of activity. Here husky crews unloaded the incoming freights, stacked high with fire logs for phosphate drying. Then the cars would be restocked with crushed phosphate to be transported either south to Tampa or north to Fernandina or Jacksonville for shipment to Europe.

Passenger trains were special, and almost everybody in town turned out when a high mine official and his stylishly dressed wife were due to arrive. Of course, there were many other passengers: the fresh young schoolmarm; Mamie back from shopping in wondrous Ocala; Johnny home from boarding school; Mr. Jones, the new grocer—you never knew whom the train carried. You just had to be there!

The engineers were often local celebrities. Certainly one of these was Tom Dunbar, whose locomotive, Sunny Jim, was known throughout the region. Dunbar was free with his steam whistle, which sang over the countryside like the voice of King Phosphate itself. Floral City was a favorite Dunbar stop. Here, Captain Tom, as he was known, would hop out of the cab and dash to the nearby Puckett home to exchange tall railroad tales for a goblet of fresh buttermilk. Once back on the platform, Tom would often dance a jig for the passengers while accompanying himself on a mouth harp. Then he'd leap into the cab, toot his ear-tingling whistle, pull the throttle, and be off. The debonair engineer left many a Floral City maiden's heart fluttering.

But by the early 1920s rock phosphate was dead, having been replaced by cheaper pebble phosphate from south Florida. Then the depot was closed and trains no longer stopped at Floral City—not even to deliver the mail. Instead incoming bags were simply thrown from the car; outgoing mail had to be placed in tough leather bags and hung on a crane that enabled speeding trains to snare them on a hook as they passed. Finally, in the 1960s rail service was permanently terminated. Soon thereafter the railroad tracks themselves were torn up, and ultimately the right-of-way was sold to the state, which converted the bed into the Withlacoochee Trail.

Today Floral City rests languidly in the Florida sun. It is perhaps best known for the Ferris citrus store beside US 41. Ferris has been a Floral City tradition since old Jim Ferris, whose uncle invented the Ferris wheel, arrived in 1925. Jim intended to convert nearby Duval Island into a millionaire's golfing paradise, but the depression bogeyed those dreams. However, Jim's son, "Doc," turned the aborted golf course into the first Ferris groves and in 1952 built a fruit stand on US 41. The stand could only be called minimal, for it consisted simply of a roof with no walls. But it laid the basis for the appealing building that now greets motorists just north of the Orange Avenue junction.

A Battle Challenge Not Accepted: Fort Cooper

From Floral City head north on Old Floral Road, which is a block and a half east of US 41. Back in the 1830s this was a military wagon path connecting Fort Brooke on Tampa Bay with Fort King, now Ocala. It edged between the Tsala Apopka marshes to the east and a dense matting of trees and underbrush known as the Big Hammock to the west. Astride it was Fort Cooper, now a state park.

This was the heartland of the vast territory allotted to the Seminoles by the Treaty of Moultrie Creek thirteen years earlier. When the American government repudiated the treaty and insisted the tribe submit to removal to the barren plains west of the Mississippi River, Seminole defiance flamed into action as their war leader, Osceola, murdered the Indian agent at Fort King, while the main body of Seminoles ambushed and virtually wiped out a column of more than a hundred soldiers led by Major Francis Dade.

After their victories, the Seminoles retired into an area called the Cove of the Withlacoochee, a virtually impregnable stronghold guarded on one side by the tangled wetlands of the Withlacoochee River and on the other by the trackless swamps of Lake Tsala Apopka.

The lake was an asset in another way, for fish abounded; indeed its very name meant "the trout-eating place."

From the cove more than a thousand painted warriors sallied north in late December 1835 to hit the force of territorial governor Richard Call as it crossed the Withlacoochee near the modern SR 200 bridge. Under a hurricane of bullets and arrows, the Americans, who had hoped to drive the Seminoles from the cove, were forced into a bloody retreat.

But the War Department realized the cove must be taken if the Seminoles were to be defeated. In January one of the nation's highest ranking generals, Winfield Scott, was given the job. Scott was certain that the army could easily overwhelm the ignorant savages, so he devised a complicated three-pronged attack on the cove.

Of course, everything that could go wrong did go wrong, and none of the divisions showed up at the appointed time—or even on the appointed day. Scott leading the largest prong of two thousand men (including a brass band) crossed the Withlacoochee with little opposition. From there he could have moved into the cove, but the incomprehensible lack of boats made this impossible, so he continued south on dry land and headed for the friendly confines of Fort Brooke on Tampa Bay. But just to prove to the Indians that he would be back, as well as to provide a resting place for his sick, Scott left a detachment of 380 Georgia volunteers to build an outpost on the outskirts of the cove.

As the main army marched off down what would become the Old Floral City Road, the Georgians must have felt great apprehension. There were so few of them, and the Seminoles were all around. The Georgian in charge had the imposing name of Mark Anthony Cooper and, in the spirit of his Roman namesake, hurriedly began erecting a fine little stockade composed of upright pine logs with sharpened tips. The men worked feverishly, knowing that only when it was completed would they be even moderately safe.

By the time Fort Cooper was finished, Osceola himself had joined the Seminoles encamped across the small lake. The Indians dared the soldiers to come out and fight. They taunted them with words and by the exposure of their buttocks, then as now, the ultimate insult. The men wisely stayed behind their wooden walls. Yet, as the days passed, food became scarce and eventually they were down to barely two ounces of meat a day. Much longer and they would not have the strength to meet an Indian assault. But after sixteen tense days

General Scott and the main army returned from Fort Brooke with provisions, and the siege was broken.

Fort Cooper remained an important station on the Tampa-Ocala army trail until 1842, when the power of the Seminoles had been broken and the war had ended. As for Mark Anthony Cooper, he went on to a distinguished career as lawyer, banker, and ultimately as a United States congressman.

 Fort Cooper State Park (admission $2 per car) is beside a lake near the old Seminole camping ground. The fort was across the water and can be reached after a twenty-minute walk down a well-traveled path through the pines and lush undergrowth. A portion of the way is along the actual military road once patrolled by angry Seminole braves. The popular park offers a total of five miles of self-guided nature trails in addition to a beach and changing rooms for swimmers. There are also paddle boats and canoes which rent for $3 per hour.

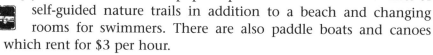

From Fort Cooper Park head north once more. When you come to Lakeview Drive in a mile or so, go a half block west, crossing the Withlacoochee Trail, to US 41. You are now on the outskirts of Inverness. This area was occupied in the 1920s by the huge sawmill and lumberyard owned by Jim Hanbury. Smoke from the mill's chimneys could be seen for many miles. Large stacks of lumber extended over several acres. The mill even had its own wood-fired locomotives constantly puffing around the yards as they moved the wood to the docks. Here they would be loaded onto the long freight trains that would tote them north to help build the nation's towns and cities.

Hanbury also threw railroad spurs into the pine lands to the west. These lines existed only until the once-magnificent trees were nothing but stumps. Then the rails would be relayed to other virgin forests that would quickly meet the same fate. Conservationists will be happy to learn that much of this land is now part of the Withlacoochee State Forest and reverting to trees once more. They may also be happy to learn that in 1925 the great Hanbury mill exploded in a colossal pyramid of flame, thereby providing Citrus County with its all-time most spectacular fire.

An Old-Time County Seat: Inverness

 Follow US 41 to Inverness, whose activity disguises the fact that the town's population is barely 7,000. Originally the federal highway funneled all traffic directly down Main Street but astute town planners have blocked off the street and rerouted US 41 into a crescent-shaped bypass. Thus downtown Inverness, although it is a county seat, has a far more tranquil atmosphere than its counterpart, Brooksville, twenty-one miles south. The feeling between Inverness and Brooksville has, historically speaking, not been the most cordial. Therein lies a tale.

No one took Inverness into consideration in 1843 when the area was included in Brooksville's Hernando County. As a matter of fact no one at all thought of Inverness, for the town would not exist until a quarter century later when "Uncle Alf" Tompkins and his wife, Fannie, shooed away the bears and other animals to start a tiny community that they called Tompkinsville. The closest post office was in Brooksville, but what did that matter, they received no mail anyhow.

Uncle Alf, who had to give away lots in order to attract settlers, ultimately became discouraged and sold out to a bunch of Jacksonville speculators. So the story goes, they considered the longings of a homesick Scot and changed the name to Inverness, which meant "at the foot of the ness," referring to Loch Ness, famous even today for its elusive "monster." The body of water in this instance referred to Lake Tsala Apopka, which, unfortunately for modern publicists, has no such watery beast.

By 1887 many persons in Inverness and the northern portion of Hernando County had become discontented making the two-day round trip over the slow sand roads to do county business in Brooksville. So they began agitating to be split off into a county of

The county courthouse in Inverness dominates Main Street.

their own. Brooksville resisted, for the town not only enjoyed being a place of importance but its merchants relished the visitors' trade. And, as for the politicians in Tallahassee, the state capital, they were not interested in dividing the proposed Citrus County from Hernando—that is, not until some local politicians indicated that the county seat would be the town of Mannfield, thereby insuring the aid of powerful State Senator Austin Mann, who had financial holdings in the area.

When Citrus County joined Pasco County in splitting off from Hernando, Brooksville's domain plummeted and the town became almost dead. Hence, for many years resentment toward Inverness burned.

Yet the saga did not end here. Inverness had still not secured the county seat, for Senator Mann and his associates were determined to keep the prize in Mannfield. Although Mannfield was centrally located, it lacked rail connections. So in 1891, with the railroad about to enter Inverness, the issue was submitted to the people of Citrus County and the vote was in favor of the move to Inverness. The Mann faction, determined to have an injunction issued to prevent the change, sent their lawyer hurrying off to the judge's home in Tampa. The injunction was signed but before the lawyer could return, a group from Inverness snuck into Mannfield and, under the cover of darkness, hurriedly loaded all the county documents into their wagons and rode off. When the lawyer showed up with his injunction the next day, there was no one to serve it to. The county seat had

The Crown Hotel has been an Inverness showplace for nearly a hundred years.

been legally moved and there was nothing Mann or anyone else could do. The senator angrily dumped his large holdings and stormed out of the county.

Now that Inverness was the seat of its own little county, it proudly constructed a cute little Victorian courthouse. But by 1912 the wooden building had become inadequate and was replaced by a far more pretentious structure of tan bricks accented by Greek pediments supported by Doric pillars. Gracing the roof was a clock tower from which melodic chimes denoted the passage of time. The most innovative element about the new courthouse was its location in the middle of the intersection of Main Street and Apopka Avenue, giving the building an impressive approach down either of Inverness' central streets. Town boosters were quick to point out that the courthouse of rival Brooksville made no such first impression. As a matter of fact, it is claimed that no other courthouse in the entire United States has been built in such an innovative manner.

As county business began to flow into town, stores were built to cater to visitors. The first was constructed by Francis Dampier, an enterprising fellow who soon realized that out-of-town visitors did not enjoy sleeping in their buggies. In 1907 he turned his store into the Orange Hotel, which became an instant success, and a few years later he sold it to buyers from New York. The New Yorkers amazed the townsfolk by raising Dampier's original building on stilts, then constructing a new and larger building beneath it as the hotel's lobby. Over the years wings were added on each side of the hotel and in 1979 a British investor remodeled it into the likeness of an old English country inn. After importing replicas of the queen's jewels, which he displayed prominently in the lobby, he changed the hotel's name to the Crown. Today this venerable hostelry, offering as fine facilities as ever, stands on Seminole Avenue off of Main Street a couple blocks west of the courthouse. Room rates run between $40 and $80 and suites between $95 and $120. For reservations call (352) 344-5555.

Main Street has assumed the appealing air of a rather quiet, early twentieth-century county seat. But this did not happen without a great deal of effort. Actually Main Street was part of US 41 and was going to be widened, causing the destruction of some vintage buildings along the street. That impelled a group of concerned citizens to descend on the state legislature at Tallahassee. Their clamor convinced the lawmakers to have the federal highway rerouted, at which time Main Street was blocked off by a low wall.

Today it is not automobiles and rumbling trucks but the old courthouse that is Main Street's focus, just as it has been for decades; its chimes still sing yesterday's melody. The county now occupies much larger quarters across the street, and the old courthouse is becoming a fine historical museum, with a curious twist. The historical association found that when they were researching the building's past as part of the effort (ultimately successful) to have it placed on the National Register of Historic Places, about the only event of more than local interest was the filming of the courtroom scene in Elvis Presley's movie *Follow That Dream* in 1961. Oddly, the movie also provided researchers with their only views of the courtroom's historical appearance.

Elvis Is Here!

The Elvis episode still occupies an important place in many local memories, for it was an exciting event in the little town. Although Elvis was only twenty-six when he and his hundred-person crew arrived, he was already famous, having attracted an enthusiastic audience of screaming young women by his provocative gyrations while singing such all-time classics as "Hound Dog" and "Shake, Rattle, and Roll." The slim, handsome, former truck driver both delighted and shocked a national audience on the popular Ed Sullivan Show in 1957 when he was shown only above the hips so as not to offend the delicate sensibilities of Sullivan's older family audience.

Inverness' Main Street looks a lot like it did when Elvis Presley was here to shoot Follow That Dream.

After the Sullivan heights, Elvis had shown that he also had a soft side when he recorded "Love Me Tender." From there he spent two years with the army mostly in Germany, returning to the U.S. and a "Welcome Home" TV special hosted by Frank Sinatra. He would became the darling of Hollywood, ultimately grinding out thirty-three cookie-cutter movies in little more than a decade. *Follow That Dream* was one of the earliest.

The world was still fresh and fun to Elvis when he came to Inverness—the weary years of drugs and alcohol were still ahead. He loved the folks of Inverness and often tossed a football with local kids on the courthouse grounds. He always found time to joke with the townspeople who served as stagehands and movie extras. At one point, upon learning that a certain extra had a crush on him, he made a special point of approaching her during a break in the shooting. "Is this the lady who wants to see me?" he asked with a smile. Then he gave her a friendly kiss on the cheek. "I nearly turned to water," Frances Castel admitted years later. A stagehand, John Bowman, who later became a newspaper columnist, recalled: "Like most people I've talked to over the years who knew him, I found Elvis to be a normal, somewhat quiet and caring person."

Possibly the most dramatic moment of the movie-making experience came late one morning when the director asked for absolute quiet. As the cameras rolled, not one of the observers dared speak. For ten minutes the hush continued. Then suddenly the siren of the fire station went off, as it did every noon. The crowd laughed uproariously. But the directors were furious and had to reshoot the entire scene.

Most of the downtown buildings predate the Presley appearance. Foremost among them is the three-story Masonic Lodge with 1910 inscribed over its entrance. For many years the building was used for community meetings and social events. Now it houses attorneys, county bureaus, and other businesses.

To see more of old Inverness drive north on Apopka Avenue. In a few blocks you'll come to the Withlacoochee Trail. Nearby is the 1910 railroad depot, now occupied by the *Tampa Tribune*. When the trains were running, several hundred persons often congregated here, some to board the trains, others to meet passengers, but most for no other reason than to watch the steamy monsters arrive and depart—it was the major source of nonalcoholic entertainment.

Of course, members of the incorrigible younger set could create their own excitement, and any handcar left unlocked overnight was sure to provide fun-loving youths, both male and female, with free moonlight excursions down the tracks to the secluded phosphate pits on the edge of town. But this was routine. Certainly the height of teenage bravado occurred one Halloween when a group of boys got the night watchman drunk, then fired up two locomotives and ran them far out on a logging spur. The next morning the muttering train crews looked to hell and high water before they found their engines.

Nearby is Suncoast Bicycles Plus where bikes can be rented at $7.50 for the first hour and $2.50 each additional hour. Tandems rent for $10 the first hour or $25 for the day. There are even kiddie trailers for rent. And for persons who desire greater exercise, in-line skates go for $10 the first hour and $2.50 each hour thereafter. It is open Monday through Saturday after 9 A.M.

For a scenic 6.5-mile side trip from Inverness, take SR 44 east, which skirts the forested solitude of Lake Tsala Apopka before reaching the Withlacoochee River. Near the bridge is Wild Bill's airboat, open Monday through Saturday 10 A.M. to 5 P.M. and Sunday 11 A.M. to 5 P.M. Wild Bill roars off on a thrilling forty-five-minute passage through forests and wetlands and past "everything that walks, crawls, slithers, swims, or flies," according to Wild Bill's wife and sidekick, Savage Susie. The cost is $11.95 ($7.95 for kids under twelve), and includes a visit to the wildlife exhibit. Across the road is the Fisherman's Restaurant, specializing in seafood and occupying a modernized 1950s inn. Windows in the rear open up on an outdoor dining area and on the Withlacoochee River beyond. The restaurant is open Tuesday through Thursday 11 A.M. to 9 P.M., Friday and Saturday 11 A.M. to 10 P.M., and Sunday noon to 8 P.M.

The Ted Williams Museum in Hernando has vivid exhibits on the life and times of this baseball legend of the 1940s and '50s.

A Legend's Farewell: The Ted Williams Museum

Now resume driving north on US 41. At the town of Hernando take CR 486 three miles west to the Ted Williams

Museum. For those who don't remember much, if anything, about Mr. Williams, he was one of the best sluggers baseball has ever produced, being the last man to hit over .400 for an entire season, in 1941. Teams playing against him had a special Williams shift, but to no avail. "I've never seen a better hitter than Ted Williams," said Joe DiMaggio, one of the many old-time baseball greats attending the building's dedication in 1994.

The museum contains seven hundred photographs as well as ample displays of baseball memorabilia. It is open Tuesday through Sunday 10 A.M. until 4 P.M. Admission is $5 for adults and $1 for kids.

The Forgotten Town of Hernando

The little town of Hernando was named for Hernando de Soto, who trod the original Indian path more than four hundred years ago. The settlement was in the heart of the phosphate area. From the surrounding open-pit mines, the rocks were mule-wagoned to the large Hernando mill, where they were crushed, washed and dried, and then loaded into railroad cars and transported to ocean freighters at Port Inglis on the gulf.

Hernando was a wild place at night. A special town official furiously rang a loud bell when the miners, several thousand strong, were tramping to town. It was a warning to women and children to clear the streets. But the mill is gone now and so are the miners' shanties, and today Hernando is a quiet, largely forgotten roadside hamlet on the shores of Lake Tsala Apopka.

Incidents on the Road to Dunnellon

As you continue north on US 41, you might be interested to learn that this was part of the route of "The Great Endurance Contest" promoted by the *Tampa Daily Times* in 1909. The contest's purpose was to determine whether horseless carriages could actually survive an attempt to travel from Tampa to Jacksonville and back. The first part of the route would be through Dade City, Trilby, and Brooksville to Inverness, where the motorists would rest after the first grueling day. The next morning it would be through Hernando and Dunnellon, then on to Gainesville and distant Jacksonville. Because most of the way was devoid of road markers, mileposts were pounded into the sand and a direction book was provided. The book seemed simple enough: "Turn right at Griffin's drug store along the RR" was the way through Dade City. And at Inverness you should be sure to "take the right-hand paved road"—the book not indicating what horrible fate would befall a careless motorist who happened to take the left turn.

Sixteen adventurous motorists volunteered for the rugged trek. They drove through sand above their hubcaps and through mud that clung like glue. They endured a constant aggravation of flat tires, motor trouble, and bumps enough to almost pop the fillings from their teeth. But there were some slightly less rugged segments such as the eighteen-mile portion from Inverness to Dunnellon, which was singled out as actually having a rock surface—although it is difficult to imagine that rocks would be much of an improvement over hard-packed sand. Surprisingly all the cars completed the circuit.

One purpose of the contest was to bring the horrible condition of the roads to public attention. It worked, as that same year the Florida legislature passed the Good Roads Act, whereby the state gave a bonus to each county for every mile of hard surfaced highway it built. The contest also illustrated the need for public restrooms. Newspapers took up this cause and one editor stormed: "In less than a year from now any town in Florida that is not provided with a restroom for women and children will be a back number, and ought to be wiped off the map." Apparently men were expected create their own facilities.

Although male opinion was solicitous toward women's restrooms, it did not carry over to ladies behind the wheel. In 1914 one newspaper ran a headline proclaiming that "Women Have No Business Driving Autos." The subtitle went on: "There Should Be a Stop Put to This Sort of Thing." And the accompanying article described the shocking story of a woman who drove herself and five other ladies from Dunnellon to Inverness. Certain male motorists watched with indignation: "It is reported that when she passed one of these parties she was driving at the rate of 35 miles per hour. Others said they had to get clear out and give them all the road to keep from getting hit." Despite such forewarnings, women to this day continue to drive autos, often even above 35 mph.

The Withlacoochee Trail parallels US 41, sometimes in sight, sometimes not. In 1892, when the trail was the bed of a railroad, the line's temporary southern terminus was Inverness. Since there was no place to turn around, the trains had to back down the tracks all the way from Dunnellon. This was a rather hazardous operation, for the cattle freely roaming the area took obvious pleasure loitering about the tracks. Often passengers were called into service as kinds of cow-cops, remembered Judge E. C. May:

I stood on the back platform and helped the brakeman yell at the cattle to keep off the tracks. We had a little air whistle which was attached to the train, and which blew when the brakeman twisted a little gadget, but it was not much louder than a boy's toy, and sometimes we had to pull the bell-cord and stop the train until we could run the cattle off the tracks.

The US 41 bridge over the Withlacoochee at Dunnellon is not particularly impressive, for we have grown accustomed to such structures. But it was not always thus. When the first bridge was built in 1891, replacing the erratic ferry, it was a big event. None other than John Dunn, who had founded Dunnellon four years earlier, was there. So too was about every dignitary who could afford clean clothes. After the windy speeches about the wonders of the modern age and the formal ribbon-cutting ceremony, a band played rousing marches while the crowd walked in slow but stately fashion over the fresh-cut wooden planks into Citrus County.

Florida's Deadwood: Dunnellon

Once the name of Dunnellon was uttered with awe throughout America, for it was famous as a center of blood and booty. First about the booty. That concerns one Albertus Vogt.

Vogt was a young aristocrat from Georgia. Although he was slightly pompous and more than a little vain, he was also tough, having been twice wounded fighting for the Confederacy. In addition, he had a business ability free from the burden of moral scruples. Vogt was the proprietor of a stagecoach line that ran from Ocala to Crystal River on the Gulf of Mexico. To enjoy his earnings, he bought ten acres along the Withlacoochee, where he and his wife, Mamie, built a home they called Rosebank.

In 1889 one of Vogt's farmhands excitedly came to him with some fossilized animal bones encased in a chalky material. Vogt had the chalky stuff chemically analyzed and learned it was among the purest phosphate ever discovered. So Vogt, in combination with John Dunn and a few others, secretly bought up thousands of acres of the richest phosphate land. Then they began mining. The phosphate, after it was cleaned and crushed, was transported to the Withlacoochee from where one of John Dunn's barges floated it down to Port Inglis for shipment as fertilizer to Europe.

As production soared, Vogt, Dunn, and the others became immensely wealthy. Vogt and Mamie entertained lavishly at Rosebank on the Inglis Road. Albertus drove horses of pure white whose harnesses glistened with gold and silver trim. He began dressing in a dandy style and soon became known as the "Duke of Dunnellon."

But Vogt was the exception. While he was reaping profits of $500 a day, his miners were trying to exist on a wage of barely five cents an hour. Most of his several thousand workers were black and lived in squalid shanty towns near the mines. Their only release from the cycle of sweat and strain were periodic carousels in Dunnellon. At these times fights and knifings were frequent.

Nearly every miner carried a weapon of some sort. There were sixteen saloons in town, most along Pennsylvania Avenue east of the railroad tracks. The largest was Big Johns Beer Gardens, where five bartenders kept the suds flowing, and a ragtime pianist attempted to pound out his version of music above the shouting, cursing, and general pandemonium. Every so often a pistol cracked. The din hardly diminished as a body was thrown into a wheelbarrow and carted off to the Withlacoochee River for the fat, waiting alligators.

Because the seven hundred white townsfolk living west of the tracks were greatly concerned that the miners would get out of control, they hired six-foot four-inch Bill Stephens as sheriff and gave him a force of twenty-five gunmen. Quick tempered Stephens, with his red leather boots and smoking pistol, was feared and hated by most black miners.

Tensions on both sides snapped during a cold spell in November 1895. It was toward midnight that two white shopkeepers in a nearby settlement were shot and killed by a pair of miners. Vigilante horsemen tracked the culprits down and hanged them on the spot. Then, when rumor had it that another man was involved in the murders, a third black was apprehended. Not quite sure of his guilt, the authorities sent him to Sheriff Stephens' jail for safekeeping.

News of the miner's incarceration spread quickly through Dunnellon's white neighborhood, and soon a mob gathered in front of the jail. When Stephens, with hardly a second thought, gave him up, the suspect was roughly hustled off to the bank of the Withlacoochee, where he was hanged. When the death dance was over, his body was stuffed into a burlap sack, weighted with rocks, and thrown into the river.

The blacks were enraged. The next evening several dozen angry miners entered town from the north on what is now US 41. What their intent was is not clear, but Stephens knew he was high on their list for retaliation. The sheriff and two henchmen waited tensely in a darkened building at the corner of US 41 and Pennsylvania. They were heavily armed and expert shots. When the blacks were close, Stephens and his men suddenly opened fire. The miners, taken off guard and not knowing from where the shooting was coming, fired back in all directions. A stray bullet hit Stephens in the ear. But otherwise the whites were protected by the building's walls. After a few moments the blacks fled, three of their number dead.

Upon hearing the gunfire, white men throughout town grabbed their weapons and indulged in an antiblack orgy of lawlessness seldom, if ever, exceeded in a small American town. The lynchings and shootings continued for several days. Bodies regularly floated down the Withlacoochee—no one will ever know how many. When the episode finally ended, "Dunnellon had lived through its darkest and most barbaric days," wrote town historian, J. Lester Dinkins.

Chief Stephens with his boys kept a tight grip on Dunnellon for seven more turbulent years. But gradually the town settled into a more orderly mode of life, and by 1902 the need for a roughneck like Stephens was over and he was unceremoniously voted out of office.

Rock phosphate from the mines between Dunnellon and Floral City dominated the world's fertilizer industry for more than a decade thereafter. But with the advent of World War I German submarines cut the shipping lanes to Europe, causing phosphate production to plummet. When the trade began again in the 1920s, the more economical pebble phosphate deposits east of Tampa displaced Dunnellon's rock variety. After a long, lingering death, the last phosphate mine closed in 1966.

Now Dunnellon, with a population of barely 2,000, is a quiet place. The town seems to be uncertain about what course to take in the future, at least pertaining to the downtown. Although the historical society is renovating the old railroad station, little else is currently being done to recall the mining era that made Dunnellon unique. The downtown cries for an injection of vigor, but the widening of US 41 back in the 1950s, which resulted in a skinny sidewalk and minimal parking, apparently detoured the central business section's revival.

For a while it appeared that Rainbow Springs, three miles north of town on US 41, would be the town's salvation. During the 1960s a joint venture including Holiday Inn turned it into a popular theme park with numerous rides. But in 1974, when the number of visitors plummeted with the completion of Interstate 75 and the overwhelming competition of Walt Disney World, the venture was abandoned.

Today Rainbow Springs is a relaxed state park that, although it contributes little to Dunnellon's economy, offers modern facilities for persons wishing to swim in the up-welling, crystalline, seventy-two degree water. The park also has forested nature trails, picnic areas, and changing rooms. Admission is $1 per person, with kids under six free.

Otherwise there is not a lot to see in modern Dunnellon. The Withlacoochee is almost ignored as an attraction. The best that can be had is a drive down Palmetto Way to the city beach, where there is a swimming area with a scenic overlook of the confluence of the Withlacoochee and the Blue Run.

There is a pleasing collection of old homes west of US 41, and at Pennsylvania and Cedar is the public library, where you can obtain a

Rainbow Springs State Park, just north of Dunnellon, is a popular local destination.

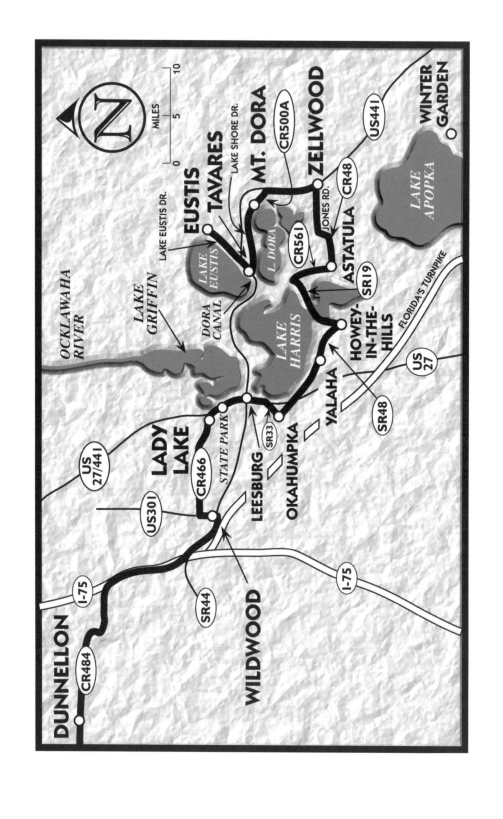

The World of Lakes and Country Towns
Dunnellon to Eustis • 91 Backroad Miles

The Song of the Road: Where the Byways Lead

The sixth exploration meanders among the towns of Florida's central valley. Most are built around lakes, and thus form the nucleus of Lake County. Each town has its own special attraction. There is Lady Lake, where The Villages, a huge retirement community, has sidewalk cafés that appeal to persons of all ages. Leesburg has a revitalized, yet still quaint downtown as well as proximity to Lake Griffin State Park, where visitors can rent canoes and glide past alligators. Howey-in-the-Hills boasts the Mission Hills Country Club with fine public golfing as well as restaurants and shops.

Then you'll drive through the Lake Apopka marsh, once the site of highly fertilized muck farms, now a touchy experiment in wetland restoration. North of Apopka are the three towns of what their boosters like to call the Golden Triangle. Mount Dora is the best known—for its antique and collectible shops have some of the state's finest assortment of bric-a-brac. Also well known is the Lakeside Inn, a modernized vintage hotel once echoing to the footfalls of the likes of Calvin Coolidge. Today it offers boating and a popular restaurant. Boats are also available in downtown Mount Dora, and trips on Lake Dora and the Dora Canal are one of Florida's more memorable experiences.

The Dora Canal can also be accessed from neighboring Tavares, seat of Lake County. Here you can visit the museum in the 1920s courthouse, although the building is still used for county business. From Tavares a beautiful lakeshore drive takes you to Eustis, the third member of the Golden Triangle. Here you can join the fishing congregation on the bank of Lake Eustis or stroll the boardwalk over the water to the historical museum or a lakefront restaurant.

The Great Canal That Isn't There

Eastward from Dunnellon CR 484 leads through the Western Valley, lowlands that would have been ideal for the Cross Florida Barge

Canal. The intended canal route paralleled the road from the Withlacoochee River for twenty miles to Interstate 75, then arched northward to connect with the Ocklawaha River at Silver Springs. In response to vociferous concerns about leakage into the precious Florida aquifer, almost at the surface here, President Nixon canceled the project in 1971. Now the route will be converted into the Cross Florida Greenway, a system of trails and recreational facilities being built slowly and piecemeal by the state and local authorities.

Waiting For the Future: Wildwood

When CR 484 reaches Interstate 75, take the expressway south eleven miles to SR 44, the Wildwood exit. From the tangle of gas stations, motels, and fast-food joints, it is difficult to picture the days when this was a dark and lonely forest. A telegraph crew, laying a line through here and asked by a clerk in the home office where they were, tapped out a message stating all they knew was it was a wild wood. The name stuck. But it is certainly wild no longer.

One reason for the activity is the exit's location at the juncture of Interstate 75 and Florida's Turnpike. Most travelers see only the clutter here. They do not realize that there is an actual town of Wildwood. To get there drive a mile southeast on SR 44, then a couple of miles due east on SR 44A, also known as Kilgore Street.

When old-timer W. C. Kilgore was carrying the mail in these parts, "the country was filled with wild game," he recalled, "bear, panthers, wild cats, wolves, deer, turkeys, and other small game—and of course I felt somewhat uneasy traveling through the country where so few people lived and there were so many ferocious wild animals." But he never went hungry. "All that you had to do was to go into the woods and kill your meal or go fishing and catch all the fish you wanted. Only a few people lived in Sumter County at that time, but they seemed to be contented and satisfied."

The isolated village that Kilgore knew suddenly burgeoned when the tracks of the Tropical Florida Railroad were laid from Ocala in 1882. Wildwood was the end of the line, so there was a turntable here where mules and brawny men pushed the engines around—much to the delight of half the kids in town. After the tracks were extended to the south, Wildwood became the most important stop between Jacksonville and Tampa. By the 1890s the surrounding farms were specializing in cabbages, and such was the richness of the soil that a single large farm could load up to thirty boxcars at harvest time. Just after the turn of the century, the mule dealers began to stock the bucking and belching contraptions called automobiles. A few decades later Wildwood's main street, the old Fort King military road, became part of the national highway system under the title of US 301. With the influx of travelers, Wildwood sprouted an impressive assortment of brick commercial buildings.

But the completion of Florida's Turnpike, and then Interstate 75 in the 1960s and 1970s, proved catastrophic to Wildwood's commercial section, which was largely replaced by the franchise businesses at the exit ramps outside city limits. The demise was nearly complete when CSX, successor to the old Tropical Florida Railroad, diminished its formerly extensive Wildwood facilities.

Today the old downtown is struggling. The railroad yards, once jammed with up to 95,000 boxcars a month, are quiet except when the nonstop CSX freights roar through town. US 301 has become so broad and busy that motorists hardly even slow down. Although a modern strip shopping area has been built near the city hall, the future commercial center is almost certainly going to move several miles south to where SR 44 is being widened as part of the plan to convert it into a four-lane arterial highway.

Nonetheless, the future looks favorable for Wildwood as a whole. Long-range plans foresee extending the turnpike from Wildwood west beyond Dunnellon to US 19, thereby offering a shortcut to Tallahassee and states to the west. Wildwood will be the center of one of the most extensive expressway webs in the state. "We're on the cusp of phenomenal growth," City Manager Jim Stevens told me. "Even though Wildwood has only four thousand people at the moment, we are going to be a major warehousing center, for you will be able to get anywhere in Florida from here." With this in mind the city has already erected a hundred-acre industrial park, with an additional three hundred acres on the planning board. It has also annexed a great deal of land to the south in preparation for a population boom.

Before leaving Wildwood, you must hear the Great Pyramid story, one of the most bizarre schemes in a state that has had more than its share of them. This off-the-wall proposal hatched by outsiders in the mid-1990s envisioned constructing a giant pyramid fifty stories high beside Interstate 75 a few miles north of town. Inside this structure would be facilities to store up to 1.3 million dead persons. The idea was that people traveling to Florida would find it easy to get off the expressway at Wildwood and pay quick respects to grandpa and grandma with hardly any interruption in their vacation. There would even be a glass-enclosed chapel at the pinnacle affording closer communication with the dear departed while enjoying a God's-eye view of the countryside. The kids would certainly enjoy it, and maybe even remember to visit mom and dad when their time came.

Most of Wildwood's elected officials endorsed the idea, noting that it would contribute $100 million to the town's economy. The only problem was that Sumter County had an ordinance against any building over two stories. When the Sumter commissioners gathered in Bushnell, the county seat, to vote on a zoning variance, the court-room was crammed with a largely hostile crowd of two hundred. After almost four hours of hot debate, the mausoleum was cremated.

The Shadow of Florida's Future? The Villages of Lady Lake

Now drive four miles north from Wildwood on US 301 to CR 466, where you should turn east. You'll find a pleasant road across pastures of the undulating Sumter upland. The vistas are long and grassy, highlighting solitary live oaks against the sky.

But the bucolic scenery suddenly ends where a development called The Villages will soon transform CR 466 into a suburban parkway. Although The Villages contains six thousand homes, plans call for it to triple in size within two decades. By then it will have spread west to US 301 and north into the next county. The development already has its own ZIP code.

To see The Villages up close, when you reach US 27/441 at Lady Lake, turn north a short distance to the entrance, which you can't miss, as they say, by the golf cart bridge over the highway. Once there you'll find yourself driving down a main street lined by build-ings designed to look as if they were constructed in the late nineteenth century—and, in case you have doubts, the dates 1872 and 1876 are inscribed on two of the buildings' facades. One shop has a sign reading blacksmith and an other calls itself the Citrus Exchange. The church resembles a Spanish mission. There is an old-style town square, where arts-and-crafts shows and other events make regular appear-ances. If you try hard, you can almost make the present vanish— except for the omnipresence of the golf carts that the residents use in place of cars. This is a fantasy world, and why not, for much of the planning was done by an experienced team from Universal Studios. To see more you can take one of the forty-five-minute tours that leave regularly seven days a week.

The Villages of Lady Lake is a family-owned company that seeks to offer its home-buyers a "return to a simpler, more relaxed and more gracious way of life," according to one of the company's brochures. Begun by Harold S. Schwartz in the 1970s as a humble trailer park, The Villages is now a community of around 18,000 persons, most fifty-five and over, who are enjoying retirement in homes that range from $56,000 to $185,000. It is oriented around golfing, and has 108 fairways—enough to weary any enthusiast. Sales literature promises "the unequaled convenience of life in a self-contained golf cart community . . . where stores, restaurants, shops, professional services and your friendly neighbors are all just a leisurely, safe and quiet golf cart ride away."

Is this where we're going? Will the day come when Florida's precious countryside is one vast, artificial park of homes and shopping centers trying to recreate a past that is gone forever? Where putting greens have replaced pastures. Where the roads bear cute, manufactured names like Happy Hammock and Dreamy Dell. Where a long vista is anything more than five homes. Where an oak is considered tall if it is higher than you can reach. Where the wild animals are earthworms and a spaniel who missed dinner.

This is not to put down The Villages. The development is well done. It's just a question of how many Florida can hold.

After you bid a moderately fond farewell to The Villages, turn back south on US 27/441 and go through the town of Lady Lake. For all the activity at The Villages, it's difficult to realize that the town's unusual name dates back to Seminole times when the Indians found an unknown white woman drowned in the small body of water just east of the modern town. For most of its existence Lady Lake was so minor that many cars hurrying along the federal highway didn't even slow down. For this reason during the 1960s the Lady Lake council appointed retiree Jim Dudley town marshal. There was no money for a patrol car, so Dudley was given a whistle and told to blow it at speeders. If they paid no attention, he was to hitch a ride from the nearest cooperative local citizen and chase the offender down. Although this was moderately effective, Dudley felt he really should have his own car. Eventually he went before the council to plead his case. So to help him with his duties, they gave him not an auto, but a larger whistle.

In four miles you'll reach Fruitland Park. During the last decades of the nineteenth century and first of the twentieth,

Fruitland was on the circuit of Estelle Swan, one of the very few woman doctors in the state at this time. Miss Estelle, as she was known, drove western Lake County's dusty backroads alone in a buggy drawn by Cadmus, her horse. In those days huge trees enclosed the paths with deep shadows. Sometimes she drove at night, when the trees growled in the wind and owls hooted in chilling cadences. Peril could fall upon her at any moment, and help was usually many miles distant. But she kept her buggy moving along the rutted byways almost until the day she died in 1926 at the age of sixty-eight.

You Say You'd Like To See Some Alligators?
The Lake Griffin State Recreation Area

When you pass CR 466A watch for the sign to the Lake Griffin State Recreation Area. There is an entry fee of $3.25 per car. The recreation area is in a live oak hammock beside an extensive marsh that is part of the Central Valley, a twenty-mile-wide basin in which Lakes Griffin, Harris, Dora, Eustis, and other smaller bodies of water have formed. The marsh supports a lush growth of sawgrass and water lilies and is as well home to an abundance of wading birds and water-loving mammals. Rental canoes at $3 per hour allow visitors to paddle along channels and out into Lake Griffin.

This canoe channel at the Lake Griffin State Recreation Area leads to Lake Griffin, which, as the sign warns, contains a few alligators.

Do I recommend canoeing? To answer that, I'll relate a conversation I had with a park ranger. Having seen a sign that read "Caution Alligators," I asked him to explain. "Oh, there are plenty of them along the canoe channel," he said. "One party just came back and encountered four." He shrugged apologetically. "They were only five or six feet long though. Lake Griffin has the highest concentration of alligators anywhere in Florida. But they don't bother you, if you don't bother them." I didn't ask him what would happen if you DID bother them.

A City Igniting: Leesburg

From the Lake Griffin State Recreation Area take US 441 a few miles south to Leesburg. When you come to Lee Street, turn right and cross the CSX tracks to Herndon. Then drive three blocks east to Sixth Street, location of the city hall, an impressive building with a proper Roman exterior. This is a good place to pause and consider the development of this city of 20,000.

When Evander Lee and his younger brother, Calvin, arrived at this wilderness site in 1857, they could see that the narrow strip of elevated land that separated Lake Griffin from Lake Harris was a natural crossroads and an excellent location for a store, which they promptly built. Their choice was good, and just eleven years later their namesake village of 150 mosquito-swatting persons became the temporary seat of Sumter County. When Lake County was lopped off of Sumter in 1888, Leesburg confidently expected to continue as the seat of government. However, the prize was blatantly stolen by Alexander St. Clair-Abrams, political boss of nearby Tavares, who won the election for his village by importing three hundred railroad workers from Sanford, plying them with beef and booze, and having them cast ballots already marked for Tavares. This began the rivalry between the two neighbors that continues to this day.

The biggest event in Leesburg's early development was the arrival of the Florida Southern Railroad in the mid-1880s. At this time a station was built near Sixth Street and the current CSX tracks. Shortly thereafter a mule-drawn trolley line was laid over Sixth's sandy base, across the low ridge, and on to the small harbor on Lake Harris—a total of a half mile. The mule was not the most cooperative beast and at least once bolted out of control and gave the passengers an unanticipated dunking in the lake. Nonetheless the Sixth Street trolley provided Leesburg with access to an economic hinterland that included not only Lake Harris, but plantations along the Palatlakaha River as far south as Clermont. This in turn gave birth to Leesburg's shopping district, which by the 1920s extended along Main Street from First to Ninth Streets. One of the most impressive buildings of that era was the tri-story Masonic Temple, where in the Palace Theater on the ground floor enthralled audiences could watch Gloria Swanson on the silent screen, her sultry actions somewhat crudely augmented by the clanging chords of an underpaid pianist in the orchestra pit.

During the Depression federal funds flowed into the city as the Works Progress Administration converted the marshy land around the old Lake Harris harbor into the beautiful Venetian Gardens. But not even the Venetian Gardens could prevent the drastic decline of downtown Leesburg, which began in the 1970s when Lake Square Mall opened along US 441 just beyond the city's eastern border. "Before the mall," City Planner Matt West told me, "downtown Leesburg was the center of the universe for this part of Lake County. We had a J. C. Penney, a Sears, the county's largest movie theater, two big grocery stores, several major car dealers, five banks—everything. After the mall, the downtown became dead and almost deserted." And so it remained for the better part of twenty years.

But in 1994, when the city joined Florida's Main Street program, business began to revive. The revival program, supervised by the

The Venetian Gardens in Leesburg emerged from marshes as a Depression-era project.

state, required that the city form an independent Main Street agency run by a full-time manager. This agency adopted the name of the Downtown Partnership and within a few years had an active membership of more than 250 businesses and private individuals. It is funded partly by the city, but mainly through membership dues, corporate sponsorship, and special fund-raising events, such as the Halloween festival when Main Street was closed off and thousands of children did trick-or-treating among the stores while live musicians played. When little feet got tired, there were ponies and a miniature train to give them free rides.

Under the partnership's capable leadership not only is the downtown renewing itself, but there is a new attitude within the Leesburg citizenry as well as within the city government itself. Prior to joining the Main Street program, Leesburg seemed satisfied to stagnate. Population projections forecast virtually no increase for at least ten years into the future. Now the city is busy annexing acreage to the east, where it is bumping heads with Tavares, and to the south, where it is reaching out along US 27. The city also intends to expand westward along SR 44, and it will soon compete with Wildwood for the new enterprises destined to sprout along that road as it is widened.

It is exciting to stroll down Main Street, which is a block south of the city hall. Although obviously much remains to be done, there is an air of expectation, for the fire of revitalization has started and everyone wonders where it will strike next. There is the old Sun Bank at 515 W. Main Street, transformed from a deserted eyesore into a showplace by LifeStream with the aid of the Downtown Partnership. The Leesburg Heritage Museum is close by at 111 Sixth Street a half block south of Main. It has organized its countless artifacts into displays, encouraged by the ubiquitous Downtown Partnership, whose offices are on the second floor. The museum is free and open weekdays from 9:30 A.M. to 4:00 P.M. Farther east on Main Street the remodeled Tropic Theater is operating once again. Other businesses are opening up and down the street. In addition, a showplace park has just been erected between Main Street and the city hall.

Now go three blocks south on Second Street across SR 44 to the Venetian Gardens. Once a marshy wasteland, it has been converted into a beautiful park with sparkling flowers, calm lagoons, and quiet streams. Pathways meander about the grounds and over arched pedestrian bridges. The eighty-acre park also has ample space for baseball fields, tennis courts, shuffleboard facilities, a swimming pool, and a public beach. And there is a launching area for boaters seeking the pleasures of Lake Harris.

Now head west from Leesburg on SR 44, which you can pick up at the Venetian Gardens. You will quickly reach US 27. Turning south on 27, you will pass a junky melange of commercial establishments that make one doubly appreciative of the downtown revival. Farther on, the road travels briefly along Lake Harris, where Singletary Park offers a scenic outlook.

The land near here was the scene of a little drama in the spring of 1999 when the Florida Game and Fresh Water Fish Commission released several whooping cranes selected especially for their strong genetic qualities to help repopulate the endangered population in this area. The birds spread their.great wings, rose effortlessly in the air, circled the officials on the ground, then, realizing they were free at last, soared into the blue. It was an exciting moment, not only for the birds, but also for the humans who had spent so much time preparing for this event.

Great flocks of whooping cranes once soared across America. But as civilization drained the marshes and plowed the prairies, their habitat was destroyed. By 1938 only a very few were left. In desperation federal officials began saving their eggs and raising the young in captivity. Then in 1993 they began releasing these cranes into the wild. Two-thirds of them died, but the program continued. It is still a chancy operation. The survival of the entire whooping crane species might depend on repopulation efforts such as these.

When US 27 reaches the CR 33 turnoff, take it a mile south to Okahumpka.

The Forgotten Saga of Virgil Hawkins: Okahumpka

To the former Indian inhabitants, Okeehumpkee referred to the "deep waters" of a spring near here. In the early twentieth century whites found that the location was ideal for growing melons, and Okahumpka became the one-time watermelon capital of the nation. At harvest time the train siding here was crowded with freight cars waiting to be loaded with juicy fruit just harvested by black workers. The melons are gone now, but many of the descendants of the workers remain, living on streets still called the North Quarters and South Quarters.

The center of the community is at the intersection of CR 33 and SR 48. On the northwest corner is a marker to Virgil Hawkins, which reads in part: "May his personal sacrifices, which desegregated Florida universities and provided legal assistance to those in need, inspire future generations." Although Hawkins is largely forgotten nowadays, he received considerable publicity in the late 1940s when he applied for admission to the University of Florida's law school. Upon being denied because he was black, he instituted legal challenges that were masterminded by NAACP lawyer Thurgood Marshall, who would one day become the first black justice on the U.S. Supreme Court. Hawkins' suit and petitions lasted ten years, with the Florida courts defying a federal order to admit him. Yet he persisted, even though his life and those of his family were threatened. Finally, he agreed to drop his charges in exchange for the state's desegregating its universities. Although Florida continued to deny Hawkins admission on the grounds that he was not qualified, Hawkins' fortitude and persistence helped establish the right of blacks to attend Florida universities.

Hawkins went on to secure a law degree in Boston, paying for his education by working as a janitor. But it wasn't until he was seventy years old that he was admitted to the Florida bar. Thereafter he opened a one-man law office in Leesburg at the corner of Orange and Second Streets. He died in 1988 and was buried in Okahumpka. By then he had been largely forgotten, his career overshadowed by that of Martin Luther King and by the highly dramatic events of the Civil Rights movement in general.

A Beautiful Bit of Bavaria: Yalaha

From Okahumpka take CR 48 east. Immediately after crossing US 27 you'll come to the bridge over the Palatlakaha Creek, the same river you visited on an earlier exploration near its source in the Clermont chain of lakes. It has squiggled through a maze of marshes, ponds, and puddles and will soon flow into Lake Harris. From there the water route leads through Lakes Eustis and Griffin to the Ocklawaha River, where it continues north until it merges with the St. Johns and ultimately reaches the Atlantic near Jacksonville. Before the advent of railroads, small steamboats chugged up and down the Palatlakaha, providing Clermont's citrus farmers with access to world markets. Long before that, ancient Timucuans dug clams along the creek, leaving a series of mounds at their village sites in which lance- and arrowheads have been found.

Continuing east, you'll traverse flat, scrubby land that apparently was once part of Lake Harris. When, in a few miles the land becomes

The Yalaha Country Bakery boasts German pastry as well as Bavarian architecture.

gently rolling, orange groves appear. Seminole Indians called this area Yalaha, which probably meant "yellow-orange" and might have referred to the corn spirit. Tribal festivals were held here annually at a sacred plot where the clay became brick-hard by the dancers' pounding feet.

Today Yalaha is gaining a reputation for its savory German bakery goods. Begun only several years ago by Gunter Herold, recently arrived from the Old Country, the bakery is a two-story, Bavarian-style building. The entry has been gaily hand-decorated with a colorful cornucopia motif. Alpine balconies enhance the second-floor exterior, and a red tile roof completes the building's quaint appearance.

Inside is a long counter, in back of which a glass wall permits visitors to see the bakers at work. The air is filled with the aroma of cooking bread, of which many various styles are available. Available too are flaky pastries—from Black Forest Cake to German Apple Pie. Luncheon sandwiches are also served either for takeout or to be eaten at one of the tiny tables inside or at one of the larger tables in the outdoor courtyard. The bakery is open Monday through Saturday between 8 A.M. and 5 P.M.

Aside from the bakery, there is not much else to see at Yalaha, except a country cemetery, which must have some importance, since it rates a road sign.

A Spanish Mission, Florida-Style: Howey-in-the-Hills

From Yalaha CR 48 turns southeast as it ascends the Coharie Terrace. The terrace originally formed as a narrow strip of wave-washed beach and dunes when the ocean level was more than two hundred feet above the current level and most of Florida was beneath the water. At one time the terrace ran down almost to Lake Okeechobee, but, as the ocean receded, erosion cut it into isolated mounds and ridges.

William Howey, developer and general character extraordinaire, was entranced by the hilly terrain and in 1916 began purchasing land here for $8 to $10 an acre. Howey was a born salesman, handsome, with piercing eyes, and an infectious air of confidence. After clearing the native trees, he made sparse plantings of citrus. Then he hyped the area as the "Florida Alps" in the gaudy brochures his sales force distributed nationwide. Soon he was his selling land for up to $1,200 an acre. With the profits he laid a golf course over the scenic hills and in 1925 incorporated the settlement as Howey-in-the-Hills, of which he became mayor, a position he held for the next ten years. At the height of activity in 1928 he attracted 10,000 visitors, many of whom recklessly purchased acreage in the speculative fever of the times. As Howey's fame spread throughout the state, he became the Republican candidate for governor. His platform included strong support for Prohibition—despite the fact that the fast-living politician and his party-loving wife, Grace, had a secret liquor vault in their mansion. Although he lost, the spunky developer ran again four years later, but was once more defeated—not surprising in the then-solidly Democratic state.

The Great Depression of the 1930s hit Howey hard. When he could not meet his financial commitments, creditors took his assets until he was left with the poorest 3,500 acres of the 60,000 he once held. After he died in 1938, his dream town also faded. By midcentury only 188 persons remained at Howey-in-the-Hills, and not a single new building had been constructed in the decades. Then Nick Beucher arrived on the scene.

Beucher had much of Howey's dash and daring. He worked at rodeos until he broke his leg, then, while recuperating, he and a buddy horsebacked nearly the entire length of Mexico just for the heck of it. In his early twenties Nick opened a cattle by-products brokerage house in Chicago. It became so successful that in 1964 he purchased Howey's old country club. Within a few years Beucher had not only converted the rundown course into one of Florida's premier golf links, but added a restaurant and overnight facilities housed in a new, spectacular Spanish-style building that he called the Mission Inn. The challenges and rewards of the Mission Inn were such that Beucher sold his brokerage business and devoted himself full-time to his Florida property.

The Mission Inn is still a work of art. In addition to having two championship golf courses, which are open to all who can pay the rather stiff fee, there is a public shopping arcade, several restaurants, and nearly two hundred deluxe overnight accommodations, all in an exotic setting of fountains, courtyards, and tile murals. The newest addition is Nickers Restaurant and Lounge, named for Nick Beucher. Located in a separate building north of the main group, it offers sandwiches and full dinners as well as an appealing view of verdant fairways and soft Coharie hills.

CR 48 ends at SR 19. A block south of the junction, at Citrus Avenue, is the old William Howey mansion. The handsome, two-story building occupies spacious grounds, and you can well imagine the gala parties that Billy and Grace gave in the ballroom that was large enough to accommodate a production by the entire New York City Opera Company. But the building is only a faded shell undergoing on-again-off-again restoration and currently not open to the public.

Heading northward out of town on SR 19, you will pass the road to the Mission Inn marina, located on Lake Harris. Here you can rent a pontoon boat that will hold up to ten persons. Smaller boats are available for bass fishing.

SR 19 passes over the narrows between Lake Harris and Little Lake Harris on a scenic, water-level bridge. This bridge replaced a rickety four-mile wooden structure that, when it was constructed during the Howey era, was the longest nonsuspension bridge in the world. Lake Harris, incidentally, was named for Ebeneezer Harris, who lived on the southern shore with his wife, Sarah, and their three sons in the 1850s. Ebeneezer was a frosty fundamentalist who allowed no one to use liquor or tobacco in his presence. Nor did he allow card playing or other frivolities. He was not above self-glorification, however, and insisted that the nearby body of water be called Lake Harris, which evidently sounded better to him than the beautiful Indian name, Astatula or "Lake of the Sunbeams." Just over the bridge is the Hickory Point Recreation Facility directly on the lake. It is a delightful spot for a picnic if you don't mind the small entry fee.

Continuing north, SR 19 passes through rolling land that was once orange groves; but now the old irrigation sprinklers are all that remain as the area waits for developers. And they will come, for the land offers home-buyers some of the most pleasing outlooks in Florida.

Trash to Treasures: Astatula

After an abrupt turn south at CR 561, you are off to the Astatula Landfill, better known as the trash dump. You may smirk, but the public does not always have the opportunity to view the immense quantities of waste material modern society generates. The entry is just past CR 448. Access is permitted between 7:30 A.M. and 5:00 P.M. every day except Sunday as part of Lake County's Trash to Treasure program. There are some treasures here, slightly used and soiled though they may be. The items that county officials believe might have fix-up value have been placed in a special area, and in it I found couches, lawn mowers, barbecue grills, bicycles, and a group of nice looking executive chairs whose only problem appears to be their slightly frayed arms. The items can be inspected throughout the month, but can be taken out on a first-come, first-served basis only on the second and fourth Saturdays. Don't get your hopes up, however, for these "treasures" are only for Lake County residents. County officials encourage the withdrawal, since it means they will not have to dispose of them in the 430-acre landfill, which will fill up soon enough anyway.

Driving farther into the landfill, you'll find a barren, surrealistic world pocked by large pits with linings of tough plastic sheets and hills of loose sand to one side. Nonburnable, nonrecyclable items are dumped in some of these holes and covered over with sand and more liners. Despite these precautions, a small amount of rainwater gets into the fill. But it percolates to the bottom, where it is collected in underground pipes and pumped to tanks where it is cleansed. Thus it is hoped the Florida aquifer is protected.

Farther back is a structure that resembles a large grandstand. Beside it is a huge pile of trash brought in by collection trucks from the county's 200,000 residents, who, if they conform to Florida's average, generate eight pounds of trash and garbage daily. This means that in one week Lake County must dispose of more than 30,000 pounds of debris! The cans, bottles, and plastics that make up around 30 percent of this total are sorted out, then compressed into large bales and sold to the highest bidder, who will truck them off for recycling and resale.

Next to the trash is a sizable heap of ashes, the remains of garbage that has been burned at the facility in Okahumpka. It contains many toxic chemicals, some of the worst from disposable diapers, and has been brought here for burial. The county employees I spoke to claimed that there is no odor at the landfill, but I regret to inform them that, if this is the case, there is a distinct aroma wafting from some unknown quarter very close by.

After visiting the Astatula Landfill, you may be asking yourself where all this is going. When Astatula fills up, another dump must be found, then another . . . and another. What do we do when all the land is occupied by trash dumps, suburban clutter, and cemeteries? Where can beauty dwell?

But condemnations are easy. Until we can find an acceptable way to make mankind vanish, we must find solutions to our environmental problems. That is not always easy, as you'll discover when you drive on into the Lake Apopka marsh.

The Lake Apopka Marsh: The Perils of Restoration

Continue south a few miles to the town of Astatula, blue-collar home to a few light industries. Here you'll pick up CR 48 heading east. This is the same CR 48 you left at Howey-in-the-Hills, for the two segments were once connected by the long wooden bridge across Little Lake Harris we mentioned earlier. You'll find the land is flat, since you are traveling across what was formerly marsh country extending to Lake Apopka, out of sight to the southeast. In three miles you come to the Apopka-Beauclair Canal, where a small dam regulates the water flowing northward from Lake Apopka to Lake Beauclair. Anglers often throw in lines from the shore and sometimes ride the eddies in rowboats. There is a parking lot beside the dam, so here is a good place to pause and hear the story of the Lake Apopka marsh.

Originally the marsh extended for seven miles along the upper lake margin. When the rains came, it became part of the lake itself, making Lake Apopka Florida's second largest body of fresh water (after Lake Okeechobee). But in 1940, during the wartime need for additional food sources, a long dike was constructed separating the marsh from the lake. Once the water was pumped from the marsh, the rich muck was converted into some of America's most productive vegetable farms. After the war, returning veterans bought many of the farms, and over the decades these fields provided Floridians with rich harvests—particularly of locally treasured Zellwood sweet corn.

A problem soon arose, however. Because the former marshland was as much as five feet below the surface of the lake, there was no drainage. The farmers then had to pump excess rainwater out of their fields and into the lake. This water was filled with fertilizer-derived pollutants, which gave rise to dense algae blooms that began turning the lake green at the same time that it killed off the fish that had once made Apopka Florida's bass capital. This pollution was helped considerably by a hurricane that killed most of the original plants when it ripped them from the lake bottom, by a severe chemical spill from a manufacturer, and by the city of Winter Garden using the lake as a convenient dump for its effluent sewage. In 1968 the problem widened when the Apopka-Beauclair Canal was dug, facilitating the flow of polluted water into Lake Beauclair, which, in turn, fed Lakes Dora, Eustis, and Griffin.

Environmentalists gradually made the public, as well as state legislators, aware of the problem, and in 1996 Florida passed the landmark Lake Apopka Restoration Act. This law allotted funds to buy out the farms and convert the area back into a pollution-filtering marsh. By 1998 $91 million had been spent and the former farm lands came into the state's possession.

So the marsh restoration began. It looked easy on paper: pump lake water back into the old fields, let the regenerated marsh plants filter the gunk from the soil, then, in five to ten years, tear down the dikes and permit the lake reclaim the whole 14,000 acres.

But an in-depth study by the *Orlando Sentinel* found many experts who questioned the wisdom of creating a marsh that would itself be polluted, at least initially. It would threaten hundreds, if not thousands, of birds. And how would it be possible to keep alligators and other land animals from entering the marsh? A *Sentinel* editorial questioned whether the buyout was a "multimillion-dollar blunder" and suggested that the farmers should have remained, but forced to adopt

The Apopka-Beauclair Canal is narrow, but it allows Apopka's polluted water to taint Lakes Dora, Eustis, and Griffin, as well as the Ocklawaha River.

environmentally sound agricultural practices. These farmers could have helped pay for restoration of the lake the way the sugar growers were helping clean up the Everglades. Even earlier a geologist hired by the state's St. Johns Water Management District, in charge of the cleanup, warned officials not to buy the land, as it was too polluted. But they refused to listen. "This was a train that was not going to be derailed," one expert complained to a reporter.

With this background, continue east on CR 48 to CR 448A, then jog left to Jones Road, where you'll resume your eastward drive. If Jones Road is not open, continue north one mile to CR 448, then turn east. The land around you was once covered with fields of Zellwood corn, the sweetest corn in the world. Thirty thousand enthusiasts would come to the annual summer festival at the nearby town of Zellwood to consume 200,000 ears of luscious corn. When the last harvest was commencing in July 1998 a *Sentinel* reporter interviewed the farm manager. "I'll tell you," he lamented, "it's going to be sad. To us, this is the best farmland in the world. . . . This is our social structure. All our friends are here." He was also speaking for the 2,300 workers who lost their jobs.

The St. Johns River Water Management District opened the dikes and permitted Lake Apopka water to reflood the farmland. Then they closed the dikes, intending to let the water filter into the soil, carrying with it the multiyear accumulation of fertilizer residue. Birds returned in numbers so great that even the Audubon Society was surprised. The first stage was an unparalleled success.

But then birds began dying. First just a few, then more, and soon the numbers had reached nearly a thousand. Realizing that they were being poisoned by the fertilizer-drenched water, the district had no choice except to dry out the marsh by pumping the water back into Lake Apopka. This, of course, made the lake even more polluted than before.

The district was "devastated," commented a retired board chairman. Nearly a hundred million dollars had been spent and the result was that prime farm land had been converted into a wildlife death trap. Jones Road was closed to the public, for the district feared that even humans could be imperiled by the toxic acreage.

So what to do? As of this writing the restoration is on hold while the situation is studied. The results are being carefully watched throughout Florida, where other projects, such as the Everglades restoration, may be in question.

Crown of the Golden Triangle: Mount Dora

The town of Zellwood is at the corner of 441 and Jones Road. The annual corn festival continues to be held one weekend in May in a large pasture several miles east of town. Although the country bands and knickknack booths are still there, the luster is gone, for it's not the same without the banner Zellwood cobs.

Now head north on US 441. Quickly you'll ascend the low Mount Dora Ridge and in a few miles more reach CR 500A. Turn left here and drive into Mount Dora, a town of around 8,000. Since US 441 bypasses Mount Dora, you'd expect it to be a sleepy backwater. But it is one of central Florida's most active locales. And therein lies an interesting story.

Mount Dora traces its beginnings to a pioneer named Dora Ann Drawdy who provided food, and even did the laundry, for a group of surveyors tramping through the pines and wire grass. Out of gratitude the surveyors, in fresh clothes for the first time in weeks, named the nearby lake in her honor. Later the "mount" was added to emphasize the fact that some of the land was more than 180 feet above sea level, which passes for great height in Florida.

The town actually got its start when newcomer John P. Donnelly emerged from the lake, having swum across it after being ousted from his raft by some boisterous alligators. Donnelly was an energetic soul who laid out most of the streets, became mayor, and, in 1893, constructed the fanciest, as well as the most garish, house in these parts.

The citizens of Mount Dora have always felt there was something special about their little town. They have an attitude that might be called snobbery if they weren't so good-natured about it. The Chamber of Commerce calls Mount Dora "the kind of place you wish you had grown up in" and extols its "quiet gentility." *Money* magazine recently declared Mount Dora one of the top three retirement towns in the entire nation.

Almost from the beginning Mount Dora was regarded as different from other Florida settlements. Then, with the construction of the Lakeside Inn in 1883, the town also assumed the role of a showplace. Wealthy visitors from the North, charmed by the lake and the surrounding hills, brought with them a respect for culture. Before the turn of the century the town joined the Chautauqua circuit so eminent lecturers, musicians, and actors could bring intellectual stimulation to otherwise isolated towns across America. One of the most thrilling moments for Mount Dora was the arrival of William Jennings Bryan, the famous orator and politician, who gave a series of programs for as many as 1,500 in the grand assembly hall overlooking Lake Dora.

Lake Dora played an important role in making Mount Dora what it is today. In 1913 boating enthusiasts founded the Yacht Club, being the first such organization located on a lake, rather than the ocean, in Florida. When the annual regattas were held, all the businesses closed so the entire town could enjoy the event. These regattas were quite a distinction for a place that didn't even have a bank and the club treasurer had to store the cash at home in an old sock until he could find time to make the day-long round-trip train journey to Sanford, twenty-five miles east.

Other institutions started in the early twentieth century still flourish. The Woman's Club, the ladies' answer to the men's Yacht (and poker) Club, was founded in 1919. A few years later the Art League was formed. It was not only the first club of its type in Florida, but was largely responsible for the establishment of the annual art festival. This midwinter display by three hundred of the nation's best artists has not only attracted nationwide acclaim, but habitually draws a two-day total of more than 200,000 art lovers.

Mount Dora's downtown has attracted an impressive assortment of small businesses offering fine-crafted items, fashion apparel, flowers, jewelry, and unusual art objects, as well as such a bevy of antique shops that the Chamber of Commerce has crowned the city "the antiques capital of central Florida." This is just not idle boasting, for readers of the respected *Florida Living* magazine recently selected Mount Dora as having the best antique shopping in the whole state.

Visiting Mount Dora in the glitter of success, you can hardly imagine the downtown as it was a few decades ago after Mount Dorans made the fateful decision to have the state reroute US 441 around, rather than keeping it running through, the town. Within a few years all nonlocal traffic disappeared. Then as both a Wal-Mart and K-Mart sprouted along the new US 441, downtown shops began to close. Soon the business section was virtually dead.

But the Mount Dora spirit remained, and the town decided to make itself over as a "bit of New England." Many storefronts were remodeled and facades received mansard roofs. The effort attracted the notice of a prominent Hollywood producer, who chose the town for the filming of *Honky Tonk Freeway*, starring Beau Bridges and Jessica

Tandy. The plot revolved around a small town, bypassed by the freeway, that painted itself pink to attract attention. The proud Mount Dorans had to swallow hard as much of their downtown became hot pink, and, although the production company tried to remove the paint afterwards, some overlooked spots took many years to fade. Furthermore, the movie itself was not a blockbuster, and Mount Dora resubmerged into such doldrums that one merchant recalled, "You could lay on the street for two hours and, believe me, there would be no tire marks on you."

At last, in desperation, the town formed the Community Redevelopment Agency, whereby a tax base was established at current levels, then ninety-five percent of future tax increases could be used to improve what the state called a "tax increment district." During the next eight years a stunning $23 million in tax increment funds helped pay for the town's facelift.

Gradually Mount Dora reached what is called "the ignition point," for as the spruced-up, New England–style downtown attracted tourists, the tourists attracted more specialty shops—which attracted more tourists—who attracted more shops, and so forth. An essential point was that, because this was a home-grown event, the glitzy chain stores that cast the pall of sameness over malls did not intrude. "Luckily," one merchant commented, "nobody had enough money to screw it up." Furthermore, because the US 441 bypass kept trucks and

Mount Dora's downtown is a superb example of revival.

high-speed travelers out of the business district, Mount Dora was able to maintain its small-town image.

So today Mount Dora is yours to enjoy, provided you don't mind an overabundance of other onlookers. Start at the Chamber of Commerce, located in the old railroad station at Alexander and Third, where you'll find more informative leaflets than you'll be able to carry. Just be sure that one of them is the walking tour (with map) of downtown. Then start strolling.

The shop area is mainly along Donnelly Street and the side streets between Third and Sixth Avenues. One of the buildings you might want to watch for is the old Princess Theater at 130 West Fifth Avenue, where Mount Dorans attended silent movies in the 1920s and '30s. Although the building is now a gift-and-collectibles store, the Princess name is still emblazoned in blue and white mosaics across the second floor, just below the add-on mansard roof. The Royellou Museum features incidents in the town's past. It is in the old jail hidden down a picturesque alleyway behind Donnelly Street off of East Fifth Avenue. The museum is open at the whim of volunteers, but try it—maybe you'll have better luck that I did. The alleyway ends across from Donnelly Park, the heart of Mount Dora, where retirees are usually working hard at shuffleboard and bench-sitting. The original shuffleboards, so characteristic of the town's genteel heritage, were built when a club was founded in the 1920s. It is said that J. P. Donnelly would never have sold the land to the city for such a give-away price were it not for prodding by certain persistent gadflies of the Women's Club.

Across the street is the Donnelly mansion, a gleaming, whipped-cream monument that this energetic man built to himself. Unfortunately for visitors, the structure belongs to the Masons and is not open to the public.

The lakefront can be reached by walking two blocks west on Fourth Avenue. Here you'll find the Yacht Club, a surprisingly unimposing building that is for members only. The even less-imposing public dock is also here, from where a pontoon boat takes passengers for one-hour, $8-per-person cruises on Lake Dora as well as three-hour, $15-per-person excursions along the cypress-framed Dora Canal. (For more on the popular canal trip see Tavares.)

Now walk to the venerable Lakeside Inn, off of Third Avenue on Alexander Street. Here you can have a snack or a full-course meal in the Beauclaire Room, a cooling drink in Tremain's Lounge, or you can just sit and do nothing at all on the long verandah that looks out on Lake Dora. There is such an air of the 1920s about the old wooden building that it would not be surprising to see one of the Inn's most famous guests, frosty Calvin Coolidge, strut past—insisting his wife remain several paces behind out of respect for the presidency. Room rates and amenities range widely from $105 to $210. For reservations and more information call 1-800-556-5016.

If you want to see another side of Mount Dora, walk a few blocks east on Third Avenue to Tremain, then south a few more until it ends at the Palm Island boardwalk. This elevated walkway leads through as dense a tropical hammock as you'll find anywhere. Signs identify many of the exotic trees and plants, and there will probably be a private naturalist or two along the route happy to point out the birds.

To leave Mount Dora, drive west on Fifth Avenue, also called Old 441, which soon edges beside Lake Dora. The Chautauqua grounds were to your right—a marker in a little park beside Old 441 at Oakland Drive commemorates the meeting site. With the coming of World War I, interest in the Chautauqua faded, and during the 1920s, radio and the movies displaced it entirely.

At Oakland, cross over the tracks onto Lakeshore Drive, Florida's most pleasant four-and-three-tenths-mile ride. Lake Dora will be on your left, with private boat docks and short piers

Lakeshore Drive between Mount Dora and Tavares is a pleasure to travel.

jutting into the ruffled blue water. Tall pines shade the roadway. On the right will be upscale homes set on broad, grassy lawns.

As the road enters Tavares, homes on the left tend to obscure the lake. When Lakeshore meets the railroad, it splits, with the lane on one side of the tracks going north and the other going south. Tentative plans envision a vintage steam train running once more along this route, as it connects Mount Dora with Tavares and Eustis, the third member of what is called the Golden Triangle. Lakeshore becomes Main Street as it enters downtown Tavares.

The Scepter of the Golden Triangle: Tavares

Tavares, with a population of around 10,000, is the second of the three little towns that comprise what is locally hyped as the Golden Triangle. As you'll see when you reach Eustis, each is surprisingly distinct from the others. For example, Tavares' Main Street is quiet and inconsequential compared with bustling Mount Dora close by. Tavares has done little with its frontage on Lake Dora, mostly because of the horribly ugly Lake Region Packing Association plant. Tavares' principal asset lies in being the seat of Lake County.

Tavares was groomed to be the capital of something right from its founding in 1880 by Major Alexander St. Clair-Abrams. The major, an egotist of the first order, named it Tavares in honor of himself and his ancestors, whom he claimed to have been Portuguese noblemen. He was an ambitious, irascible, and unscrupulous man who had married wealth and was determined that the settlement he was laying out should not only be the seat of the new county he was about to form by grabbing pieces of Sumter and Orange Counties, but should replace Tallahassee as the capital of Florida itself.

St. Clair-Abrams was successful in creating his new county, which was named Lake after the numerous bodies of water that graced this part of the state. He also obtained the county seat for Tavares—although only after four heated elections that left nearby Leesburg fuming, as we have seen. Not only was he thwarted in establishing his town as the state capital, but, when a devastating fire burned down most of the buildings he had constructed and the big freeze of 1894–95 wiped out the citrus industry, St. Clair-Abrams himself stomped out of Tavares and resettled in Jacksonville, having lost a fortune on his venture.

But Tavares did not wither away; its role as county seat saved it. When the massive courthouse went up in the 1920s, Tavares assumed an almost imperial presence amid the rustic villages of Lake County. In those early days county judges and juries executed the laws without state interference, as when death by hanging was decreed for one John Revels, who murdered his wife and brother for doing him wrong when he was in the slammer for stealing hogs. Accordingly, a two-story gallows was erected on the courthouse grounds, and at the proper time a crowd gathered to see the noose put around Revels' neck. Then the trapdoor was jerked open and Revels dropped to his doom, his death agonies hidden from the frustrated onlookers by a wooden fence around the gallows' lower portion.

Over the years the once-impressive courthouse seemed to become dated. Thus an extensive lattice-work screen was installed over the facade. But this ill-conceived "modernization" has been removed, and the exterior cleaned and restored. The interior too has been renovated and is open to the public. It is a thrill to stand in the lobby and gaze up at the high-vaulted ceiling. The small, nicely done, two-room museum on the ground floor has historic photos as well as displays of arrowheads and other artifacts left by the forgotten tribes who once inhabited the area.

In 1976 a second courthouse was built beside the old one. The new building's odd, circular shape caused it to be nicknamed "the round-house." It was so out of whack with the old courthouse that it caused shudders in all but the most staid observers. Now both buildings have given way to a still newer, third courthouse a half block west on Main Street. The round-house has been demoted to the administration center.

Now drive west on Main Street to SR 19, where you should turn right. You will quickly reach US 441, where you should head

The old (left) and newer courthouses in Tavares make a stark contrast.

west. In less than a mile you will pass over the Dora Canal and reach a roadside park on the shore of Lake Eustis. The park has pavilions, picnic tables, and a marvelous view of Lake Eustis, which, along with Lakes Dora, Harris, and Griffin, are actually part of a single extensive depression bounded on the east by the Mount Dora Ridge and on the west by the Sumter Upland.

Continue on US 441 a very short distance to the bridge over the Dead River, linking Lake Eustis with Lake Harris to the south. The original crossing was via a railroad trestle connecting Leesburg with Tavares. The structure's completion was the occasion for a festive picnic on the riverbank.

Immediately over the bridge on the right is a road leading to Heritage Lake Tours, which conducts narrated one-hour boat rides along both the Dead River and the Dora Canal. Other such tours are offered by Captain Charlie, a salty old Coast Guard veteran of World War II. Captain Charlie charges $10 for a ninety-minute excursion. His boat pulls out at 10 A.M, 1 P.M., and 3 P.M. every day of the week.

If you like quiet waterways bordered by lofty cypress that shelter countless birds and provide the setting for numerous alligators, you must take the boat trip on the Dora Canal. The mile-long channel has been called Florida's most beautiful waterway—and with good

The Dora Canal has been called, with good reason, Florida's most beautiful waterway.

reason. It occupies the bed of a stream that St. Clair-Abrams' workers straightened out so steamboats from Tavares could reach Lake Eustis, and, from there, Jacksonville via the Ocklawaha and St. Johns Rivers.

Although the railroad put an end to the canal's economic use, pleasure craft and sightseeing boats continued to glide along its placid waters. It became such an attraction that in 1938, when a logging company threatened to fell the precious cypress along its banks, local citizens heatedly expressed their concern and persuaded the company to deed a strip of land along the canal to the county for preservation. Because of them we are able to enjoy the priceless glimpses of Florida's natural beauties as they existed when the land was new and unspoiled.

The Third Piece of Gold: Eustis

From the Dora Canal bridge take US 441 east a mile and a half to Lake Eustis Drive—watch for the stoplight. Then turn left. This is another scenic lakeside road similar to the one between Mount Dora and Tavares, but not so built up. The route skirts some orange groves before hugging the lake where piers and boat docks protrude periodically into the water. Bald cypress hung with Spanish moss grace the road (which in Eustis is called Lakeshore Drive).

Seminoles often hunted along the lakeshore. Although the first whites to penetrate the region called the lake Sinufke for an Indian leader, after the Seminole War it was renamed for Colonel Abraham Eustis, a rough disciplinarian who was respected, nevertheless, for establishing the rigorous discipline necessary to combat the Indians. It is easy to understand why the Seminoles loved this area, and it is probably with regret that you'll reach the terminus of the short road at Bay Street in downtown Eustis.

Eustis, with a population of around 15,000, is the largest member of the Golden Triangle and is one of the fastest-growing cities in Lake County, despite lacking the tourist appeal of Mount Dora or the governmental facilities of Tavares. It does have a regional hospital, the Florida-Waterman, but this is being transferred to Tavares. It has the Lake County Fair Grounds, but this will soon be relocated to Groveland. It also has a beautiful waterfront, which, fortunately, cannot be removed. And Eustis is making the most of it.

The citizens of Eustis have long prized their lake. As early as 1912 they constructed a covered pier eighty yards into the water, at the end of which was a roofed pavilion where dances and concerts were held. These events were so popular that the townsfolk decided to convert their marshy lake front into a three-block-long public park. Everyone realized it would be a tremendous undertaking for the little town. First a seawall would have to be constructed into the lake as far out as the pavilion. Then a dredge would have to pump lake-bottom sand equivalent to 950 railroad cars into the enclosure. Still Eustis embarked on the program and, after six years, it was finally completed.

The new park at the foot of Magnolia Avenue was named for E. L. Ferran, whose department store at Bay Street and Magnolia had long been a community focal point. The park was such an instant attraction that a year later William McClelland built an ornate band shell there, which he named in commemoration of his wife, Alice. The shell originally faced the town, but the buildings bounced the sounds back, so the WPA eventually moved it to its current location, where it still treats audiences to musicals, plays, and social events. The shell has aged so gracefully that it has been placed on the National Register of Historic Places.

Ferran Park, also on the National Register of Historic Places, is active in many other ways. Most days men and women install their portable chairs along the seawall for a whirl at fishing and neighborliness. During summer it is abuzz with children frolicking in its pair of swimming pools. As the town began to cherish its heritage, a historical museum was made out of the charming 1910 Clifford-Taylor

Eustis' waterfront is a popular fishing spot.

House at 536 N. Bay Street. It is open Tuesday through Friday from 1 to 5 P.M. and Sunday 2 to 5 P.M. Admission is free.

Nonetheless Eustis wanted to do more. So the town voted a $6 million bond issue and in 1998 completed a 1,500-foot-long walkway over the water from Ferran Park north to the Clifford-Taylor House. Immediately property values along that portion of the lakefront soared, and even before the walkway was completed an old brick building, once a feed store, was converted into a handsome eatery called Sunsets, from its appealing western view of Lake Eustis.

But a waterfront alone does not make a downtown, and Eustis' central business section along Magnolia Avenue between Bay and Grove Streets is still trying to recover from its decline during the 1970s and '80s as large shopping centers sprouted along the US 441 bypass. Eustis has tried to fight the trend. In the mid-1990s it joined the state's Main Street program and did a major streetscape of Magnolia Avenue, including the installation of brick walkways and bush and tree plantings. And, most innovatively, it put a traffic divider on Magnolia, which allowed the conversion of one end of the two-block business section into traffic going east and the other end going the opposite direction. Then the age-old Ferran's Department Store, which had advertised itself as the store with the squeaky floors, converted itself into the trendy Moonlight Grill.

So Eustis, often called simply the "other city" of the Golden Triangle, is positioning itself for resurgence. Will it succeed? There is a tense wait for ignition.

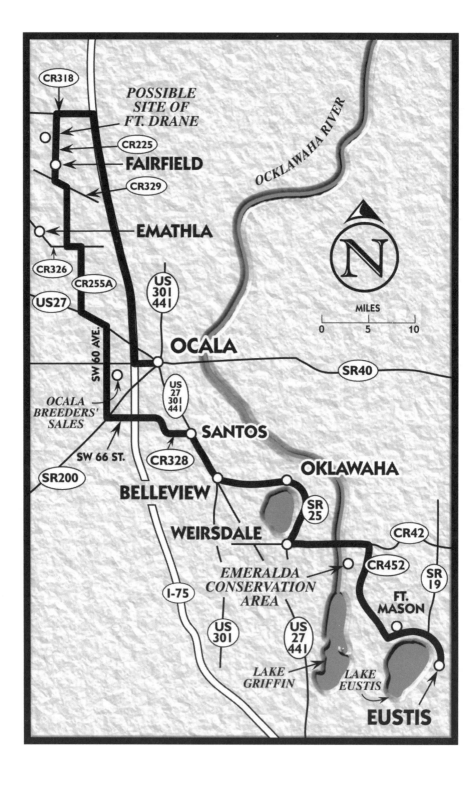

Loping Among the Thoroughbreds

Eustis to Ocala • 94 Backroad Miles

The Song of the Road: Where the Byways Lead
his exploration heads north from Eustis through the Emeralda Marsh, a bird and wildlife sanctuary reclaimed from former farm land. If you have fishing gear, you can try your luck in some of the backwaters. Next you'll pause at Lake Weir, where the notorious Ma Barker and her renegade son met their well-deserved, bullet-ridden ends in 1934.

Beyond Lake Weir the road ascends gently onto the Ocala Platform, whose limestone bedrock feeds the lush grass that nourishes some of the nation's premier thoroughbred race horses. You'll take byways along picturesque pastures where spirited horses sometimes prance almost up to the roadside. You can stop at the Ocala Breeders' Sales facility, site of world-famous horse auctions. Here you can lunch at the Champions Restaurant overlooking the workout area.

Entering Ocala, you'll find a proud town in the process of renovating its central business area. The new growth is exemplified by the restaurants blossoming around the old courthouse square.

The Steamboats Don't Stop Here Anymore: Fort Mason

Driving north on SR 19 from downtown Eustis, you'll quickly come to a fork where you should take CR 452 to Fort Mason. Although the fort was a minor outpost during the Second Seminole War, it later assumed some importance when it became a port during the steamboat era. Orange growers sent their fruit here, where it was loaded on shallow-draft steamers that wound their way from Lake Eustis along Haines Creek to Lake Griffin, then down the treacherous Ocklawaha to the St. Johns and Jacksonville. The trip was slow, arduous, and subject to tricky water levels, so it is not surprising that when the railroads began linking the region with Jacksonville, Fort Mason went into a deep decline.

Invasion of the Aliens: The Dreaded Medflies

North of Fort Mason the somewhat higher land of the Mount Dora Ridge provides suitable drainage for the growth of oranges. During the 1940s Eustis was known at the "Orange Capital of the World," a title that periodic freezes eliminated. Indeed, this is about as far north as citrus can grow with any certainty that the trees will last long enough to bear fruit. But even if the groves are not hit by freezes, they are subject to other catastrophes. One of these is the dreaded Mediterranean fruit fly, or medfly.

Because the entire citrus-growing portion of Florida is fearful of the medfly, traps are set at strategic areas to determine if any of the insects are about. In the spring of 1998, when some medflies were discovered in a trap a few miles northeast of Fort Mason, the news was treated almost as if alien invaders had landed. An instant quarantine was slapped on the thirty-five-square-mile citrus area around Fort Mason. No fruit was allowed out except that in sealed containers determined to be free from medfly adults, larvae, or eggs. Even homeowners with ornamental citrus trees were forbidden to give the fruit to friends outside the quarantine area. Meanwhile spraying units fanned out and, with military precision, repeatedly riddled the underside of every citrus tree with medfly poison. And once a week helicopters roared overhead as they coated fields and farms with a sticky solution of malathion and molasses. "The Agriculture Department has declared all-out war," trumpeted one newspaper. That was true, for it was absolutely imperative that the medflies not be allowed to spread into the rest of the state. Florida's entire multibillion dollar citrus industry could be at stake.

The operation continued for many weeks in order to kill all the medflies over at least two of their thirty-day life cycles. At the end of this period no more were found. So the danger passed—at least for the time being.

But there will always be some peril to the citrus trees, whether it be medflies, frosts, or root-borer weevils, competition from Brazil, or whatever. Yet perhaps the worst threat to the groves along CR 452 is from an entirely man-made source called urban sprawl.

While we are speaking about citrus, you may be interested to learn that, in order to produce fruit, each blossom has to be fertilized by pollen carried by honey bees. These bees are, in effect, itinerant workers, for they do not reside in the groves but are transported here by professional beekeepers. Each winter up to 200,000 hives are brought to Florida from as far away as California. While the season lasts the bees flit among blossoms, which have about the most delicious fragrance in creation. When the blooming season wanes, the bees are tucked away into their hives and transported off. Then, behold, when they next take to the air they are amid say, apple blossoms in Michigan. It's a constant paradise. Do any creatures on earth have better lives?

Problems in Paradise: The Emeralda Marsh

Now CR 452 leaves the orange belt and gently descends into the Central Valley that was once part of a wetland connecting Lake Griffin to the west with Lake Yale immediately east. Tradition has it that the area was originally called the Emerald Marsh, after the almost limitless expanse of grasses. Today it is known as the Emeralda Marsh and is part of a conservation area administered by the state.

You can take a pleasant little sojourn through the marsh by turning west onto Goose Prairie Road three miles past Fort Mason. Continue a few miles to Emerald Island Road, then follow it four miles through the marsh and two more miles back to CR 452. Although this is not a spectacular drive, on your way you will probably discover, particularly during the winter, large flocks of ring-necked ducks, as well as sandhill cranes and other water fowl. You may also see such rare birds as bald eagles, wood storks, limpkins, and snowy egrets. Fishing is also available, especially along the Yale-Griffin Canal, if you have gear and a license.

Idyllic as Emeralda may seem, there is a disquieting mystery here that concerns scientists. After the restoration of the marsh in 1993, wildlife managers stocked the ponds with bass and waited for accolades from anglers. But the bass did not reproduce, and when scientists examined them, they found that the males had abnormally high female hormones and females high male hormones. One explanation was that in reclaiming the outlying farmland, the fish were subjected to harmful fertilizers such as DDT. These poisons may also be drifting into Lake Griffin, where less than five percent of the alligators' eggs are hatching, and there have been unexplained deaths of turtles and snakes. Should this be the cause, the ironic results of the state's attempt to save the wetlands and the lake would prove to be their undoing.

An Eyesore With a Story: The Blesy Dairy Farm

Back on CR 452, continue north along the Mount Dora Ridge until CR 452 ends at CR 42. On the corner is Blesy's Dairy—but it's not the sort of dairy you're likely to have seen before. You'll find no pasture with sparkling grass and placid ponds. This is an agribusiness where 1,600 Holstein cows, crowded together on less than three hundred acres, have long since trampled the vegetation into grime. The cows live on imported feed consisting, at least partly, of leftover grain from the Budweiser brewery in Jacksonville as well as peels and pulp from nearby citrus plants. After the feed passes through the cow, the manure is collected, turned into compost, and sold to the Black Cow fertilizer company. When a cow's milk production wanes in three or four years, she meets her final destiny on McDonald's grills.

It is easy to criticize farms such as Blesy's, for they are eyesores that we wish were somewhere else. But it does no harm to learn a little more about the people who run it.

When Mike and Ellen Blesy bought the spread in 1984, it was just what Mike had dreamed of, having grown up on a dairy farm in New York state. He liked the Florida weather and wanted to be close to a good source of feed, which was the vast muck farms around the Emeralda Marsh. Mike does a good deal of the work himself, although he has the help of thirty-five employees. "When you're dealing with animals," he told me, "you have sickness and other health problems. They must be monitored and looked after all the time." Blesy breeds his own calves, and he personally fertilizes the cows by artificial insemination. He is present at the time of birth, when Caesarean operations are sometimes required.

Mike is proud of his farm and of his daily milk production, which runs about 12,000 gallons, much of which goes to schools. His two sons help him, and he hopes they will eventually take over.

So this is the Blesy farm. At least now it has a human side. But it's still an eyesore.

The Ocklawaha Crossing

After turning west on CR 42, in a few miles you make a gradual descent to the Ocklawaha River. Originally these lowlands supported live oaks of "ponderous size," noted an early traveler. But plantation owners had their slaves fell the oaks and plant sugar cane instead.

The land around the modern little bridge once belonged to Major Thomas Starke. Because the major had a ferry boat here, the crossing became known as Starke's Ferry, a name it still bears. Tom Starke was a staunch secessionist. Following the Civil War, he allowed his home to become the temporary hideout for former Confederate Secretary of War, John C. Breckinridge. It was a dangerous decision, since Starke could have been imprisoned for harboring a fugitive. But Breckinridge, in disguise, soon made his way to the coast and from there sailed in an open boat to safety in Cuba.

After the Civil War the Ocklawaha was frequented by steamboats. This may seem incredible, given today's usually low water level, but these were specially adapted, shallow-water vessels that could run on less than a foot of water. Some of the more boastful captains even claimed that they could sail on a heavy dew. But, fortunately, they were never called on to do so. The steamboats would proceed up Lake Griffin to Leesburg, and, when a canal was cut up Haines Creek, to Eustis.

Beyond the Ocklawaha SR 42 passes out of Lake County and enters the Ocala Platform. There are scenic vistas here and some of the last large-scale orange groves you'll see as you travel into a new climatic and geographic area.

Bullets in the Night: Lake Weir

At the small town of Weirsdale, turn north on SR 25, which was US 441 before modern 441 was built three miles west. SR 25 recalls the days when travel was more leisurely and the roadway did not cut through the land forms but curved gently around them. Just past Eastlake Weir, another tiny town, is the entry to Hampton Beach State Park. If you're in the mood for a swim, you'll enjoy a dunk in Lake Weir. There are also picnic tables. The lake is where many people from Ocala go for recreation. It was named after its discoverer, Nathaniel Ware, who may not have appreciated the altered spelling.

The area around Lake Weir was the site of many pre–Civil War plantations. Among them was that of Colonel Adam G. Summer, who raised prize cattle on the rich pastures just west of the lake around the town of Summerfield, named in his honor. Colonel Summer also owned a mansion on the western shore of the lake. Upon the conclusion of the Civil War, he too gave refuge to John C. Breckinridge, who would soon move on to the nearby Starke plantation. Breckinridge spent a pleasant week with Summer, during which they swam in the lake.

When the railroad came to Lake Weir in the 1880s, a post office was built at the village of Oklawaha, a mile or two beyond the park (the postmaster apparently dropping the "c" from the spelling for simplicity). With good transportation available at last, the beautiful lake with the sandy bottom began to attract vacationers, who stayed at one of the small hotels or in second homes along the water.

The Roaring Twenties brought an ambitious developer to Lake Weir. His plan was to construct a model city on the northeast lakeshore with a fashionable hotel, country club, and golf course. He also intended to dig a four-mile canal to the Ocklawaha River, which would give yachtsmen access to the lake country to the south as well as the scenic river expanse to the north. But the depression sunk these plans.

Bad times or not, the lake maintained its appeal, and in November 1934 who should select this attractive, yet isolated, place for a hideout than the notorious Ma Barker and her wild son, Freddie. Ma, Freddie, and the other boys of the Barker mob had enjoyed full gangster lives up to this time—this involved robbing banks and shooting people. But, when they kidnapped one of the Hamm Brewing family, this brought them to the attention of the FBI. So the gang had been on the lam ever since. To throw the feds off their trail, the gang had divvied up the ransom and split for the time being. Ma and Freddie decided to disappear into one of Florida's remotest vales, renting a secluded cottage on Lake Weir under the name of Blackburn.

At first the villagers in the hamlet of Oklawaha found the Barkers good neighbors, particularly the waitresses at the local bar, where Freddie left juicy tips. But the locals did not appreciate it when Freddie took his machine gun to the lakeshore and whanged away at the ducks. Soon they began suspecting that there was not something quite right about these newcomers. So they contacted law enforcement officers, who found that the Blackburns were dead ringers for Ma and Freddie Barker.

Before dawn on January 16, 1935, fourteen heavily armed federal agents quietly surrounded the Barkers' residence. When the chief called called out for the Barkers to come out with their hands up, Ma and Freddie answered with a round of bullets. With that the feds opened up with all they had—which was plenty. They riddled the house for forty-five minutes, then kept up intermittent fire for another five hours. When they cautiously entered the house, both Freddie and Ma were punctured corpses.

Curiously, although the home had more than 1,500 bullet holes, in addition to pounds of lead embedded in the walls, it was fixed up and sold. Today it is virtually indistinguishable from the many residences set back from SR 25 along Lake Weir after you pass the community building. Understandably, because the owners do not care to have sightseers poking around, they do not publicize the home's location. So be contended just to drive along and let your imagination create the gunfire.

West from Lake Weir, SR 25 has been straightened and has become uninteresting. Even the landscape has deteriorated into scrubby pines and auto repair shops.

The Town That REALLY Went Dry: Belleview

The Belleview area was once a favorite Seminole meeting place called Nine Mile Pond. During a lull in the Seminole War the Indians invited officers from Fort King to attend a feast at the campground. It was a friendly affair where a huge fire illuminated the bronze dancers far into the night. The Indians ardently desired to make peace if only the Americans would leave them alone. But hostilities soon resumed.

In 1982 Belleview had a disaster that brought the seriousness of pollution to the national fore. At this time there were no regulations about underground fuel storage tanks and it was discovered that petroleum had leaked into the wells from which 7,000 residents pumped their water. Emergency cleanup took eight months, during which time Belleview had no water except that which was trucked in from Ocala.

The incident caused Florida to examine the situation, at which time it was learned that the state had 120,000 underground tanks, many potential polluters. Thereupon the legislature decreed that all steel tanks, being rust-prone and subject to leaks, must be replaced by fiberglass or double-walled tanks. It was a program which, including the cleanup, will take several decades and cost a staggering sum estimated at $3 billion.

Now turn north on US 27/301/441. Although the highway follows the route of the old Fort King military road, there is little to remind you of the days when it was a lonely dirt path edging through a dense forest in the heart of Seminole country. In three miles the highway splits near the village of Santos as it goes around a forested area. This was originally designed to be a temporary bypass until the completion of a bridge over the never-completed Cross Florida Barge Canal.

Gateway to Nowhere

The demise of the canal is one of the more interesting, yet most neglected, sagas of Florida's past. To learn more about it turn into the wooded area at the northern end of the bypass and proceed to the parking area at the rear of the sheriff's headquarters. Then walk down the short path through the woods. Ahead you'll see two huge stanchions and a massive cross-beam that look like an oriental gateway to eternity. Instead, the structure was an abutment constructed in 1935 to carry US 301 over the canal, the overgrown excavation of which can be seen from the path.

A canal across Florida had its conception as far back as Spanish times, almost as soon as it was learned that Florida was a peninsula. John Quincy Adams and Andrew Jackson considered it, as did Calvin Coolidge and Herbert Hoover. By the time Franklin Roosevelt came to office in 1933 a total of twenty-eight surveys had been completed; one route was finally selected as the best. This route would take Atlantic ships from Jacksonville up the St. Johns River to the Ocklawaha. Then they would proceed up the Ocklawaha to near Ocala, where a thirty-mile cut across Marion County would take them to the Withlacoochee River near Dunnellon, from where they would reach the Gulf of Mexico. Not only would shippers thereby diminish their sailing time around Florida, but they would avoid the sometimes treacherous seas off the Florida Keys.

The bridge pylons of the Cross Florida Canal remain a dark and mysterious monument to what can never be.

Such a canal appealed to Roosevelt, who saw it also as a depression-fighting enterprise. He turned its construction over to the Works Progress Administration, which wasted no time in getting started, as its function was to furnish work for the unemployed. Soon teams of men were erecting a large supply depot and construction headquarters beside US 301 three miles south of downtown Ocala. Called Camp Roosevelt, it seemed to herald a new future for this depressed, landlocked area of the state.

Jacksonville and central Florida were jubilant. The

chairman of the Jacksonville Chamber of Commerce called the upcoming canal "one of the greatest events that could possibly happen to the people of this state," and promised that it would bring "happiness and prosperity to all." A church celebration proclaimed it a "holy enterprise." A politician nominated the canal as "the outstanding achievement of the century." In towns from Palatka to Ocala and Dunnellon talk was mainly about the canal and the great days that were beginning. People were so certain that economic boom times were about to commence that at one meeting of the Marion County commissioners, there were ten applications to open bars in and around Ocala.

Camp Roosevelt became jammed with workers and earth-moving equipment. At the same time that excavation of the canal started, forms were laid for the tall piers that would be needed to elevate US 301 over the waterway. The cement was poured and, when the forms were removed, a cross-beam was attached. Then work was started on a pair of second abutments. The canal seemed unstoppable.

But opposition was developing. Even within Florida many elements were opposed to the canal. Businessmen in Miami and Tampa complained that the canal would give Jacksonville shippers an advantage. Citrus farmers along the route worried that the ditch would drain water from their groves. Many towns were concerned that the canal would become brackish, despite assurances that locks at both ends would keep seawater out, and this saltiness would filter down to the precious Florida aquifer from which they drew their drinking water.

Nonetheless, President Roosevelt continued to support the canal, as did Florida's influential senator, Duncan Fletcher. When the canal needed more funding in the early part of 1936, Fletcher, with tears in his eyes, begged his fellow senators to approve it. But the appropriation was defeated in an extremely narrow vote. Thus work ground to a halt. Camp Roosevelt was deserted for the better part of a year until its buildings were utilized by the University of Florida for police courses.

Although construction had been stopped, the dream of a waterway across Florida still flamed in many hearts. During World War II it was promoted for national security, but the manpower was not available. Again in 1956 agitation resumed; this time all sorts of advantages to the state were stressed, including the assurance that the transportation of beer by ships would save thirsty consumers forty-two cents per case.

At last, in 1964 the advocates seemed to succeed when work was resumed. As did FDR before him, President Lyndon Johnson reignited the endeavor by setting off the initial blast of dynamite. This time construction was begun at both ends, rather than at Ocala near the center. On the Gulf of Mexico side, the 150-foot-wide canal was dug for ten miles to the Inglis Locks, as long as two football fields, completed in 1970. On the St. Johns River side, a dam was built at Rodman to create a navigable reservoir out of sixteen miles of the Ocklawaha River and nearby the Buckman Lock was constructed to raise barges and other boats to the reservoir's level.

But now a strong environmentalist movement materialized. Not only were concerns raised about the wildlife that had been destroyed by the reservoir, but even greater fears were expressed over the old question of saltwater seepage into the irreplaceable Florida aquifer. Furthermore, economists showed that the canal would not be utilized by most shippers. So in 1971 President Richard Nixon ordered construction stopped. After both Gerald Ford and Jimmy Carter refused to resume work, the project was at last pronounced officially dead. The federal government then gave the long, narrow strip of land designed for the canal to Florida, which in 1993 initiated long-range plans to turn it into a cross-state greenway. Currently the 110-mile greenway corridor has been divided into six regions, in each of which state agencies are currently working with local governments and private organizations to determine how best to utilize it. Plans have been developed, and in some places construction begun, on biking and hiking paths, boat launches, and facilities for swimming, fishing, and canoeing.

But the pylons remain as a gaunt gateway to nowhere except the past. It was a time not really so distant, for many persons alive today can recall Franklin Roosevelt and the bleak years of the Great Depression. We call it a simpler age, but, in reality, the question of how to recover from such an economic meltdown has never been solved outside of complete mobilization for a major war. This is, of course, a cure worse than the ill.

And so the gateway stands, mute and mysterious, a reminder of yesterday—and ominously, perhaps, as a warning of possible tomorrows.

Roaming Through Horse Country

From the canal site take CR 328 west. Almost immediately you'll be traveling through wide, green pastures with brown board fences. Most of these spreads are horse training and boarding farms.

The owners take great pride in their farms, and most have freshly painted buildings and fences. The horses, a majority of which are thoroughbreds, are given workouts in the mornings, so, if you are there then, you may see some being put through their paces. Often horses trot up to the roadside, for they are predominantly friendly creatures. The farms along here are some of Marion County's finest and the Country Club of Ocala, which you will pass, is one of the area's more exclusive facilities.

Why is the land around Ocala so favorable for raising horses? The explanation goes back sixty million years to when the western third of Marion County tilted upwards to form what geologists call the Ocala Platform. This upland, by bringing the underlying limestone to the surface, became the basis of a rich soil that contrasted sharply with the poor acidic soils forming in other parts of the state. By the recent past, the Ocala Platform was supporting a lush hardwood forest known to early pioneers as the Big Hammock. They began converting the land to pastures, for it was obvious its rich grass would support fine herds of cattle, as well as the handsome horses they imported from England. But the Civil War thwarted these ventures, and the region's development did not really start until the early 1970s.

Today the equine industry is thriving, and more than a thousand horse farms grace the land south and west of Ocala, which has become

Prosperous farms line the backroads south and west of Ocala.

known in equestrian circles as the Lexington of the South. Although Florida is not quite ready to dispute Kentucky's preeminence in racing, Florida's horses are winning a goodly share of national events. Furthermore, Marion County has recently attracted three of the world's most prestigious thoroughbred training centers, placing it on the same level in this respect as Lexington and Newmarket, England, and Normandy, France.

If you would like to visit one of the horse farms, phone the Ocala/Marion County Chamber of Commerce at 352-629-8051 to find out which are currently open to the public. Some will permit visitors to drive almost at will down the narrow lanes bordered by rail fences and out to the almost limitless emerald-green pastures where the horses frolic, when they are not trotting over to check out the humans. If you are there before nine, you can watch the horses being worked out around the half-mile tracks. Often you can roam through the stables and communicate with the thoroughbreds close up.

Many employees will tell you about their jobs. I spoke to one man who was leading a horse. "This is a teaser," he told me. "When we want to see if a mare is ready to mate, we bring the teaser past her. If her tail goes up, she's ready. A good mare will usually give birth four years out of five. But she's through by the time she's eighteen."

From another employee I learned what a pampered life a thor-

Some horse farms permit visitors to drive along their rustic byways.

oughbred lives. After he awakens, he enjoys a breakfast of the finest oats. Then he is lovingly groomed and stroked. Around eight a rider strolls him around the barn to limber up. This done, he is led to the track, where he jogs for a quarter mile, then gallops for a half mile. Next it is back to the barn where a groom bathes and walks him until he is cool. Now he lounges in his just-cleaned stall until his lunch of oats and sweetfeed is served. Around one he is turned out to pasture for relaxation after his hard day. When twilight falls, a groom gently bandages his legs for overnight protection.

You'll find it a pleasure to meander through horse country. So continue on CR 328 as it bends north following an ancient Spanish land grant. Osceola and the Seminoles had one of their chief settlements near here. Then the road turns west once more as it becomes SW 66th Street. But don't let the urban-sounding name concern you, for this is still horse country. Two miles after passing Interstate 75 the road reaches SR 200, where you should jog left then head north on SW 60th Avenue, which also is country despite what they call it.

In two miles you'll see the Ocala Regional Airport on your left. This is a big deal, for the facility is a federally sanctioned Foreign Trade Zone, which means that foreign goods can be brought in, stored, worked on, and exhibited, then exported without paying U.S. duties.

Across from the airport is the Ocala Breeders' Sales Company, a cooperative owned mainly by local horse people. This is an impressive operation, as you can see if you drive around the grounds—for which there is usually no admission charge. Most of the time thoroughbreds and their riders are everywhere, for the stalls can accommodate up to a thousand horses. There is also a 1,100-seat auditorium for shows and horse auctions as well as a mile-long racetrack with a grandstand for spectators.

The co-op's main purpose is to provide facilities for the breeders and raisers to show off their thoroughbreds to buyers from all over the world. The average two-year-old horse sells for around $80,000. But special horses command a half million dollars. Although buyers take a chance, the gains can be huge: The 1997 Horse of the Year retired with earnings of $1,727,000! The public can attend the auctions held at various times throughout the year. To get current dates phone 352-237-2154.

But there is more than cold cash involved, since a person who has raised a special horse often grows fond of him. For this reason, during the January through March racing season, the Teletheater, housed in the grandstand, shows simultaneous broadcasts of races at the premier parks around the country. Former owners place bets and cheer for their horses.

The company's Champions Restaurant, in the grandstand's second floor, affords an excellent view of the workout racetrack. It is open to the public every day except Tuesday from 11 A.M. to 4 P.M. Champions serves full dinners as well as sandwiches or soft drinks. On Saturdays during the winter a company official greets visitors between 9 and 11 A.M. with coffee, donuts, and a feed bag full of information. At other times you may browse the company store with its extensive line of saddles, bridals, blankets, and countless other equestrian accessories.

The Ocala Breeders' Sales is in the heart of horse farm country, as you will see as you continue driving north on 60th Avenue. The road ends in two miles at US 27, where you should turn west a mile to CR 225A. Then proceed north once more. You are now on or near the vanished military road used by troops in 1835–36 during the Second Seminole War. Three American armies marched down this once-lonely gash in the forest to do battle with Osceola's warriors on the banks of the Withlacoochee River. Two were defeated. The third never located the the main body of the wily Indians.

Ocala has many horse competitions.

Osceola was a complicated man: often warm and friendly, but deadly as an arrow when aroused. It was he who murdered fellow Seminole Charlie Emathla, who counseled his fellows to avoid war and accede to the American demand to resettle beyond the Mississippi River. Emathla's body was left to rot on the forested path that is now CR 326, which you come to three miles beyond US 27.

Yet few persons nowadays know Emathla's story, for all thoughts hereabouts are on horse farms. This is such prime land—rolling, fertile, and scenic—that it is swarming with real-tors. Prices for choice spreads run around $12,000 an acre, triple what they were just fifteen years ago. A farm of twenty-five acres with a four-bedroom home and an eight-stall horse barn will sell for around $600,000.

The For Sale signs thin out the farther you travel from US 27 and soon you'll be able to enjoy the bucolic countryside without their disconcerting babble.

CR 225A stops at CR 329, but you can pick up CR 225 (without the "A") a half mile west. Then, continuing north, you will quickly come to Fairfield, which consists mainly of a convenience store and a couple of churches that hardly interrupt the horsy land-scape. However, echoes of the Seminole War also persist, for Fort Drane formerly stood on a knoll a mile north of Fairfield.

During its brief existence Fort Drane was unquestionably the most important site in Florida. The fort owed its existence to Colonel Duncan Clinch, who had a sugar plantation nearby. Built under the direction of Captain Gustavus Drane, the fort consisted of a twelve-foot-high, rectangular palisade one hundred and fifty yards long and eighty yards wide with a square blockhouse on the east corner. It was hardly completed when the murder of Emathla caused frightened settlers to jam into it.

Soon the settlers were joined by soldiers, whose tents covered every available space within the walls. The officers used Clinch's two-story plantation house as their headquarters. On Christmas Eve, 1835, the army under Clinch's command marched south to do battle with Osceola but returned in defeat. Clinch's casualties were placed on blankets spread on the frigid earth, for, incredibly, the army had provided no cots—and little else to treat the sick and wounded, which eventually rose to two hundred. Then in February 1836, General Edmund Gaines arrived with eleven hundred men. Osceola defeated him too, and Gaines retreated to Fort Drane with more wounded.

Now it was the turn of General Winfield Scott, who marched into Fort Drane with two thousand men and took over from Gaines early in March. Scott brought all the pomp of his position, which included an entire military band. There were now more than three thousand soldiers at the fort, so many that most had to camp outside the walls. They built what amounted to a hut city, using wood and branches from the surrounding forest. "It was a beautiful sight from the fort," wrote a young medical assistant, "— the view of the camp fires at night."

After General Gaines and his dispirited men left, the number of troops was reduced. Clinch departed too, resigning from the army and retiring to another plantation he owned in Georgia. Then Scott moved out as part of the too-complicated, three-pronged attack against the Seminoles that we encountered when visiting Fort Cooper.

For troops remaining at Fort Drane life was not easy. The food turned rancid during the torrid summer and the mosquitoes became voracious. When disease broke out, the hospital tent became so full of groaning men that crude lean-to shelters had to be thrown up against the palisades. After the commanding officer himself took ill and died, the fort was evacuated. The last wagon had hardly disappeared, when Osceola and his jubilant warriors put the hated place to the torch. Yet, ironically, Fort Drane may have had one last card to play, for legend has it that here Osceola contracted the malaria that would contribute to his death eighteen months later.

CR 225 terminates at CR 318, represented on maps as the settlement of Irvine, but which in reality is just an antique shop. Interstate 75, upon which you'll reach Ocala, is due east. But if you're here Wednesday through Saturday after 5 P.M. or Sunday between 11 A.M. and 3 P.M. I'd suggest a one-mile jaunt west on CR 318 to the Ocala Jockey Club, one of the area's finest restaurants. It is on a 600-acre horse farm with spectacular views from its knoll-top perch. It's popular, so you should consider making advance reservations: 352-591-5966.

Ocala lies fourteen miles south on Interstate 75. Take the SR 40 exit into the center of town, where you'll find the old courthouse square and the town's trademark gazebo.

Ocala

Ocala occupies one of Florida's oldest historical sites, its first European visitor arriving in 1539. This was Hernando de Soto, who happened to be accompanied by six hundred fighting men and a pack of attack dogs. This crew had bullied its way up the ancient Indian trail that we know as US 301, attracted to the Ocali segment of the far-ranging Timucuan tribe by tales of a golden city akin to those de Soto had helped loot in South America. De Soto did find a town, large by Indian standards, of several hundred flimsy dwellings. But no gold. Nonetheless, since the inhabitants had fled, he made camp here for several weeks, long enough to consume all the maize and beans they had just harvested. Then he enslaved the few Indians he was able to catch and used them as unwilling porters as he headed north toward his ignoble demise three years later.

By the time the Americans arrived three hundred years later, the Ocali were gone, having succumbed to European diseases and devastating raids by the Creek tribe instigated by the English in Georgia. In their place was a branch of the Creeks known as Seminoles. The newcomers had not wanted to be here, but the Americans had won the First Seminole War in north Florida and, as a result, the Indians had been forced to relocate in central Florida. The Americans, for their part, agreed to erect a post there to furnish the Seminoles with supplies for a short time while they resettled. This supply post, named Fort King, was constructed in 1827 along an ancient Indian path on what would become the eastern outskirts of Ocala.

For a decade and a half, Fort King was one of the most important places in the Florida Territory, as the military presence helped keep the lid on the discontented Seminoles. It was on an elevation overlooking the forest, surrounded by a wall of twenty-foot-high timbers with a blockhouse at each of the four corners. "In the center," noted one officer, "stands a two story building occupied by the soldiers, on top of which is a cupola in which is posted a sentinel who announces the approach of a man by ringing a huge cow-bell. . . . There are about sixty men here."

Imposing fort or not, when the Indians learned that the Americans planned to violate the treaty and ship them off to reservations in the west, they decided to revolt. On December 28, 1835, their leader, the fiery Osceola, and some warriors concealed themselves behind the thick growth of trees that encircled the fort. When the commander and a fellow officer emerged for their evening stroll, the Seminoles caught them in a fusillade of gunfire that left the commander dead. Then Osceola scalped him and disappeared into the gloom. At almost the same moment other Seminoles were massacring a column of 108 soldiers whom they had ambushed at what has become the Dade Battlefield State Historic Site, which we visited at Bushnell. Thus began the Second Seminole War.

Fort King, as a center of army operations, was the nexus of a half-dozen military roads radiating into Seminole lands. When, after seven long years, the Indians were defeated and most of them removed to the West, these roads rapidly evolved into the main pioneer routes to the fertile lands that became Marion County.

One of the first settlers in what is now the central part of Ocala was Alexander McLeod, whose son related how his father had reached the site in 1841, having driven his cattle and hogs for miles through the pines and live oaks. He made camp on the lonely knoll where the courthouse was to stand. There he found a lone Indian dying of wounds he suffered from a fight with one of the area's many panthers. McLeod nursed the Indian as best he could, and, when he died, buried him beside the old oak tree that stood at the southeast corner of courthouse square.

McLeod had stumbled on a location more choice that he realized and, although in 1844 Fort King became the seat of newly formed Marion County (named for General Francis Marion of Revolutionary War fame), almost immediately plans were made for a permanent county seat where downtown Ocala now stands. David Bruton headed the surveying team, and for thirty days he and his chain men tramped through the woods slapping at mosquitoes while keeping wary eyes for panthers. Bruton received a dollar a day; his chain men received far less. Together they laid out the downtown streets as we find them today and assigned a central lot to be the county square. Within a few years a modest two-story courthouse was built in the square, along with a tiny log jail beside it on the northwest corner.

The parcels of land not belonging to the county were sold off at public auction. Josiah Paine paid $67.25 for the block of Main Street (now SE First Avenue) along the east side of the square. Here he constructed the Ocala House, which, rebuilt and expanded over the years, developed into the town's premier hotel.

The Ocala House also became the local headquarters of the H. L. Hart stage line. Arrival of a stage was heralded by echoing blasts from the driver's bugle, soon accompanied by the rumble of the heavy Concord coach and the sharp clatter of its four horses' hooves. Coaches—one from Palatka and the other from Tampa—arrived every Tuesday and Friday evening. This was a big event, and Ocalans usually gathered along Main Street to watch. The weary travelers spent the night at the Ocala House, where they often regaled the townsfolk with information about the world beyond. Then, at seven the following morning, it was "all aboard" and the bumpy, two-day journey resumed.

After 1867 Ocala was not so isolated from current events, for in that momentous year the telegraph line was extended from

Gainesville along the stagecoach route. Travelers found the endless line of telegraph poles so unusual that they called the route that is now US 441 the "Wire Road." These wires led to the Ocala House, which became the center of news when the telegraph company established its office there.

A decade and a half later came more big news: a railroad at last had laid its tracks into Ocala, thereby enabling the town to gain commercial access to the outside world. The first train arrived on the track down Osceola Avenue bedecked with flowers and with a brass band blaring triumphantly on one of the flat cars. From the station passengers were escorted along a paved walkway through a garden to the east entrance of the Ocala House. After registering, they could enjoy juleps on either the long piazza that looked down on the garden with its bubbling fountain and subtropical plants or the front piazza that afforded a vista of the square, always lively with persons coming and going from the courthouse, the public well, or the shops that had sprung up around the square.

Modern visitors will find that Ocala is in the process of rehabbing its old downtown, located on SR 40 (Silver Springs Boulevard) at Magnolia Avenue, which is four blocks east of US 301/441. Although it has been more than thirty years since a courthouse graced the

Downtown Ocala shows its prosperity.

square, the site has become a pleasantly landscaped park, complete with a replica of the old gazebo from which bands once serenaded and such political bigwigs as William Jennings Bryan held audiences in sway. The ancient oak tree where Alexander McLeod's Indian may be buried is long gone, but his bones possibly still rest, perhaps uneasily, somewhere in the park.

One of the best restorations has been done on the 1885 Marion Block, across from the gazebo on Broadway. Currently occupied by a popular casual restaurant, the Marion Block once boasted Ocala's first electric elevator. The third floor was the site of the town's most festive balls, in addition to featuring amateur plays and what passed for opera. Other times white performers darkened their faces and presented black-folk caricatures called minstrel shows.

One block west on Broadway, at the corner of Magnolia, is an eye-catching, three-story rehab. Although it now houses another of Ocala's trendy restaurants, it was constructed as the staid First National Bank. Just down Magnolia are more rehabbed buildings, culminating with the 1941 Marion Theater, representative of the art moderne style so popular at the time. Ocalans flocked to the theater not only to view the latest movies but also to enjoy the cool marvel of air conditioning—for the theater was the first building in town to have it. Today the Marion has been converted into the Discovery Science Center, oriented toward young people.

The rehabbed Marion Block once hosted parties and musicals in its third-floor ballroom.

The illustrious Ocala House, once occupying the entire block on SE First Avenue opposite the courthouse square, is gone forever. It has been replaced by the jarringly modern structure occupied by the Chamber of Commerce. A Chamber spokesperson explained the out-of-place architecture with a mental shrug: "They did things differently in the 1970s."

The large Concord building across from the park on Silver Springs Boulevard appears modern, but is a facade over an older structure. Close by, the One Professional Centre has a small belfry from which chimes ring out just as in the old days. "I remember that in the still of the night," recalled Sybil Bray, "one might clearly hear the striking of the big clock in the dome atop the courthouse. It gave me a sense of security." What does it matter if the chimes are digital recordings? One cannot always choose the most ideal links with the past.

A faint shadow of bitterness lingers about Ocala, for many believe the town has received short shrift over the years. There are still those who resent the University of Florida's being located in Gainesville, when Ocala had claim to an institution of higher learning before its neighbor to the north was even founded. And Ocalans begrudge the fact that they were denied becoming a major inland port when the Cross Florida Barge Canal, championed by Franklin Roosevelt and Lyndon Johnson, was canceled by Richard Nixon submitting to pressure from environmentalists and interests from the port of Miami. Most discouraging of all, Ocala was at the top of the list as the site of Disney World until Walt flew over Florida and happened to see that Florida's Turnpike and the yet-uncompleted Interstate 4 met near Orlando.

Yet Ocala looks to the future. New businesses have found the city's environment extremely friendly, and the Ocala-Marion County Economic Development Council has been active in the area's promotion. The city has several industrial parks as well as a foreign trade zone, resulting in tax advantages favorable to companies doing international business. In addition, Ocala has won the prestigious All America designation, granted to only a few U.S. cities each year. Recently Ocala received the coveted Sustainable Community award from the state. The decision was based on Ocala's programs to preserve historic sites, revive the downtown, attract new businesses, and manage its growth in a responsible fashion. This award gave Ocalans a special satisfaction knowing they snatched it from under the nose of their larger archrival, neighboring Gainesville.

"There has always been a rivalry with Gainesville," a prominent Ocalan told me. "Both cities are part of the north central region, which we feel is different from the rest of Florida. Even towns as close as Eustis and Mount Dora are different. We have a regional development council that includes the surrounding counties, but Ocala's and Gainesville's are the most important. So it seems as we are always in the midst of friendly competition."

Ocala has had an aggressive business attitude from early in its development when it found itself in the center of a rich farming and livestock area. By the end of the nineteenth century many of its merchants had become wealthy. They tended to construct their homes along the tree-cooled streets in the town's southeastern section, now a historic district. A drive along Fort King Street, which is a block south of Broadway, reveals many of these Victorian- and Queen Anne-style homes. Of particular interest is that of John Dunn at the southwest corner of Alvarez Avenue. Dunn was an energetic entrepreneur participating in whatever field promised profits. He started as a lawyer, but turned to developing subdivisions on Ocala's outskirts. Soon he also owned a large orange grove. Then, as the greenbacks accumulated, he began making loans on real estate. Next he entered politics and went to the Florida legislature as a senator. When he returned to Ocala, he became president of the Merchants Bank. Upon hearing rumors of a rich phosphate strike to the west, he quickly became involved financially, and ultimately gave his name to the new mining town of Dunnellon. It is strange to think that such a dynamic individual is gone, yet the wooden shell where he made his plans and lived his dreams remains.

Fort King Street leads, not surprisingly, to the site of the old fort just beyond SE Thirty-Sixth Avenue a few miles east of town's center. What IS surprising is that virtually nothing has been done with the fifteen-acre site except to put up a plaque. Over the years plans have been discussed, but the fort's wooden foundations rotted away so completely that no one is certain as to the structure's precise location.

Now return to SE Thirty-Sixth Avenue, then head north along the Municipal Golf Course to SR 40, Silver Springs Boulevard. This is, again not surprisingly, the road to Silver Springs. Turn right and watch for the Civic Theater at 4337 and the Appleton

Museum adjacent to it. They are Ocala's showplaces. The Civic is the second largest community theater in Florida. The Appleton is known for its pre-Columbian artifacts and oriental art, and is open Tuesday through Saturday from 10 A.M. to 4:30 P.M. and Sunday from 1 to 5 P.M. Admission is $3, but kids under twelve are free.

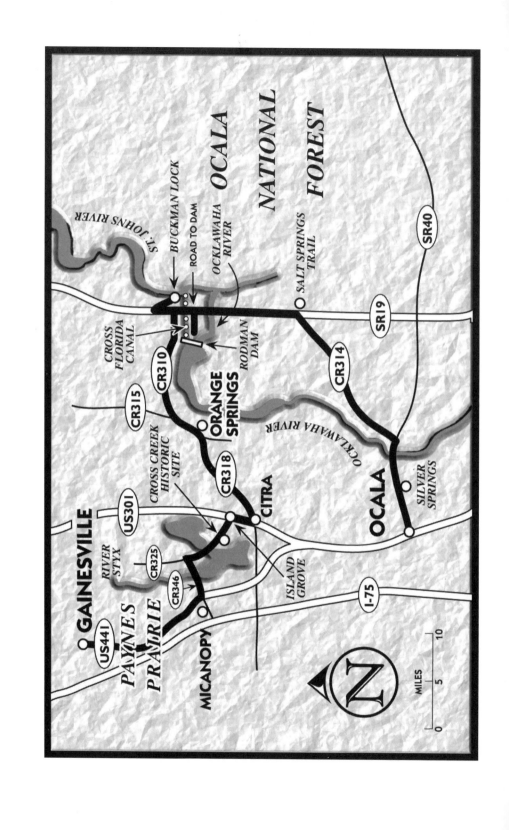

The Forest, the Creek, and the Wide Prairie
Ocala to Gainesville • 103 Backroad Miles

The Song of the Road: Where the Byways Lead

After a brief stop at Silver Springs, the eighth exploration heads into the Ocala National Forest, an unusual environment of sand hills and stunted pines also known as the Big Scrub. This was the site of Marjorie Kinnan Rawlings' Florida classic, *The Yearling*. It is also home to a variety of unusual plants and animals, and the nature trail at Salt Springs will take you past many of them—including alligators. The northern limit of the national forest is the Ocklawaha River, where you'll visit the controversial Rodman Dam, which fishermen love but environmentalists want to breach.

Beyond Rodman is Cross Creek, where Marjorie Rawlings lived in the 1930s in order to absorb the atmosphere of rural Florida. Her home and grounds are now a state historic site. The rustic setting still captures the flavor of long-ago Florida.

From here the road leads across almost deserted wetlands to the little town of Micanopy, once an important Seminole village, now a charming backwater settlement well known for its old buildings, many of which have been converted into antique shops. Near Micanopy is the exotic Paynes Prairie State Preserve, a spacious grassland extending for miles. Hiking trails offer you the opportunity to penetrate this strange world reminiscent of the Great Plains.

Sparks and Sparking

SR 40 leads to Silver Springs, which is just six miles from downtown Ocala. This road was originally a rutted dirt path down which oxen groaned as they hauled heavy wagons heaped high with much-needed supplies to Ocala from the boat landing at Silver Springs. Later, after a rail line was constructed, log-burning engines rattled along the route, the sparks from their stacks having the unfortunate tendency to set the wooden rails on fire. During the bicycle craze of the Gay Nineties, young men with flowing mustachios and fair damsels in colorful bonnets peddled along the road on their way to picnics and sparking at Silver Springs. Their conduct, particularly that of the young ladies astride bicycles, shocked the more straight-laced older generation. The bikes and trains are gone now, but the old railroad bed has become the center parkway of the modern highway.

The Beauty of the Deep: Silver Springs

PAY TOLL AHEAD   Admittedly Silver Springs can hardly be considered a "backroad," as it attracts thousands of visitors a year. The entry fee to Silver Springs is stiff, about $30 for adults and $20 for kids, and were it not for the downright beauty of the springs (and the fact that it's directly on our way), I'd go directly to neighboring Ocala National Forest.

Silver Springs is large even for Florida, which boasts one-third of the nation's first magnitude springs. Enough water gushes out of the park's fourteen major apertures in twenty-four hours to supply two gallons for every man, woman, and child in the United States. Not only that, but the water is among the purest in the world.

The springs have long had their appeal. Ten thousand years ago prehistoric Indians trod the shores and, presumably, swam in the cool water that bubbled up so mysteriously from the blue caverns below. Because the climate was cooler then, these ancient tribes hunted many animals no longer found in Florida. Among them were bellowing mastodons that crashed through the dense covering of trees. The forest around the springs must have been an exciting place when the hunters fought the huge beasts, but often the hunters succeeded, their arrowheads having been found around here among the bones of

Glass-bottom boats take sightseers across the fascinating water caverns at Silver Springs.

fallen prey. In historic times the Timucuan people dwelt beside these sweet-water pools. Here they planted their crops, raised their families, lived their lives, and, ultimately, buried their dead in the earthen mounds that were once so common in the area. Much later the Seminoles had a village here—until they lost their second war with the Americans in 1844 and were packed off to desolate reservations beyond the Mississippi.

The springs were important in early travel, for their wide runoff, which flowed into the Ocklawaha River seven miles east, enabled Ocala's merchants to send the products of the surrounding farms all the way to Jacksonville.

Eventually the springs' beauty attracted national attention. Hubbard Hart's stage coaches began pausing there so the passengers could savor the attractiveness of the place where silver shells danced in the crystalline, up-welling water. In warm weather few could resist taking a dip in the refreshing springs. So great was the interest that it wasn't long before Hart invested in steamboats to carry tourists on memorable two-night journeys up the Ocklawaha. Soon a hamlet sprouted beside the placid water, with three stores, a post office, and a modest hotel to accommodate Hart's passengers.

Until 1878 visitors had to be contented to peer into the springs from over the side of row boats rented from the hotel. But in this year one Hullam Jones brought forth a new kind of boat with a rectangular glass pane covering a cutout in the hull. This glass bottom, by eliminating ripples, gave tourists unparalleled views of the wondrous depths.

Over the years Silver Springs maintained its popularity. Movie-makers added to its fame in the 1930s and '40s with the shooting of six Johnny Weissmuller Tarzan films. In 1946 the springs were the site of *The Yearling* with Gregory Peck. More recently, episodes of such TV series as *I Spy* and *Sea Hunt* were made here.

Silver Springs has always hovered between being a naturalist's gem and a tourist snare. It still does. Although glassbottom boats glide quietly over the azure water, pausing patiently over the pulsating, prismatic springs, the emphasis has shifted to the areas downstream where imported animals roam purposelessly over fenced areas that in places have been worn bare by their ceaseless pacing.

Unless you have an overwhelming interest in the springs or the animals, you will may find the admission price to the park rather intimidating. But plenty of people do go and enjoy themselves. It is open every day from 9 A.M. to 5:30 P.M.

A Stage Awaiting the Actors

Three miles beyond Silver Springs on SR 40 is the turnoff to the Ocala Boat Basin. When the basin was built, expectations were that this would become a major point on the Cross Florida Barge Canal. It was here that Ocalans anticipated realizing their cherished dream of becoming linked with the Atlantic Ocean as well as the Gulf of Mexico. They looked forward to the day when yachtsmen from all over the hemisphere would dock at the basin. Boosters were convinced that hotels and recreational establishments would grow up around the basin. But the dreams died when the canal project, begun with such fanfare by Franklin Roosevelt, was terminated by the quiet stroke of Richard Nixon's pen. Now the basin is frequented by fishermen, boaters, and picnickers who seem to rattle around the ample stage that was set for different actors.

The Controversial River

Just beyond the boat basin SR 40 passes over the Ocklawaha River on a bridge constructed at an unusual height to accommodate the traffic of the Cross Florida Barge Canal, which was to enter the river near here. The water level was designed to be much higher than now, for the river was to be flooded as part of an elaborate plan that envisioned three sets of dams and locks. Two were actually constructed, one at Eureka, fourteen miles downstream, and another at Rodman near where the Ocklawaha discharges into the St. Johns, resulting in the conversion of sixteen miles of the Ocklawaha valley into the Rodman Reservoir. Another long reservoir was to extend from Eureka to just south of the SR 40 bridge, from which point the canal would cross the rolling land of Marion County to the Withlacoochee River, also impounded, and on to the Gulf of Mexico.

Although work on the canal was halted in 1971, the dams at Rodman and Eureka remained, and that at Rodman, especially, has become the subject of a fierce, ongoing controversy. Environmentalists charge that as long as the Rodman obstruction remains, the ecology of that part of the river valley cannot be restored. But economic interests retort that the impounded lake has now become popular for its bass fishing. "If you want to light some REAL big fires around here," a spokesperson for the Ocala/Marion County Chamber of Commerce warned me, "just mention the question of the Rodman dam." We'll continue the story when we visit Rodman.

Now knowing something about the controversy surrounding the

Ocklawaha, you may be looking forward to viewing the river. But the bridge is very high and the land below so overgrown with trees that it is impossible to see it.

You're not missing much, for today the Ocklawaha is just a sluggish stream. Yet once it ran fuller and faster, and guests at the old Silver Springs Hotel loved to take sailboats along its surging channel. "We went ten miles down the famous Ocklawaha and back," went an 1887 newspaper article quoted by Sybil Bray in her engaging booklets, *Salty Crackers*, "and one could not imagine a more thoroughly tropical scene, the boat lined with gay people, chatting and leaning lazily over the sides, all intent on enjoying the hour and scene. . . . The water of the river . . . is clear, and you can amuse yourself watching the fish, snakes, turtles, etc., all swimming in the depths below."

Steamboats and barges also moved along the river as they carried goods and passengers between Silver Springs and Palatka. The steamboats were a way of life for the folks living in cabins along the valley. Kate Randall reminisced about those days with Sybil Bray: "I recall that everyone on the river knew the sound of the whistle on each boat that cruised the Ocklawaha River. From far away, one might hear a lonely whistle in the night and say to themselves, 'Here comes the Sharp Shooter, the Okeehumpkee, or the Hiawatha.'"

The Wonders of the Big Scrub

The Ocala National Forest begins across the Ocklawaha. The wild, sandy landscape here is in vivid contrast to the manicured horse farms west of Ocala. This is because you have left the fertile Ocala Platform and have descended into an acidic region known to geologists as the Osceola Low. The soil is not conducive to agriculture, as Marjorie Kinnan Rawlings' heart-rendering novel *The Yearling* makes so very clear. And because no one thought this desolate Big Scrub had any value, it was set aside as the Ocala National Forest in 1908—making it the oldest such forest east of the Mississippi River.

A park museum is located on SR 40 just past CR 314, a road you'll take in a moment. Although the museum is not large, it contains interesting displays about the forest, which is not comprised of the towering trees one would expect. Instead, the sandy soil can only support scrawny underbrush and the world's most extensive stand of sand pines—with crooked trunks rarely more than fourteen inches in diameter. Nor are these pines very tall, for when they gain much height, their root system, anchored in sand, is incapable of preventing them from toppling over. The museum also contains displays of local animals. I should also mention it has a good collection of Sybil Browne Bray's *Salty Crackers* booklets, thoroughly enjoyable remembrances of Marion County's yesterdays.

Now head back a short distance on SR 40 toward CR 314, where you'll turn right. But while you're still on SR 40 you might be interested in learning that the road has been placed on the Florida Department of Transportation's timetable for conversion into a four-lane, high-speed connector between Interstate 75 on the west and 95 on the east. The Florida Audubon Society warns that these plans raise concerns as to "whether a viable national forest can exist if such a deadly structure is built."

Drive north on CR 314. Much of the road was originally hacked through the wilderness by Colonel Alexander Fanning, a fiery, one-armed man, as he marched federal troops to battle during the Second Seminole War. Although this is the heart of the Ocala National Forest, you may be disappointed with this assortment of scrawny trees and undistinguished underbrush. Yet the Big Scrub has been called Florida's most unique ecosystem, so it merits some attention.

This sandy world was created as a dune-island during an interlude in the Ice Age when the ocean level was much higher than today. The sand is almost pure quartz carried here by wind and ocean currents from the eroding Appalachians in Georgia and Alabama. Sand pines, the dominant tall plants, are particularly prevalent on the ridges. Beneath them

The road through the Ocala National Forest meanders past low-growing sand pines.

are smatterings of sand live oaks, with saw palmettos, needle-leafed rosemary, and lyonia bushes dotting the ground. Where the soil is better the sand pines give way to longleaf pines, standing tall and erect, with dense clumps of wire grass below. In other places compact stands of dwarf live oaks form umbrella-shaped growths called "oak domes."

This is an inhospitable place for farming, but early settlers tried nonetheless. Author Marjorie Kinnan Rawlings lived with such a family for several months during the 1930s as they tried to scratch a bare subsistence from this unyielding soil. Even when they managed to grow a saleable crop, the lack of through-roads forced them to mule-wagon their harvest down the sand path to the steamboat port of Volusia fifteen weary miles east on the St. Johns River. Here they had no choice except to barter away their pitiful earnings for seed, tools, clothing, and the other basic necessities of frontier life. Rawlings captured the struggles of one family, as seen through the experiences of the twelve-year-old son, in her excellent book, *The Yearling.*

As you drive along, don't be surprised if you see some areas that have been recently burned, for the role of fire is one of the most interesting aspects of the Big Scrub. Until recently the park department did everything possible to prevent forest fires, and, when one occurred, to keep the burned area to a minimum. But, as the years went by, the forest floors became tinder from decades of debris. It was a self-defeating cycle: the longer fires were prevented, the more litter accumulated and the greater became the menace of future fires. The explosiveness of the situation was brought home by the savage fire storms in Yellowstone Park.

Now the forestry department actively pursues a policy of "prescribed burns," where park employees actually start small fires, which are carefully controlled. These burns remove flammable ground clutter, and, in doing so, clear the area for the growth of the shrubs that deer and other animals depend on for food. The scrub plants are not permanently injured by the fire, for the oaks resprout from extensive root systems and rosemary returns from seeds previously deposited in the soil. Furthermore, fires are vital in the scrub's perpetuation, for sand pine cones require severe heat to release their seeds.

On the drive you'll also observe areas where all the trees have been removed. Government policy permits the harvesting of up to thirty percent of forestry trees by private timber companies. This not only brings in revenue to help maintain the national forests, but is beneficial to the forests themselves, for the cut area is reseeded, and eventually a new generation of healthy sand pines is created to take the place of the old trees. However, some naturalists criticize this reseeding policy, claiming that, since the trees are almost all sand pines, they do not recreate a well-rounded habitat suitable for many of the scrub animals.

Alertness is required to spot the scrub animals. You may be lucky and see a shy bobcat. Alligators, always dangerous, can sometimes be discerned around the ponds. Flying squirrels often leap across the upper branches of the sand pines, which are also home to a variety of colorful woodpeckers. Endangered scrub jays feed on acorns beneath the oaks. Occasionally eagles, with wingspans up to eight feet, soar overhead. Their nests are in the taller pines or the large cypress that grow around the water pockets. These are treasured birds, and to molest them or their nests can result in a fine of $20,000 and/or two years in jail!

Threatened black bears also roam the Big Scrub. They are not normally aggressive animals, and unprovoked attacks on humans have never been documented in Florida. They forage over large areas in search of wild grapes, acorns, and insects. An adult bear can require a territory nine-by-nine miles square, and when things get really tough he can set out on an expedition that might take him up to many miles from his home base and cause him to cross busy highways. So be wary as you drive: the Ocala National Forest is a particularly active area for bears.

In eighteen miles CR 314 ends at SR 19. Just south on SR 19 is the parking lot for the Salt Springs Trail where a path leads a mile to an observation platform over the Salt Springs Run. Here you can often observe eagles and osprey riding the upper air currents while egrets and a variety of herons tread the shallows below. Alligators are also common. There is no charge to use the trail, and it is open to the public seven days a week, night and day.

Alligators are not animals to fool with, and it is against the law to feed them. There have been at least six instances when they attacked humans, one of the latest being a swimmer at Ocala Forest's Juniper Springs. "I saw the head coming toward me, then I saw its mouth open," recounted James Morrow. "Next thing I knew my head was inside the gator's mouth. He started shaking me like a rag doll." Then the twelve-foot monster pulled Morrow underwater, preparing to drown him and eat him at his leisure. But, miraculously, the gator let him go and swam off. "I think my mask saved me," Morrow said. "If I hadn't had it on, he could have put one of my eyes out or punctured my jugular."

Marjorie Kinnan Rawlings camped just downstream with two friends in the 1930s. It was a beautiful location, and, when the full moon rose, she felt herself to be among the most favored of all mortals. But, she wrote, "that night was hideous," due to mainly to the immense swarms of mosquitoes. "We built up the camp fire to make the smoke to drive them away and the smoke was more annoying than the mosquitoes. Hoot owls settled in the oaks over our heads and cried jeeringly all night. Wood roaches came in and awakened us from our spasms of slumber with their sharp nibbling on our ears."

From Salt Springs, SR 19 leads north through the Ocala National Forest along the Ocklawaha Ridge, which, although it is barely perceptible, is enough to separate the Ocklawaha River to the west from the broad St. Johns a short distance east. Eight miles from Salt Springs, the ridge gives way to a wide swampy area where the Ocklawaha River, braided and overgrown, makes its sluggish way to the St. Johns. For centuries a magnificent cypress forest grew here. But during the early 1900s the trees were felled, formed into long rafts, and floated to the St. Johns River where they ended up at the voracious Wilson mill at Palatka. Within four decades the entire forest had vanished.

To Destroy or Not To Destroy: That Is the Question

A couple of miles farther on is a sign to the controversial Rodman Dam. The entry road is rather scenic as it first passes through a thick growth of pines, then along the crest of the dam's earthen retaining embankment, from which there is an excellent view of the reservoir stretching far off into the blue distance. The dam itself is a surprise, for despite all the furor, it is a relatively small structure with just four spill gates controlling the flow out of the reservoir. The

The fishing is good in the turbulent waters below the controversial Rodman Dam.

churning water has become such a favorite fishing site that the state has provided a public pier, boat ramp, and picnic area as well as restrooms. Another picnic area is on the north side of the dam beside the reservoir itself. Here there is also a boat launch, for the sixteen-mile-long reservoir has been attractive for its bass fishing almost as soon as it began filling in 1968.

Despite the dam's appeal, it is a manmade alteration of the natural ecosystem that environmentalists find an abomination. They have opposed the dam since the days of the Cross Florida Barge Canal. Although they stopped work on the hated canal in 1971 and finally buried it forever when the land was turned over to the state for conversion into a 110-mile-long series of recreational strips, the dam, the reservoir, and the Buckman Locks nearby remain.

The environmentalists' goal is to breach the dam, eliminate the reservoir, and restore Ocklawaha as a free-flowing river. They thought they had achieved their goal a few years back when Democratic Governor Lawton Chiles came out in their favor. But supporters of the dam, led by Gainesville's determined state senator, George Kirkpatrick, prevented the $3 million needed for the dam's destruction from being included in the budget. Kirkpatrick's triumphant Republican supporters gleefully renamed the dam after him.

So what position should a responsible person take on this complicated issue? Standing on the pier and watching the people fishing, it seemed a shame to destroy the dam. But turning to look down the Ocklawaha, it seems an equal shame that such a beautiful stream has been blocked by the dam. Then, driving on the embankment and looking over the reservoir's turquoise expanse, it may seem a crime to empty it. But when you muse about how beautiful the valley must have been before being flooded, you may think it a crime that such a place no longer exists.

The Rodman Reservoir impounds the waters of the Ocklawaha River.

When you consider the several million dollars that would be needed to remove the dam, it may seem that the funds could be better spent on schools or housing or highway improvement. But when you learn that a study indicated it would be cheaper to destroy the reservoir than spend the money to constantly maintain it, you may switch you opinion once more. But, again, how do you know that such a study was accurate?

It may be that your feelings will go one way, then the other, until all you can do is shrug your shoulders and give thanks that the decision is not yours. Whatever they do it will be right. Or will it be wrong?

More of the Great Debate: The Buckman Lock

Back on SR 19, the road passes over another of the large bridges built to permit passage of the anticipated canal boats and barges. Below, the waterway stretches in both directions as far as one can see. In two miles you'll come to a side road leading to the Buckman Lock. While the Buckman Lock has not taken on the clamor of the Rodman Dam, it is also marked for destruction if the environmentalists have their way. It is a huge piece of masonry designed to lower vessels from the reservoir to the level of the St. Johns. It is almost ridiculously large, given the fact that its only use now is to give passage to fishing boats. Environmentalists estimate that it costs the taxpayer around $140 for each boat's round trip. Furthermore, in recent years nine endangered manatees have been crushed to death in the lock or drowned in the floodgates. On the other hand, if the reser-

The Ocklawaha River below Rodman is broad and clear as it heads toward the St. Johns and the Atlantic Ocean.

voir remains, the lock is essential for fishermen from Palatka and other marinas on the St. Johns as well as for boaters from lakes as far distant as Eustis and Dora on expeditions to Jacksonville.

The Joys of the Vanished Ocklawaha Valley Railroad

Now return on SR 19 to the junction with CR 310. This is the site of the town of Rodman. During the first quarter of the twentieth century a community of several thousand grew up around a large sawmill and turpentine still that operated here. The Ocklawaha Valley Railroad carried logs to the mill. Nearby was a busy hotel and two stores. There was also a church and a school for the whites and a separate church and school for blacks. But when the timber gave out, the town utterly vanished.

Now head west on CR 310 up the Ocklawaha flood plain. The river has been submerged in the Rodman Reservoir, which is out of sight, except for a brief moment, to the left. This is the route of the old Ocklawaha Valley Railroad, completed in 1912 to connect Ocala with Palatka.

The railroad was one of those friendly little lines where the train crews knew most of the passengers. During strawberry season, when the plants grew profusely along the railroad embankments, the engineer would often stop so the passengers could clamber out and gather the luscious fruit. The engineers were family men who often let their children ride in the cab. One of these was little Sybil Bray, who later wrote her recollections in the series of delightful booklets entitled *Salty Crackers*:

> I was my daddy's girl and I stayed with him in the cab of that old engine. . . . He let me ring the bell and blow the whistle. My daddy loved his job and loved old engine 101. He kept her clean and shining. The brass flambeaus and the knobs on the end of the steer horns just above the light were kept polished until you could see yourself in them . . . [From] far in the distance, as the sun's rays would hit the engine, it glistened, and everyone would say, "Here comes . . . No. 101."

The railroad made most of its money hauling timber to the Wilson mill at Palatka, so as the woods gave out, the Ocklawaha Valley line began to have financial difficulties. In 1917 the owners decided to remove the steam trains and use gasoline busses on the tracks. These busses were as strange contraptions as ever sputtered down American rails, for they were actually two busses with their rear ends welded together so they would need no turntable when reaching either of their destinations, since the driver could just rev up the front engine and they were off again. "Oh, I'll tell you," recalled Sybil Bray, "you should have taken a ride on that little passenger car, if that's what you could call it. Trash, sand and twigs would blow into your face and eyes. They would destroy a hairdo. It was an exciting ride."

When CR 310 ends in eight miles, turn left on CR 315, and in six more miles you'll arrive at Orange Springs. The railroad promised great things for Orange Springs, which which celebrated its completion in "a day to be remembered," according to Sybil Bray. "All kinds of ice cream was churned. AND . . . there were also 'spirits' by the barrel! Oh, it flowed so freely. All the local politicians were there and the more they ate and consumed the greater the campaign promises. . . . The gala affair lasted well into the wee hours of the morning"—when, we may assume, everyone was either asleep or quite drunk.

But the railroad is gone, now and the little town has become a sleepy place once more.

Incidents on a Country Lane: Marjorie Kinnan Rawlings

At Orange Springs turn west on CR 318, which leaves the Ocklawaha flats to traverse higher, slightly rolling terrain. Marjorie Rawlings may have been driving on this road alone late one night as she returned from a rugged hunting trip with some of her male friends in the 1930s. Exhausted from forty hours of tramping through woods, she fell asleep at the wheel. Suddenly her car crashed into the forest and, while she sought to gain control, it flattened saplings yet somehow dodged larger trees. When the car finally ground to a halt, Rawlings saw that she needed help to extricate it. So she stumbled to the highway and staggered two miles back toward the Ocklawaha before she was able to flag down a motorist. Working with him, she managed to get the severely damaged vehicle back on the road. Then she drove the remaining fifteen or twenty miles to her home at Cross Creek through a dense fog that terrified her even more than the crash. "For weeks after," she recalled, "a road swam ahead of me and suddenly ended, and the trees poured in on me, and I was damned in the fog."

To get home Rawlings would have turned north at the hamlet of

Citra on US 301, at this time a narrow two-lane road, until she reached the even smaller settlement of Island Grove. Here she would have taken the deserted, gravel side road that now is paved and goes under the designation of CR 325 to her humble cracker dwelling four miles farther on.

It was most unusual for a young single woman to live alone in the virtual wilderness. But Marjorie was an unusual person. Born in 1896, she grew up in Washington, D.C. At the age of twenty-three she married Charles Rawlings and moved to Rochester, New York. Here she wrote a women's column in the local newspaper dutifully entitled "Songs of the Housewife."

The seminal event in her life occurred in 1928 when Charles and she purchased a rundown Florida farm near a little stream called Cross Creek in north central Florida. Marjorie was assured by Charles that he would do all the heavy chores required to make the neglected home and adjacent acreage livable and productive. But Charles was used to gentler tasks and not only skipped out after a year, but divorced Marjorie to boot. It was a devastating blow that left her depressed and on the verge of a breakdown. "Life was a nightmare," she wrote. Even her dog, a citified Scotty, hated it and turned into such a mean cur that she had to give him to friends in the city. Marjorie rented out a small house in the rear to a series of black and white tenants who were supposed to help with the work, but often only gave her more problems. These transients made her feel vulnerable, so she sometimes slept with a pistol beside her pillow.

Marjorie Kinnan Rawlings' rough farm home is now a state historic site.

Despite the difficulties, she managed to plant a rather extensive citrus grove. At the same time she tended a prolific vegetable garden in her backyard. And she began selling some of her stories. The recognition, to say nothing of the money, was welcome. The inspiration for her writing was Florida itself, which, possibly to her surprise, she began to love.

The road past her home became an integral part of her life:

> Folk call the road lonely, because there is not human traffic and human stirring. Because I have walked it so many times and seen such a tumult of life there, it seems to me one of the most populous highways of my acquaintance. I have walked it in ecstasy, and in joy it is beloved. Every pine tree, every gallberry bush, every passion vine, every joree rustling in the underbrush is vibrant. I have walked it . . . in despair, and in the red of the sunset is my own blood dissolving into the night's darkness. For all such things were on earth before us, and will survive after us, and it is given to us to join ourselves with them and to be comforted.

The loose group of homes that went under the name of Cross Creek belonged to five white and two black families scattered at lengthy intervals along the southeastern portion of the road to Island Grove. They referred to Rawlings as "the Young Miss" and believed that she would be gone shortly. When they realized that she intended to stay, most of them became her friends.

The road northwestward from her home ran through a thick hammock before crossing the bridge over the creek itself. Along here the road was not much more than a frail ribbon of civilization passing hesitantly through what Rawlings called "the great mystery of Florida." On her walks she heard eerie calls of creatures unknown, the rustle of forces beyond her ken, the presence of the past: "I was most stirred, I think, by knowing that this was Indian and Spanish country, and that Vitachuco, chief of the Ocali Indians, was embroiled with the Spaniards somewhere north of the present Ocala—and it may have been here."

Often Rawlings walked in the other direction. Here she had a strange and moving experience with a neighbor's dog: "The dog and I first met on a warm June evening. I was walking east along the Creek road, a little later than usual. The sun had set. I remember feeling lonely. I was a little uneasy, as well, for, moccasins and rattlers cross the road in the twilight." Then she encountered the dog. He had the build of a police dog but also dirty yellowish fur and the drooping tail of a mongrel. He was sulking down the road in a wolfish manner with his head down. Rawlings understood instantly that he was a catch-dog used to round up hogs. He had been kicked and beaten and fed the most rotten of scraps. But he accepted it all, for that was the only life he knew.

When Marjorie, craving a companion, called to him, he came uncertainly. "I touched his rough coat," she wrote. "I pulled one ear. He rubbed his nose briefly against me in a gesture of acceptance. A feeling of friendliness passed over us in the dusk." Then he slouched off.

The next day Marjorie was back on the road. When she passed the neighbor's farm she yelled, "Here, boy," on a whim. The dog came sauntering out and they walked for a while, companions in the twilight. After that it became almost a ritual. If Marjorie was late, the dog would be waiting in the middle of the road for her.

But one day Marjorie acquired the high-bred pointer puppy with which she had long planned to replace the obstreperous Scotty. The pointer was a balm to Marjorie's loneliness and she wanted to train her specially. So she temporarily ended her walks down the road, and, instead, romped with her puppy through the leafy greenery of her orange grove.

Several weeks later, she led her pointer on a leash down the road. The yellow dog scented her and dashed from the farm. "He was insane with joy. He jumped against me, he went taut proudly, introducing himself to the puppy. He dropped his forelegs to the ground and shook his head, inviting the new dog to play. The puppy barked shrilly and tugged at the leash. Discipline was hopeless. There was nothing

Cross Creek still flows languidly near Rawlings' former home.

for it but to drive the catch-dog away." Marjorie made a menacing gesture: "He looked at me unbelieving and did not stir." Then she threw gravel at the yellow dog and continued her walk, dragging the puppy after her. The catch-dog watched with bewildered eyes. When he started to follow, she shouted "with as much sternness as I could manage to bring from a sick heart, 'Get back!'" From then on she kept shooing the yellow dog away until he understood that for some reason they were no longer friends. It may have been harder on Marjorie than the yellow dog: "Now we pass as though we were strangers. I am ashamed to face him, having used him in my loneliness, and then betrayed him."

Rawlings kept track of this and the scores of other simple, yet ever so poignant, incidents of life along a little country road during her thirteen years there, and used them for a series of books that brought her fame as well as such friends as Ernest Hemingway and Eleanor Roosevelt. Her most successful book, *The Yearling*, published in 1938, not only won her a Pulitzer Prize, but was turned into a blockbuster movie starring Gregory Peck and Jane Wyman. Then in 1941, the year she married Norton Baskin and moved to St. Augustine, her memoirs, entitled simply *Cross Creek*, came out. With its evocative writing, haunting imagery, and timeless descriptions of country life, this book became an instant Florida classic.

Rawlings' productive years ended when she left Cross Creek, although she kept the home as an occasional retreat. Perhaps the inspiration left when she no longer had the vibrant country road to stimulate her imagination. Nor could it have helped when one of her neighbors, Zelma Cason, brought what seemed like an endless succession of lawsuits against her for invasion of privacy in "The Census" chapter of *Cross Creek*. The court ultimately found Rawlings guilty but fined her only a nominal penalty of one dollar plus court costs. Nonetheless, her days were increasingly unhappy, and she turned ever more often to the bottle for comfort. In 1953 she died of a cerebral hemorrhage at her cottage near St. Augustine.

Cross Creek has become something of a shrine for those who treasure Rawlings' writings, and is now a state historic site. Admission to her home is $3 for adults and $2 for children six to twelve. It is open Thursdays through Sundays between 10 A.M. and 4 P.M., when tours are given—except it is closed for maintenance and repairs August and September. Although a visit to Rawlings' home is valuable for an understanding of her writings, just as valuable are the grounds, which are free and available year round. Here you can wander through a portion of her replanted citrus grove. "The green growth," she wrote, "seems, not vegetation, but sea, emerald green, with the light seeming to come from high distant earthly places down through the luminous waters." Sometimes, when the moon was gleaming she would dance beneath the trees with her pointer darting at her heels.

As for the road, it is paved now and not nearly as quiet as during Rawlings' day, for, ironically, her fame has opened it up. Yet it is still just a country lane that goes nowhere in particular. Its essence remains much as it was during Rawlings' life, particularly in early morning and on toward evenings, which were her favorite walking times. Perhaps, if you stroll along it, you'll agree with her: "We need above all, I think, a certain remoteness from urban confusion, and while this can be found in other places, Cross Creek offers it with such beauty and grace that once entangled with it, no other place seems possible to us, just as when truly in love none other offers the comfort of the beloved."

From the Rawlings Historic Site take CR 325 northwest toward the Cross Creek bridge. Rawlings liked to walk along the row of magnolias that bordered the road, especially in April when the trees glowed with their creamy blossoms. But one day she saw to her horror that all the lower branches had been sawed off. Upon investigation, she learned that commercial pickers had gathered them to decorate funeral wreaths. "The destruction seemed to me a symbol of private intrusion on the right of all mankind to enjoy a universal beauty," she lamented. "Surely the loveliness of the long miles of magnolia bloom was more important to the living than the selling of the bronze, waxy leaves for funerals of the dead."

The modern bridge is not the same one that Rawlings knew, and neither is the creek. In her day the creek was bordered by wild blackberries, which she gathered each spring. The water of the creek, which connects Orange and Lochloosa lakes, was higher then and Orange Lake was treasured for its bass fishing. But the lake and Cross Creek are much lower now, due partly to a sinkhole that opened beneath the lake's surface and partly to the diversion of water to Paynes Prairie, which we shall visit shortly.

Crossing the River Styx

Just beyond the bridge is the junction with CR 346. Take this road west, and pause when you come to a small bridge. This spans the River Styx. No one knows the origin of the strange designation, but Rawlings surmised that it came from a spiteful citizen of the nearby village of Windsor, settled by English expatriates nearly a hundred years earlier. To her it would not have been surprising if the swampy area dismayed the English families, homesick for the lovely British uplands.

Despite its name it was, and still is, a beautiful place. Yet when Rawlings guided her horse across the former shaky bridge, she felt an uneasiness, particularly after a great white heron rose before her like an angel of death. But the Styx meadow was beautiful, especially when the wild iris in bloom formed a blue tapestry for miles. Rawlings and her future husband, Norton Baskin, would go to the Styx each spring to gather some of the flowers. "The egrets are nesting when the iris blooms," Rawlings wrote in Cross Creek, "and fly up from their feeding like bursts of white spray as our splashing disturbs them."

As you continue west on the little-traveled road, you might smile with Rawlings: "It is not given to many to cross the Styx and live to tell it."

An Antique Village: Micanopy

In a few miles CR 346 ends at US 441, where you should jog south to Tuscawilla Road, then head west to Micanopy (accent on the third syllable). At Ocala Street the main road makes a sharp turn north as it becomes Cholokka Boulevard. But you should continue a half block down Ocala and watch on the left for the John Jacob Barr House in front of which stands a large oak that legend has was the site of Chief Micanopy's tribal councils.

Originally this location was inhabited by a segment of the Timucuan tribe, who favored it because it was on high ground close to the Alachua Savanna, today called Paynes Prairie. This savanna supported a rich growth of grass that attracted a large and varied assortment of animals. These animals allowed Timucuan huntsmen to provide the tribe with ample sustenance. The Timucuans lived in permanent, circular homes composed of upright pine saplings bound together with branches. This skeleton was coated with wattle, which is clay mixed with straw and roofed with palmetto leaves.

Spanish friars from St. Augustine found the Timucuans, with their affable, inquisitive dispositions, ideal for conversion, and soon they included Micanopy in the chain of thirty or forty missions that reached for 200 miles, past Tallahassee, and eventually attracted up to 26,000 members of the Timucuan and neighboring Apalache tribes.

Very little is known about the Micanopy mission, for Franciscan records are sketchy and the actual buildings have long since become one with the earth. But there would have been a church, of course, and a school where the friar (there was usually only one to a mission) taught the wondering Timucuans the doctrines of sin and repentance, and the meaning of the death on the cross.

But the future was not kind to the Timucuans. Because they were also taught love, peace, and submission, they were no match for the British and their fierce Creek allies who were expanding southward from South Carolina. Between 1702 and 1706 the aggressors conducted a series of raids against the Timucuans, the ruthlessness and devastation of which have seldom been matched in the history of the New World. Not only were the missions destroyed but up to 12,000 Christian Indians were hauled off as slaves for British plantations, where they vanished from history. The few Timucuans who survived fled to Cuba with the Spanish in 1763, when Florida was incorporated into the British Empire.

The Timucuans were virtually forgotten by the time William Bartram and four British traders reached Micanopy in 1774. The area was now inhabited by the Seminoles, an offshoot of the Creek tribe known as the "wild men." The night of the traders' arrival, Chief Cowkeeper gave them a great feast. As Bartram described it, "the ribs and choicest fat pieces of the bullocks, excellently well barbecued, were brought into the apartment of the public square, constructed and appointed for feasting. [Then] bowls and kettles of stewed flesh and broth were brought in for the next course." Bartram also noted that the young Seminole women were "by no means destitute of charms," and, though some of the traders undoubtedly partook of these charms, Bartram leaves it to our imagination whether he was one.

By 1821, when Florida became American, Cowkeeper's memory lived only in Bartram's writings. In his place was a descendant named Micanopy, a rotund little man, who was chief of the Alachua branch of the Seminoles. The cluster of buildings was now known as Micanopy's town. Two years later, as a result of a treaty forced on the tribe, the town was no longer within Indian territory and Micanopy and his people had to trudge southward. The chief, who undoubtedly felt great resentment, later fought for his homeland during the Second Seminole War. Towards the conflict's end Micanopy was captured under a flag of truce and shipped off to the

Seminoles' new reservation on the dry plains beyond the Mississippi River. Although the Americans had treated Micanopy unfairly, even treacherously, they continued to honor him by keeping his name on the little town that gradually became a trade center for cotton planters.

Now proceed up Cholokka Boulevard into the main part of town. These buildings were once busy places, and each has its story to tell. One of the first buildings, for example, was the 1906 bank, two stories of brick. John Jacob Barr constructed it for the ages, but it failed during the Great Bust of 1927. Farther on is Otis Feaster's building. Rising three stories, it was Micanopy's pride when it was in its prime. Almost everyone in town stopped regularly at Feaster's general store, if not to purchase supplies, at least to savor the latest gossip. During jamborees Feaster's third floor rocked to squeaky fiddles and the rhythmic stomp of square dancers. If festivities got too raucous, the upper set was likely to depart, preferring more genteel soirees in their stately homes, such as the pillared Herlong mansion, a short distance south, which now has been

The old town of Micanopy has gained sudden fame as an antiques center.

turned into a deluxe bed-and-breakfast.

The past rests comfortably about Micanopy, and today few people care that a railroad no longer runs into town or that US 441 has bypassed it. True, during the 1970s and '80s it seemed that the downtown would be frequented only by phantoms. But growing interest in antiques in the '90s allowed shopkeepers to return, and the town revived to the point that it now boasts nearly two dozen fine antique dealers.

For those who wish to learn more about Micanopy, the historical society is located in the former Thrasher warehouse across the street from the Herlong Mansion. For those who crave gewgaws and edible goodies more than antiques, there are several sandwich and souvenir shops.

Micanopy's Herlong Mansion, now a bed-and-breakfast,
offers a glimpse of a genteel way of life.

The Wide, Wide Prairie

Now continue on Cholokka Boulevard to US 441 and head   north. In a mile you'll come to the Paynes Prairie State Preserve's Lake Wauberg Recreation Area. For an admission of $3.75 per car you can get an overview of the prairie from a video and displays at the Visitors' Center, then take the half-mile trail to an observation tower looking across the almost boundless grassland where William Bartram once watched Seminole horsemen pursue fleeing deer. Longer trails are also available for persons with more time and/or vigor. The recreation area is open from 8 A.M. until sunset seven days a week.

The prairie, named for a Seminole chieftain, is one of Florida's most important geological, as well as ecological, areas. During excavations for Interstate 75, which also crosses the prairie a mile to the west, thirty-million-year-old fossils of horses, saber-tooth cats, and other land animals were discovered. These are the earliest indicators of Florida's emergence from the ocean, for all fossils of a prior date are whales, sharks, and other sea animals.

The fossils were part of the extensive layer of limestone beneath almost all of Florida. As portions of this limestone dissolved, the over-lying ground cover collapsed to form the sinkholes and springs with which we are familiar. Paynes Prairie, which is nine miles long and up to seven miles wide, was the result of a coalescence of many sink

Paynes Prairie, an environment completely unique in Florida, is a state preserve.

holes. Only one of these, called the Alachua Sink, is of great enough depth to reach the Florida aquifer. When the sink plugs up, the entire prairie turns into a lake. This happened early in the 1870s, and a body of water formed of sufficient depth to permit a steamboat to run between Micanopy and Gainesville. After two decades, the plug suddenly flushed out, the water gushed down the sink, and the lake vanished within two years. As for the steamboat, it was abandoned where it ran aground, and its rotting hulk was probably that which was discovered by astonished workmen constructing US 441 across the prairie decades later. Only the anchor remains as a relic in Micanopy's central parkway.

For countless centuries the rich grass supported deer and other game. When the Spanish arrived, they realized the prairie was also ideal for raising cattle, so in 1645 the Marquez family established La Chua ranch here, using Timucuan Indians and slaves as cowboys. La Chua beef not only helped feed hungry St. Augustine but the hides were shipped to Cuba in exchange for manufactured supplies and rum.

The Marquez family lived on the prairie in a hacienda sufficiently large to accommodate at least four servants, including two women, for we know that French pirates coming overland from the Suwannee captured it in 1682 and held the owners and servants for ransom. The loyalty of the Timucuans was proved when they ambushed the pirates and rescued the captives. Nonetheless, the British-Creek depredations that ultimately ruined the missions also doomed the Spanish ranches, of which La Chua was the largest; by the time William Bartram arrived a hundred yeas later the ranchers were gone. However, their cattle, now wild, remained to provide the Seminoles with barbecue feasts, one of which the British traders found so savory.

Later, American farmers wanted to turn the prairie into farmland, so they built a series of canals to drain the prairie of its wetness. But they were not successful, and after the site was purchased by the state in the 1970s, water was actually routed into the depression from the area around Cross Creek in order to preserve this precious environment.

Today Paynes Prairie is much as it was when nature, not human beings, determined its ecology. The state has done an admirable job of keeping people at bay, while allowing them to partake in the region's uniqueness. There are ample places to view the grassland. The tower and pathways at the Lake Wauberg Recreation Center are one. Bolen

Bluff, beside US 441, has a mile trail that loops along the prairie's rim, which you can use at no charge. Farther on, after US 441 dips directly into the prairie itself, there is turnout where a raised boardwalk goes a short distance into the grassland. Another fine view is from the rest park on Interstate 75 northbound. In addition there is a state trail that begins beside Gainesville's hard-to-find Boulware Springs at 3300 SE Fifteenth Street and continues eastward for sixteen miles. Much of the path skirts the prairie as it follows an abandoned railroad right-of-way to Hawthorne. A short side path not far from the Boulware trail head leads to the Alachua Sink, where water continues to drain into the porous limestone that underlies the basin.

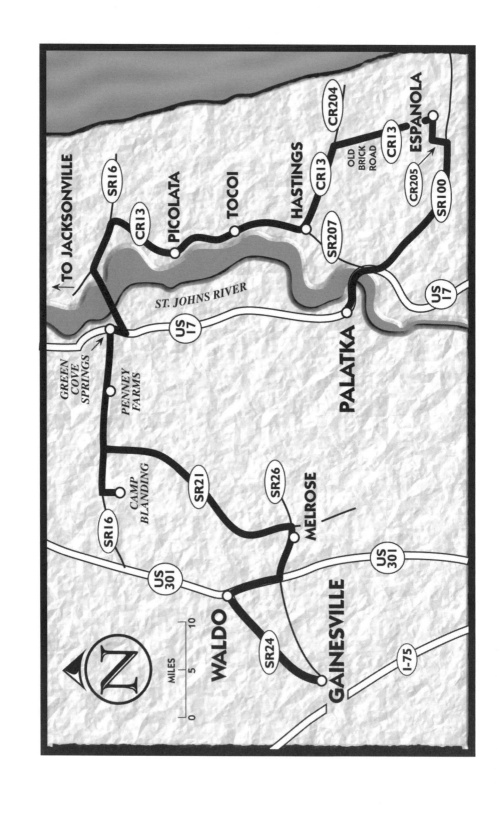

The City of the Future and the River of Music
Gainesville to Palatka • 131 Backroad Miles

The Song of the Road: Where the Byways Lead

This exploration begins in Gainesville with a drive through the University of Florida's beautiful campus. Then it's to the town's central business area, in the midst of a renovation to keep up with its regional competitor, Ocala. After a tour of the showplace, Thomas Mansion, you'll travel to Waldo for an exciting pass-through of a genuine speed trap. From there it's into pecan country along the old Bellamy Road, first constructed as a stump-pocked, pioneer cut through the wilderness in the 1820s.

Next it's northward through scrubby land to Camp Blanding to learn the exciting the story of American paratroopers in World War II while inspecting a genuine C-47 plane that carried some of them to Normandy. A barracks nearby has been converted into a military museum.

After that the way leads east to Penney Farms, where in the 1920s department store magnate J. C. Penney founded a retirement community that still thrives in the original Norman-style cottages set amid acres of grass and stately magnolias. Just down the road is Green Cove Springs on the St. Johns River. The spring, which attracted hordes of health-seekers during the steamboat era, still bubbles in the town's spacious riverside park.

From here you'll turn south on a road that hugs the river as it wends past Picolata, beloved by composer Frederick Delius, who incorporated the music of the St. Johns into several of his compositions. At Tocoi, another river hamlet, you can try your luck catching large mouth bass from the shore or simply enjoy watching for manatees.

Next it's on to Hastings, center of a rich potato farm area. Nearby you can drive fourteen miles down a little-known segment of the old Dixie Highway, with the original bricks and granite curbs still in place. The route is through largely deserted country that enables you to imagine being back in the Roaring Twenties and on your way to Miami to make a fortune in land speculation.

You'll end this exploration at Palatka, another picturesque former steamboat town on the St. Johns.

Gator Glory: Gainesville

It is natural to compare Gainesville and its regional rival, Ocala, particularly if you took the last exploration. *Florida Trend* magazine calls them "yin and yang," meaning whatever one is, the other isn't. Ocala is horses and retirees; Gainesville is government agencies and the youth-oriented university.

Although both are seats of counties that are roughly the same population, Ocala boasts a strong manufacturing base and is an active distribution hub, whereas Gainesville has a concentration of small, high-tech research firms. Ocala has excellent medical facilities, due partly to the age of its population, and has seen a large influx of doctors over the past dozen years. On the other hand, Gainesville's public school system is among the best in the nation. Because the two towns are only thirty-six miles apart, they often view each other with suspicion and watch carefully to see which might be gaining a competitive edge. For example, they would both have gained from establishing a regional airport somewhere between them, but what *Florida Trend* terms "parochialism" prevailed and the much-needed facility was never built.

The rivalry goes back to the days when the state was trying to decide where to build the University of Florida. Ocala was an early center of higher learning, with the establishment of the East Florida Seminary there in antebellum days. After the Civil War, the seminary was relocated to Gainesville, arousing the ire of Ocala citizens, who carried the dispute, unsuccessfully, onto the floor of the state legislature. The loss of the seminary cost them dearly when it became the forerunner of the University of Florida.

The university, established in 1905, is what fuels Gainesville's economy. Over the years the state has poured more than a half billion dollars into the construction of the university's 850-building campus, making UF one of the ten largest universities in the nation. The university continues to generate large sums: in 1996–97 alone it attracted $250 million in research and training grants. With a student population exceeding 40,000, young people are major supporters of many Gainesville businesses. The students come from more than a hundred countries, giving Gainesville a cosmopolitan aspect rare in central Florida.

If you took the last exploration, you'll be entering Gainesville from the south on US 441, also called SW Thirteenth Street. The university borders the road on the west. A good place to turn in is at SW Second Avenue, where there is an information booth with campus maps. Driving west from the booth on Union Road, you'll quickly reach Century Tower, the campus' centerpiece. Forty-nine bells at the summit ring out concerts at noon. They are played by a sweating carillonneur who must climb almost two-hundred steps to reach the keyboard. Next to it is the auditorium, with its impressive Gothic front. The auditorium is used for religious services, as well as for concerts and lectures. Across Union Road is the Plaza of the Americas, where twenty-one live oaks were planted in 1931 representing the Latin American countries attending the Pan-American Conference held on campus that year.

Continue on Union Road for one block until it ends at Buckman Drive, then go a block south to Stadium Road and proceed past the rear of the Ben Hill Griffin Stadium. Football has become a passion at the university and it is usually with trepidation that other teams meet the Gators in howling confines of Griffin Stadium, which locals lovingly call the Swamp. Particularly lively is the rousing rivalry with the Florida State Seminoles, based at Tallahassee. One climax of this rivalry occurred during the 1996–97

The University of Florida's football stadium becomes a familiar landmark during the fall season.

season, when Florida State beat the Gators in a game most thought would decide the national championship. Tallahassee was so elated that "National Champions" was printed on Florida State specialty license plates.

But, incredibly, the two teams met again on New Year's Day, and at this encounter the University of Florida won. Although the victory led UF to claim the national championship, naysayers at Florida State protested that UF had merely evened the series. Although the UF license plates that followed acknowledged a new champion, the old FSU ones were not recalled. So for the year Florida had two national champions. Perhaps that's the way it should have been.

Now turn right on North-South Drive to University Avenue, where you should head east past the front of the stadium, with its long row of tall palmettos. The impressive facade was added as part of the extensive 1990 expansion. At this time the stadium was renamed in honor of citrus magnate Ben Hill Griffin Jr., who had made sizable contributions to the school's athletic facilities.

When the campus was originally laid out, the land where the stadium now stands was an open field. The university began at Eighteenth Street, where Thomas Hall went up 1906. Within a few years Flint Hall was built opposite Sixteenth Street and Anderson Hall opposite Fifteenth. These buildings, which helped make up the original campus, are easily visible from University Avenue.

Of course, Gainesville is more than just the university. The town had been around for nearly half a century before the state decided to build on its western outskirts. Gainesville's initial growth dates back to 1859, with the arrival of the Florida Railroad, which was one reason the tiny settlement changed its name from Hog Town to the more dignified Gainesville. Edmund Gaines, who was so honored, was one of the most aggressive generals during the Second Seminole War. He gloried in battle, and when a Seminole bullet shattered some of his teeth, he simply spat them out and muttered to his men, "It's mean of the redskins to knock out two of my teeth when I have so few!" Though his blood was flowing, he kept on fighting.

Gainesville's rail connection enabled the town to become the marketplace for the surrounding countryside and the seat of Alachua County. Cotton was a major agricultural product. Truck gardens were likewise extremely valuable, and in 1904 alone enough melons were exported to fill 130 railroad cars.

The corner of Main Street and University Avenue was the heart of the little town. Here the ornate Alachua County Courthouse sat proudly in the center of a square, around which were prosperous businesses, as well as a goodly number of taverns. Horse buggies usually lined the streets, and water from the horse troughs was used to prime the hand pumps from which the citizens obtained their own drinking water. Not surprisingly, sickness was common, although no one seemed to know why.

In its heyday the square could be a wild place. At night, especially on the weekends, drinking and brawling were so common that after one fight in 1882, the newspaper commented laconically that nothing deadlier than an axe was used. Another incident involved four pistol-packin' drunks who staggered from one of the many taverns and started shooting wildly. Everyone, including the lone policeman, ran for cover. The quartet weaved along the square knocking the glass out of at least one store before they stationed themselves near where the Hippodrome Theater now stands. There they had a jolly time shooting and cursing until the whiskey ran out. Then they stumbled off and, as far as the records go, were never heard of again.

The post–World War II construction of suburban malls and strip shopping centers devastated the downtown. The county tried to make the square more attractive by ripping down the old courthouse and replacing it with a modern and much larger building in 1960. It was to no avail and gradually the area became something of a skid row.

But today Gainesville's downtown is being resurrected. The impetus was probably the 1980 conversion of the abandoned old post office into the Hippodrome State Theater. The Hippodrome "created a certain level of activity and a physical anchor to downtown," remarked the director of the Community Rede-velopment Agency. "It spun off a level of quality." And quality was what the downtown needed a strong dose of.

The rebirth of Gainesville's downtown began with the conversion of the old post office into the Hippodrome State Theater in 1980.

Then a few investors cautiously began to develop nearby buildings. The old opera house became a casual eatery. A rambling office building that wrapped around the sides and rear of the Hippodrome became retail stores, offices, and restaurants. A lot more has to be done. But Gainesville has gotten the downtown classified as an enterprise zone, which permits a lightening of taxes. The momentum seems to be there, and today businesses are returning to the city's traditional heart.

To reach the downtown take University Avenue to SE First Street (which is two blocks beyond SW First Street—it can be confusing until you understand the system). As you turn right you will see the Hippodrome State Theater, impressive with its six tall Corinthian columns, squatting where the street ends. Constructed as a post office in 1909, it was scheduled to be torn down before the thespians saved it.

Nearby are many buildings that are part of the downtown's renaissance. The 1887 refurbished Opera House building is at the southwest corner of SE First Street and SE First Avenue. (It was far easier to remember them when they were simply Market and Hay Streets.) White entertainers with black paint on their faces once gave minstrel shows on the second floor stage. Diagonally across the street, in a park

setting, is the 1925 Bethel gas station, whose hand pumps serviced many a Model T Ford. Across First Avenue is the Star Garage, built in 1903 as a horse stable, but now divided into modern offices.

Yet, for all the praiseworthy effort, one disappointment about the downtown is that the bland, post–World War II county building has gobbled up most of

The mansion of William Thomas, elected Gainesville's mayor in 1901, is open to the public

what was once the

tree-shaded courthouse square. Thus Gainesville lost what could have been a cornerstone of its resurrection. Although Ocala also tore down its old courthouse, at least the park remained.

The people with money lived in stately mansions on the sedate northeast side. Gainesville's finest home was that of William Thomas, who went by the title of "major," although he had never served in the military. Thomas would earn a handsome income as a banker, land developer, and retailer. He became Gainesville's mayor in 1901 and was one of the most influential figures in obtaining the university, the first building of which was named in his honor. In 1909 Thomas purchased a mansion at 302 NE Sixth Avenue and moved in the following year. It must have been quite an experience for his wife, Kathryn, who gave birth to a baby girl the day after they settled in.

The Thomas family lived in the mansion for fifteen years. Then in the 1920s, when their five children had grown up, and with William and Kathryn now rattling around the vacant rooms, the couple converted the home into a plush hotel, adding a three-story wing that brought the guest suites to ninety-four and included three dining rooms and four lounges. The major named the hotel after himself, and although he died in 1943, for many years thereafter the Thomas Hotel remained an attractive destination for tourists as well as for Gainesville's high society, who frequented it for balls, weddings, and other gala events.

But by the early 1970s the building had fallen into disrepair along with the rest of central Gainesville. To save the once-splendid structure from demolition, the city purchased it. Then civic groups, using local and federal funding, began the loving restoration that today has made the building a showplace once again, open to the public. Taking the free self-guided tour lets you see how the good life was enjoyed by a wealthy small-town gentleman and his family. The center is open Monday through Friday from 8 A.M. to 5 P.M. and Saturday and Sunday from 1 to 4 P.M.

Running the Gauntlet: Waldo

Leave Gainesville on University Avenue (SR 24) and head toward Waldo, fourteen miles northeast. It is not Waldo's flirtation with history that has made it one of the better-known towns in northern Florida, although it was on the state's first railroad line— along which Union raiders based in Jacksonville tramped in a brief and unsuccessful attack on Gainesville during the Civil War. No,

Waldo's fame does not rest on this solitary occurrence so long ago. On the contrary, the town's glory is much more recent, for this village of around a thousand has achieved national recognition from none other than the American Automobile Association, which proclaimed it one of America's three champion speed traps—the other two being close neighbors and fierce competitors Lawtey and Hampton.

If Waldo had prayed for an ideal auto snare, it could not have done better than SR 24. This is a football road, carrying an immense number of cars flooding into Gainesville from the Jacksonville area almost every autumn Saturday. Even better, US 301 comes down from the north, bringing Yankees and other foreigners into the jaws of Crackerville.

When the two highways were four-laned, Waldo hardly figured into the road-builders' calculations. Although the broad highway led traffic through the center of town, Waldo's businesses did not profit by it, for its tiny downtown had long since stagnated. The town was in desperate need of revenue, and it was far more agreeable to collect the needed funds from motorists passing through than from the town's own citizens. Hence, ticketing became a major industry, so much so that during a single month in 1995 Waldo's eight industrious police officers wrote 799 traffic tickets. This was a staggering number, for the average small town on a primary highway wrote barely four hundred tickets for that entire year. Therefore the AAA began stamping large warning letters on its trip tickets. (As of this writing Waldo is still on the list.) In addition, many Florida newspapers, getting hold of the story, gave little Waldo additional publicity.

With this preface, you must be curious to see what a real, honest-to-goodness speed trap looks like. I must admit I experienced a strange tingling sensation as I approached the infamous little town. Rarely can one challenge the fates with such minimal personal effort.

My first intimation that the game had begun was a sign posted out in the country, which apparently was within the village limits, saying something about the speed limit being strictly enforced. With this disclaimer, the limit dropped, for no apparent reason, from 65 mph to 45. Then, in barely a quarter mile, and still out in the country, the limit sunk to 35. Of course I braked, for I was on to them. But I still scanned the roadside nooks for lurking Waldo tax collectors. I noticed that most other Florida drivers were doing the same. But many out-of-state cars passed me—some going 36, even 37. Speeders, every one!

Now the four-lane highway arched through what Waldo considered downtown, but what looked to most drivers like a virtually deserted relic of the 1920s. There was no reason for them to suspect that the speed limit had now plunged to 15. Ah, what an ideal trap. The cops could have ticketed a dozen of the outlaws around me. But they only nabbed one, at least that I saw during my ten-minute sojourn. Now that's restraint.

I got through Waldo without incident, but the excitement had gotten into my blood. So I turned and ran the gauntlet once more, this time veering off on US 301 in the center of the metropolis. I saw a cop eye me—and the adrenalin flowed. Oh, how he wanted to write a ticket. But I was going below the limit. I could feel his frustration. But that's the way the game goes. I was the better man and he knew it. I left Waldo on a mental high.

So what kind of income does Waldo make from its money machine? The minimum speeding fine is $55. It rises to $130 for 10 to 14 miles per hour over the limit, and to $155 for 15 to 19 mph over. So if the tickets given out average, say, $100 and should Waldo continue writing around 4,500 yearly, it would bring the village almost half a million dollars annually. No wonder Waldo cannot give up what it quaintly call its "strict traffic enforcement."

But now for the good news, sort of. Conditions at Waldo, Hampton, and Lawtey got so bad that in 1998 the Florida legislature passed a law stating that a town could not issue a ticket, only a warning, if a motorist was going no more that five miles above the posted speed limit. It is not much of a concession, but at least it's something. And the following year the AAA's Foundation for Safety got permission to paint a series of ninety stripes across SR 24 at the entry to Waldo as a warning to slow down. So what was the response of Waldo's police chief? "After the speeders get used to it," he mused laconically, "they will probably continue speeding." And, if they do, Waldo will be waiting.

Dodging the Stumps: The Old Bellamy Road

Driving south from Waldo on US 301, you are on a low, sandy rise called the Trail Ridge. Originally it may have been a trader's route, but during the decades-long conflict between the Spanish in Florida and the British in Georgia it became a pathway of terror as the warlike Creek allies of the British raided the more peacefully inclined Timucuans, many of whom had turned Christian under the guidance of the Franciscan missionaries. By 1706 the Creeks had killed most of the Timucuans or carried them off as slaves. By then the Spanish missions, as well as the once-prosperous Spanish ranches, lay in ruins.

In five miles you will reach SR 26, where you should turn east for six miles to Melrose. On the way you'll pass groves of pecan trees, indicating that, although you are still in Florida, the heart of pecan country in Georgia is not far distant.

You are now on the route of the old Bellamy Road, Florida's first federal highway constructed between 1824 and 1826, only a few years after the territory was acquired from the Spanish and while the land was still Seminole hunting grounds. The road's purpose was to connect Florida's principal town, St. Augustine, with its muddy, new territorial capital, Tallahassee. Congress allocated a picayune $50 per mile to construct a road twenty-five feet wide through the virtually uninhabited wilderness. Nevertheless the job was taken on by John Bellamy, who owned a plantation near St. Augustine.

Bellamy and his slaves began hacking westward from St. Augustine. Some of the time he followed the old trail that had connected the town with the former Spanish missions. But that path did a great deal of meandering, so usually Bellamy relied on an Indian guide to show him the most direct route through the thick pine forest. Although there were few if any funds to pay for the Indian's service, Bellamy must have thought liberal swigs from the barrel of rum he kept in his mule wagon would buy his loyalty. But the Indian ran off one night. After Bellamy tracked him down, he chained the Indian to his own ankle during the day and to a tree at night—so much for the rights of labor.

Axe-men did the chopping, and the dead trees were simply piled up at the side. The stumps were not removed—why bother, for the drivers would get used to dodging them and in a few years they would rot away. There was little or no attempt to form a road bed, or to raise the way above wet areas. Where the streams were impossible to ford bridges were constructed. But they were narrow, wobbly things that travelers tried to avoid when at all possible. With the minimum amount of actual road building, Bellamy's choppers·were often able to move ahead a quarter mile in a single twelve work hour day. To help quell mutterings against the hard labor, Bellamy dolled out liberal draughts of rum each evening.

Crude as it was, the Bellamy Road served as a major pioneer route for thirty years, until Jacksonville displaced St. Augustine as north Florida's major city. With the rise of the railroads in the 1880s, the road was virtually abandoned; today it exists only in a few disconnected segments. Melrose contains one of these, SR 26, still referred to here as the Bellamy Road.

The hamlet of Melrose had a brief flurry of prosperity in the 1880s when a canal was opened at the western end of Santa Fe Lake, permitting steamboats to haul the local citrus all the way to the railroad at Waldo. The rail-steamboat connection also permitted Northern tourists to spend the winter at one of the Melrose's waterfront resorts. But the great freeze of 1994–95 ended the citrus trade, so the steamboats and the tourists no longer came and the town slid into an economic decline from which it never really recovered.

Now turn north on SR 21 from Melrose. The way is through gently rolling pine lands. The soil is almost pure sand: the remains of Ice Age deposits left by Atlantic breakers on the windy beaches.

One of the pleasures of driving the backroads is that the unhurried atmosphere gives you time to ponder the big, important issues of life. So consider that now you are crossing into the gum-chewing portion of Florida. According to a recent *Newsweek* article, the demarcation line runs directly across the very land over which you are driving. Gum-chewing may seem frivolous, but there may be something deeper here, for putting a foreign substance into your mouth and working on it, perhaps for hours with both your tongue and your teeth, is an extremely personal act. Why do so many of these people do it? What does it reveal about their inner beings? How do they differ from the nonchewers just south of the line? I'm sure you'll try as ardently as I did to find an answer to these vital questions.

Meanwhile SR 21 goes through an area of many lakes. It should be beautiful, but, for the most part, houses line the shores and the only thing appealing about Lake Geneva is its name. When you reach SR 16, turn west for a couple of miles to the Camp Blanding entrance.

Memories of a War: Camp Blanding

Although Camp Blanding is currently a training site for Florida's National Guard, the main interest to casual visitors is the memorial park, just outside the main gate. Here there are tanks and artillery from America's twentieth-century wars. The park's focal point is a two-engine Douglas C-47 Skytrain. This workhorse plane did everything from delivering military supplies to transporting paratroopers on jumps deep in enemy territory. The paratroopers were elite units, and many were trained at Blanding. An audio reenactment of an actual operation in Normandy lets you appreciate the danger these men went through. You can even hear the deadly rattle of Nazi machine guns.

Camp Blanding's remoteness from population centers made it ideal for the confinement of German prisoners of war. The first several hundred prisoners arrived in September 1942. These were men taken from some of the submarines that were torpedoing ships so fast off the Florida coast that many beaches had turned black with oil. They were an arrogant group, firmly convinced that the Nazi legions, then sweeping across Russia, would soon dominate Europe. In November of the following year soldiers from Rommel's vaunted Afrika Korps began arriving. They too were haughty men, disrespectful of America's fighting strength as well as of the prison guards. Just before Christmas they staged a riot that was put down with difficulty.

At the height of Camp Blanding's use as a POW compound, there were 1,200 former German soldiers and sailors here, plus another 3,000 in scattered branch camps. Although the camp was enclosed by a double barrier of barbed wire fences, there was little concern about escapees, since not only would it be impossible for them to get back to Germany, but they were warned that any escapee would find himself at the mercy of the FBI, which the Germans equated with their own utterly ruthless Gestapo. When one escapee was found hanging from a tree near Lake Okeechobee, their fears seemed confirmed—although American authorities claimed he was a suicide.

The mood of the camp changed during 1944 as less doctrinaire prisoners entered the compound. These men had been taken during the Normandy campaign and knew that the war was lost. From then on the prisoners were much easier to handle, and, as American and British forces began driving into Germany itself, movies shown to the POWs of the Nazi death camps opened many eyes to the dreadfulness of Hitler's regime. The revulsion was so deep that the Germans themselves took up a collection to aid the survivors of these camps.

Camp Blanding's museum features a C-47 Skytrain that transported paratroopers during World War II.

The C-47 and other outdoor exhibits are available for inspection every day from 8 A.M. until dusk. Admission is free. Additional historical exhibits are in an adjacent World War II barracks that has been turned into a museum. It is open between noon and 4 P.M. seven days a week, with no charge.

The Failure That Succeeded: Penney Farms

Now head back east on SR 16. In seven miles the road is suddenly lined with magnolia trees, their shiny leaves glowing as if each one had been individually polished. This is the pleasant setting for Penney Farms.

It was not like this in the beginning. The farms involved the broken dreams of none other than J. C. Penney, whose undertakings were otherwise so successful that his gigantic retailing chain is today the fourth largest in the nation.

James Cash Penney was born in 1875 on a cattle ranch in Missouri. The son of a Baptist minister, Penney called his first store The Golden Rule. Through hard work and a strict adherence to high moral principles, he rapidly expanded to a total of two hundred stores by 1920.

While business matters had gone smoothly, Penney's personal life had been marked with tragedy. As a young man he had fallen deeply in love with Berta Hess, a beautiful woman devoted to his success. She worked with him in his first little store, and, even after a son was born, she often had the baby sleep under the counter while she waited on customers. In 1910 Berta had her tonsils removed, a routine operation. But on the way home she was caught in a chilling rain and developed pneumonia. While Penney knelt at her bedside, Berta died. It was a shock from which he never really recovered.

Nine years later, at the age of forty-three, Penney wed Mary Kimball. By now he was a prosperous merchant, and two years later the happy couple bought a winter mansion on Belle Isle in the Miami area. Mary, a vivacious, outgoing woman, loved to entertain, and even installed a large pipe organ in the home where some of the top professional musicians gave concerts for the Penneys and their numerous guests. But after just three and half years of marriage, Mary suddenly died of what the doctors called "acute indigestion," which was probably food poisoning.

Penney had difficulty understanding why a second beloved had been taken from him. "It has brought me into a closer realization of the power of God," he wrote a friend. "It has also made me feel that I have not rendered the service to my fellow man that I should have done."

With this in mind Penney formed a corporation with business associate Ralph W. Gwinn, and in February 1925 they purchased at public auction a huge spread of desolate, abandoned farmland in Florida's Clay County. Penney intended to turn it into a scientifically managed community of individual farms for persons who were willing to work hard, who had at least the minimum of funds to keep them going the first difficult year, and who satisfied his high moral criteria.

This was not to be a welfare project, for each settler at Penney Farms would be expected to make his farm a going enterprise and ultimately to purchase the land at a small profit to the corporation. Since this was to be case, it was in the interest of both Penney and the farmers that they succeed. To this end Penney established the Institute of Applied Agriculture staffed by experts whose duties were to determine what plants would produce the finest crops, what was the proper combination of fertilizers to use, what sort of crop rotation was best for the soil, as well as solutions to the many other factors that would enable the farmers to obtain maximum yields. To further the scientific approach, extension courses in the latest agricultural techniques would be offered at the nearby University of Florida.

Penney was convinced that the same good business practices and spirit of dedication that he had utilized to rise from near poverty to unbounded prosperity would, when applied to agriculture, enable his farmers to also prosper. They, in turn, might become inspirations for farmers across the nation.

The first families arrived in October 1925, and by February their number stood at forty. Most had been recommended by managers of Penney stores who knew them personally. In addition, each had been interviewed by Penney-Gwinn Company executives to be sure each was the type of person needed to make this experiment succeed. There would be no drinkers or smokers among them, and they must have had farming experience.

Everyone was brimming with enthusiasm, and quickly a sense of camaraderie developed among the families. By the fall of 1926 they had planted a variety of crops and fruit trees, and most had chicken coops. A general store had sprung up, providing a convenient gathering place. At about the same time a school had been built, and eventually 150 rambunctious children were in attendance.

These were also good times for J.C. Penney, for that same year he found love once more. Caroline was her name, and although she was twenty years younger than he, they formed a personal bond that was to last until the end of Penney's long life.

Penney was immensely pleased when he made his regular visits to the farms. Everything seemed to be going so well. Soon the community even had electricity, carried to it over the new powerlines from Starke. More families continued to arrive, many attracted by company ads that extolled the community's prosperity.

Penney believed that God himself was guiding him after a voice at four in the morning told him that he should also provide retirement facilities at the farms for missionaries and ministers. Accordingly, in the summer of 1926 Penney established the Memorial Home Community, which he dedicated to his mother and father. Immediately work started on a church as well as scores of dwelling units to be constructed in an appealing Norman-Gothic architectural style.

The church commanded most of Penney's attention. The great interior arches were carved from carefully hand-hewn wood, and the roof was lovingly laid with orange-colored tiles from Georgia. The building was crowned by a massive tower, which, rising three stories, became a visual symbol of the religious principles guiding the community.

Penney was at the church for what was called the "Dedication of a Dream." Giving flowery speeches were Governor John Martin and U.S. Senator Duncan Fletcher, as well as retired ministers from sixteen

The church so dear to department store magnate J. C. Penney still graces the Penney Farms retirement community.

different denominations. After the ceremony, Penney and Margaret Sangster, a journalist with the *Christian Herald*, lingered in the church. It was a moment that approached the sublime. "I could feel the force of character of Mr. Penney's parents," Sangster wrote. "Even though the church was empty, I knew that it was in truth crowded."

Fortunately for Penney, this moment of triumph was not marred by knowledge that the seeds of disaster had already been planted. For many settlers had neglected their farms in order to take the much-higher-paying construction jobs involving the church and the retirement homes. When the buildings were completed, a return to farm drudgery had little appeal. This discontent was intensified by plummeting farm prices that sent such a staple as potatoes from $12 a barrel at the start of 1927 to just $4 by 1928.

And that was not all. The Penney-Gwinn Corporation completely underestimated the huge amount of fertilizer the sandy soil demanded—and for which the farmers had to pay. Nor did they provide the expected expertise in marketing the crops.

In retrospect, J. C. Penney himself had almost foreordained the failure by his original purchase of such infertile acreage. His otherwise acute business sense must have been clouded by the fact that he could obtain the land so cheaply at an auction.

Penney was extremely distressed as the farming colony began to deteriorate. By 1928 the men and women who had come with such high expectations and gratitude were bitterly complaining to him. "Who wants to fight bugs, suffer extreme heat, and lose money crop after crop," wrote usually cheerful Margaret Calder. "Your articles in the Magazines are very enticing but to be fair you should tell the people how much fertilizer they have to use . . . we know of people who are here now and would love to move, but they sank their all into this year's potato crop and they were left so short that they have not money enough to get out, and that is a crime." Strong words, to accuse Penney of a crime—he who had already put hundreds of thousands of his own money into the failing project.

As families began abandoning their farms, it became clear that the noble project would fail without Penney's financial intervention. But by 1929, when the securities market made its catastrophic crash, Penney himself was on a horrible downward slide. He had put most of his stock up as collateral for loans, and, because its value had collapsed with the market, he could not meet his obligations. As the Great Depression deepened, Penney sold one asset after another, but in 1932 was forced to declare bankruptcy. By that time the farm homes were deserted and the fields had gone to weeds. The land was sold to Foremost Dairies, which converted it into pasture and timber.

As for the retirement community, Penney was no longer able to help subsidize that operation, which was separate from the farms. This was a tremendous blow to the elderly couples, who now had to pay monthly maintenance fees, and thirty-two virtually destitute families had to leave. Many of the rest barely survived from the sparse produce from their bug-infested vegetable gardens.

The tragic end of the Florida dream was nearly as severe a blow to J. C. Penney as to the participants. Yet the Memorial Home Community survived under the *Christian Herald*. Penney, who gradually rebuilt his finances, made sentimental pilgrimages to the church almost every year until the frailties of age prevented him. He died in 1971.

Today the retirement community thrives. Each of the quaint homes of the Penney era is occupied by couples enjoying their golden years. The church continues to be the community centerpiece, and the ringing chimes create a sense of peace and well-being. The church rests at the end of a long parkway lined with palms and magnolias planted about the same time as those that grace SR 16. This is not a gated community, for it is far from city-bred turmoil, so you can drive along its tranquil streets whenever you wish.

Continue east on SR 16. The original road was the creation of J. C. Penney, who, in order to have it built from Green Cove Springs, purchased the entire issue of bonds that financed it.

Steamboat Memories: Green Cove Springs

From Penney Farms it is six miles east on SR 16 to Green Cove Springs, a town of 5,000 and the seat of Clay County. One of the first public buildings you'll see is the former county courthouse just across the CSX tracks at Walnut Street. This is an old, weathered building dating back to the era when the forerunner of the CSX deposited hundreds of excited tourists each winter at the station. From here carriages transported them down thriving Walnut to the bevy of large hotels fronting the St. Johns River and the fabled health spring that had attracted them. It is difficult to imagine the courthouse when it was sparkling and lively, for today it is unoccupied, except for a musty historical museum that is open at the convenience of volunteers (which at this writing is Sunday between 2 and 5 P.M.). Today the drive east on Walnut is past many empty stores, although you'll probably have to wait at the Palmetto Avenue stop light, where there is usually not enough traffic to warrant even a slow down.

Excursionists of yesteryear sought the luxury of the Qui-Si-Sana Hotel, whose name meant "health is here," referring to the mineral spring that welled up just beyond the hotel's eastern portals. The Qui-Si-Sana shell still stands at the corner of Walnut and US 17, but it is in disrepair and its glory days are long gone. Indeed, it was all the little town could do to obtain money from a state grant to repair the roof of the 1907 dowager.

The spring still flows gently up from a deep cavern, on the walls of which the sunlight forms glittering blue patterns. The water has a high mineral content, including sulfur, chloride, nitrate, iron, and calcium. The faint odor of hydrogen sulfide floats downwind. Although its medicinal powers have not been proven, many locals come weekly to fill their jugs with the liquid that has only the faintest sulfur flavor.

Yet a hundred years ago it was not so quiet, as people from all over the United States and Europe crowded beside the spring or splashed in the enclosed swimming pool, which was always at a pleasant seventy-eight degrees, even during the chilliest days of January. Here, according to an 1874 visitor, the crippled, the rheumatic, the dispirited, the feeble gathered "in the hope that by daily ablution in the clear blue waters of the spring, and by long inhalation of its sulphurated fumes, they might at last—'restore to wintry age the greenness of its spring.'"

People from all over the world came to Green Cove Springs to enjoy the hoped-for medicinal benefits of water issuing from this spring.

The town dock at the end of Walnut Street extended far into the St. Johns. During tourist season it was alive with steamboats that had made the four-hour cruise up from Jacksonville. This was a pleasant trip, with bands providing the entertainment and the river providing the scenery. A good-sized steamboat could hold more than a hundred passengers. Chugging along at up to twenty miles an hour was enough to cause a refreshing breeze to waft over the vessel. A night sail was special, with torches lighting the dancing waters. And under a full moon, there was no more beautiful place on earth than the St. Johns.

Green Cove's heyday faded as the railroads built ever farther south to carry pleasure seekers to warmer climes. By the First World War the steamboats were rotting and most of Green Cove's hotels had been torn down or converted into boarding houses. Soon only the Qui-Si-Sana remained.

Today the spring flows to a modern public pool, where Grovians relish its warm temperature as well as whatever health benefits it might impart. It is open to the public at a nominal fee, but only during the summer when lifeguards are available. The runoff ravine is landscaped and is a treasured part of the block-square riverside park, where picnic pavilions overlook the river. The Walnut Street pier has been extended four hundred feet into the river, and more boat slips have been added. But the old Qui-Si-Sana and the nearly deserted downtown await renovation and revitalization.

So the town is calling out for benefactors with ideas and capital. Are any out there listening?

Wilderness Symphony: Picolata

From Green Cove Springs drive south on SR 16. After crossing the St. Johns on the mile-long Shands Bridge, continue south to CR 13, which will lead you over Six Mile Creek, where there is a country-style restaurant with a scenic pavilion overlooking the surprisingly broad stream. A short distance farther south you'll come to the community of Picolata.

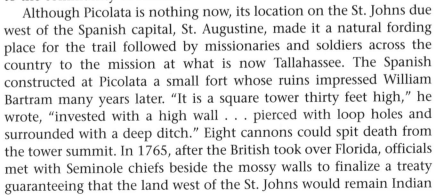

Although Picolata is nothing now, its location on the St. Johns due west of the Spanish capital, St. Augustine, made it a natural fording place for the trail followed by missionaries and soldiers across the country to the mission at what is now Tallahassee. The Spanish constructed at Picolata a small fort whose ruins impressed William Bartram many years later. "It is a square tower thirty feet high," he wrote, "invested with a high wall . . . pierced with loop holes and surrounded with a deep ditch." Eight cannons could spit death from the tower summit. In 1765, after the British took over Florida, officials met with Seminole chiefs beside the mossy walls to finalize a treaty guaranteeing that the land west of the St. Johns would remain Indian forever. The "forever" held only as long as the English ruled Florida, which was barely eighteen more years.

During its rule the British government encouraged its subjects to settle in Florida, and a year later William Bartram started a plantation on the east bank of the river six miles south of Picolata. Billy, as he was called, was hardly qualified to brave the frontier, for he was only twenty-seven years of age and had no experience in farming or in managing his six slaves, who scoffed at working for such a mild-mannered, bookish person. He lived in what one visitor called a "hovel," where he suffered greatly from the heat and from a fever he contracted. No wonder he soon dumped the project and, after his father willed him a goodly sum, took to travel and intellectual pursuits that would earn him the respect of scholars and historians.

After the Americans took over, Picolata enjoyed a brief resurrection when it became a ferry-point on the Bellamy Road. But with the advent of railroads in the 1870s Picolata drifted into the pleasant backwater that it enjoys today.

Highway 13 around Picolata offers one of Florida's most agreeable drives. Although the ancient fort has vanished, the smooth-flowing St. Johns remains. Overhead, large trees form a fluttering, green umbrella. The few homes on large lots across the road do not intrude. This fragment of beauty is so brief that you may want to park and stroll leisurely along the shoulders.

The road through Picolata recalls the days when young Frederick Delius roamed the St. Johns River country.

Given Picolata's serene splendor it is not surprising that composer-to-be Frederick Delius chose to temporarily settle here to manage his father's orange grove in 1884. The twenty-two-year-old Englishman let the oranges rot on the trees while he visited the homes of former slaves to absorb the throbbing rhythms of their music, the likes of which had seldom reached European ears. When he returned to the Old World, he incorporated what he had heard along the St. Johns into such compositions as "Night on the River," "Songs of Sunset," and, most of all, "Florida Suite." Although in his last years he developed progressive paralysis and blindness, memories of his sojourn at Picolata never left him.

Neither did appreciation for Delius leave Florida, for the site of the orange grove has been purchased by Jacksonville University, which has installed a sign beside CR 13 at the private sand road leading to the site. The university moved the composer's small frame house to a place of honor on its campus, where an annual Delius Festival is held at the beginning of spring.

"Long Reaches of Green": Tocoi

From Picolata CR 13 leaves the river for a few miles, but returns as it approaches Tocoi. During the Spanish era Tocoi was a favorite site for transporting cattle from La Chua and other ranches to the St. Johns' east bank. From here the animals were driven to St. Augustine over a trail now followed by CR 214.

After Florida became American, a long pier was constructed into the river to accommodate the steamboats and sailing vessels that frequented the St. Johns. For persons wishing to go to St. Augustine, wooden rails were laid along the old cattle path, and horse-drawn cars were installed. The horses plodded along so slowly that they usually took four hours to

The protected cove in Tocoi has made this a favorite crossing of the St. Johns River since the days of the Spanish.

complete the fifteen-mile journey. One of the passengers in 1873 was none other than Harriet Beecher Stowe, who had written the anti-slavery *Uncle Tom's Cabin* two decades earlier. But the Civil War was over and Mrs. Stowe and her husband now owned a winter home at Mandarin, twenty-five miles downriver. Often accompanied by her husband and twin daughters, Stowe made many excursions on the St. Johns River, where she became acquainted with the Tocoi railroad: "To us this bit of ride through the Florida woods is such a never-ceasing source of interest and pleasure, that we do not mind the slowness of it, and should regret being whisked by at steam-speed. We have come over it three times; and each time the varieties of shrubs and flowers, grasses and curious leaves, were a never-failing study and delight. Long reaches of green moist land form perfect flower-gardens." She enjoyed watching male passengers leap from the train to gather blossoms, then clamber back on board and present them to the ladies.

Today the long pier is gone and the wooden railroad exists only in Stowe's *Palmetto Leaves*. But the village is still as slow paced as when horses ambled leisurely off through the flowered trees toward St. Augustine. If you're not in a hurry, you can have a sandwich on the veranda of the general store. The calm river will be almost at your feet, and you might even spot a lumbering manatee or two, providing you're there in the winter when they prefer the warm river to the cold Atlantic. For a longer stay, the Tocoi Creek Fish Camp and Lodge, owners of the general store, have motel units on the St. Johns.

You may be surprised at the width of the river, which is several miles across. Actually the lower St. Johns is hardly a river at all, but more a long estuary to the Atlantic. It actually has a tidal flow, whose brackish currents allow such salt-loving creatures as shrimp, tarpon, snook, and even stingrays and sharks to swim far inland. The annual shrimp run, which begins toward the end of August and lasts for five or six weeks, is an exciting time. The shrimp, after maturing in protected backwaters, swarm downstream to spawn in the Atlantic. When the run is at its height, recreational shrimpers using cast nets can fill a five-gallon bucket in a few hours.

Potato Country: Hastings

The three miles south from Tocoi show off one of the prettiest riverscapes in Florida. The scenic turnout at Riverdale is marred only by a distant smokestack. After the road leaves the river to avoid a swampy area, it reaches a belt of great fertility famous for potatoes, as you may guess when you come to a crossroads called Spuds.

Potatoes are not a native North American plant, but were originated in Peru, providing Inca warriors with the sustenance to erect their remarkable Andean Empire. The conquistadors took them to Europe, where, because they gained a reputation for curing impotence, their price reached near-astronomical heights. From there the Spanish and English brought them to North America, where they eventually fulfilled their destiny: to be greased up and sold as McDonald's French fries. Today the average American wolfs down seventy-two pounds of potatoes each year.

Three miles past Spuds, CR 13 enters Hastings, named for Tom Hastings, who founded the settlement in 1890 to produce potatoes for fancy hotels in St. Augustine. The town held a memorable celebration in 1914 when the Dixie Highway opened through town. This was a big event: the completion of America's first interstate, which ran from the Midwest all the way to Miami. Everyone decorated the horses and buggies for the occasion and paraded along the fabulous road that was actually bricked!

Red Brick Road to Never-Never Land: The Old Dixie Highway

Almost the entire original Dixie Highway has long since been replaced by modern roads. But a fourteen-mile segment of it actually exists, and cars can still be driven over it. Take CR 13 about ten miles east from Hastings to a solitary street sign on your right that says "Old Brick Road." Turning south you will find yourself on a narrow, nine-foot-wide brick path through largely uninhabited second-growth timberlands. There are few signs of civilization, not even utility poles. Old Brick is slow, but it is still in use and even has an official designation of CR 13.

Somewhere along the line get out of your car and examine the bricks. They have the markings placed on them when they were wet clay and still unbaked. Most were made by Graves in Birmingham, Alabama. They vary in color from distinctly reddish to brown to nearly black, the tint depending on how much shale was mixed in. The variations give the roadway a pleasing appearance. Notice the cement curbs that protrude no more than a few inches above the bricks. They had to be low because, as the pavement was too narrow to permit cars to pass, one had to drive over the curb and wait on the shoulder.

Although the Old Brick Road is virtually deserted today, in former years it was thronged with jalopies toting maw and paw and the young 'uns to what everyone believed would be paradise. It was the Red Brick Road to the Emerald City. They rocked down this very highway—honking, cussing, laughing, sweating—phantoms of wealth dancing on their steaming car hoods. Many had their entire life savings stashed in their frayed suitcases They planned to invest it in Florida real estate and let it ride into the stratosphere. With their new wealth they'd buy a mansion on Biscayne Bay and a yacht, and spend the rest of their lives in this blissful land of Oz.

But the bust of 1926 ended their dreams of Florida fortunes and sent the same horde rattling back north, the jangle once in their pockets and dreams once in their souls left with the binder-boys at Miami.

The Old Brick Road would have many stories to tell if it could speak. But it's quiet now, the past secreted away in the silent bricks. As you drive through the solitude, perhaps you'll hear whispers of what was.

At the approach to Espanola there are a couple of signs that you may find ironic. The first reads "Reduced Speed Ahead" and the second "35 mph." How fast do they think a person drives on the bumpy old road?

 At Espanola, which consists mainly of a community house and a cemetery, take CR 205 south to SR 100, where you should head

The original Dixie Highway still exists as a county road a few miles east of Hastings

for Palatka, twenty-four miles west. SR 100 is one of the principal timber routes, and there are almost always long trucks hauling pine trunks to the huge Georgia-Pacific mill at Palatka. You'll probably see a truck or two being loaded in a cut-over field along the way. The forests are owned by private companies, some of whom reseed the clear-cut areas; others let the pines reseed themselves, which they seem to do quite efficiently. Within fifteen or twenty years the trees will be tall enough to be harvested once more.

SR 100 eventually merges with US 17, and together they enter Palatka by way of a high bridge across the St. Johns. At the foot of the bridge there is a Holiday Inn that has a restaurant, as well as rooms, with excellent views of the river. (Reservations: 800-465-4329.)

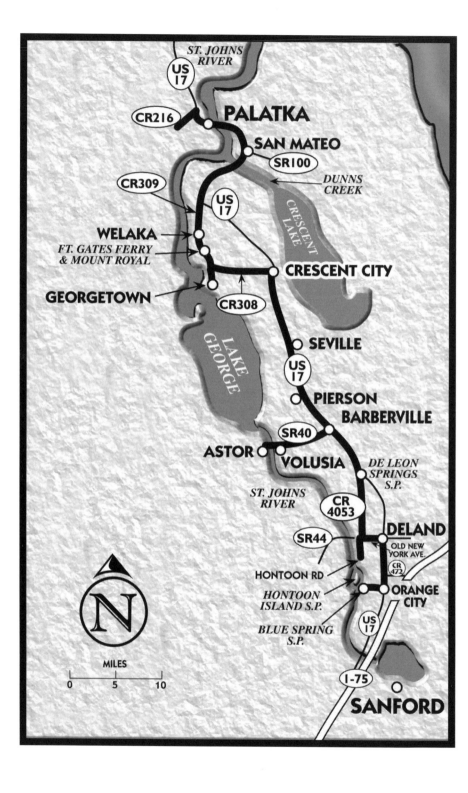

The Pleasures of the River Road

Palatka to Sanford • 124 Backroad Miles

The Song of the Road: Where the Byways Lead

Before you take the open road on this last exploration, you'll want to spend a little time in Palatka. During the steamboat era this was the queen city of the St. Johns River, and many buildings of that era remain. Later Palatka became the location of a huge timbermill. The Georgia-Pacific Corporation still has an impressive plant where visitors can watch great mechanical claws unload the large timber trucks in a single grasp.

Then it's southward along the river, perhaps stopping at the Bass Haven Lodge in Welaka for breakfast or lunch while looking out on the water near where Confederate cavalry defeated a Union warship in one of the Civil War's most unusual battles. Farther on you can take the old Fort Gates ferry for a rather primitive, but most pleasant river ride. Nearby are the remains of the Mount Royal mound, once sacred to the now-vanished Timucuan people.

Leaving the river temporarily, you'll drive to Crescent City to stop at the venerable Sprague House inn and restaurant, known for its pair of stained-glass windows depicting a stage coach and a riverboat. Farther down the highway you'll pass through fern country, with hundreds of netted greenhouses. A side trip will take you to Astor on the St. Johns. Canoes are for rent here—or you can just enjoy the food and the river view from the second floor balcony of the Blackwater Inn.

More canoes are for rent at DeLeon Springs State Park, where you can also swim in the spring-fed pool. Hontoon Island State Park, just down the road, also has canoes as well as a lookout tower that presents a windy vista of many miles. At Blue Spring State Park you can board a pontoon boat for a narrated cruise on the St. Johns, or can also swim in the clear, cool water of the spring run. And winter visitors are thrilled by the dozens of manatees that make the spring their temporary home.

The Town That Steamboats and Cypress Built: Palatka

Compared with its county seat neighbors, Gainesville and Ocala, Palatka is a laggard. One reason is that, with a population just 10,000, the town has a much smaller financial base for revitalization. And the income level of surrounding Putnam County is significantly below that of Alachua and Marion Counties.

But Palatka was not always this insignificant. During the prehistoric era the location was well known to the Indians, who called it the pilatka, or "fording place," and often held canoe races here. British traders constructed a major post called the Lower Store, just south of Palatka and it was from here that William Bartram set out in 1774 on his historic trip to the Native-American settlements at Micanopy. Six decades later, during the Seminole War, the American army converted Palatka into the hub from which men and material, transported by steamboat from Jacksonville, were dispatched to the military posts that were scattered strategically throughout central Florida.

Once the Indians were gone and the interior opened, Palatka became the northern terminus of Hubbard Hart's stagecoach line that ran through Ocala and Brooksville all the way to Tampa.

During the Civil War Lincoln's military advisors considered Palatka vital to control the St. Johns and thereby prevent supplies from reaching the Confederate armies. After Palatka fell to Union forces based in Jacksonville, it became the key port for Union gunboats. At its height up to five thousand federal troops were stationed in Palatka, one of their barracks being the St. Mark's Episcopal Church, which still stands at the corner of North Second and Main streets.

Palatka's halcyon days came immediately after the Civil War. Hubbard Hart again led the way when he started a steamboat line that ran not only down to Jacksonville, but also up the Ocklawaha all the way to Silver Springs. It took a day and a half to reach that natural wonder, but the numerous sightseers agreed it was worth it. Hart also built the Putnam House, which instantly became Palatka's finest hostelry. As his profits continued to mount, Hart developed Palatka Heights on the bluffs a few blocks back from the waterfront from which residents gained pleasing views of the town and river. Here he constructed his own residence: a two-and-a-half-story mansion that still stands at 1220 Kirby Street.

By now the riverboat era was in full flower. Docks and piers bristled along what are now Memorial Parkway and First Street. A half-dozen or more times a day the town echoed to the whistle of an incoming vessel. Each steamer brought excitement: goods from far away, visitors from distant places—maybe relatives long since seen. And when a boat pulled back into the water, it carried the bounty of the country-side: heavy bales of cotton, bulging crates of oranges, and stacks of fragrant pine lumber. The riverboats also gave the villagers the oppor-tunity to travel to Jacksonville or even Savannah, which was many days by land but only forty-five hours by steamer. Isolation finally was a thing of the past. One recollection illustrates:

> We are glad to see [each steamboat] gliding up and down our river. It seems to give life to everything. The merchants move with quicker step. . . . Individuals feel its influence, the community feels it, and the streams of life course their way with quicker pulsation.

A trip on the St. Johns was a joy. The boat could clip through the water at fifteen miles an hour, creating a cooling breeze on the hottest Florida day. For special occasions the line hired bands, often Italians with concertinas and beautiful voices. Even without professionals someone was always strumming a banjo while others sang. A boat could carry as many as 150 passengers, so anyone could find compan-ions of his or her liking. And when the moon came up and silver danced on the wavelets—ah, could paradise be sweeter?

Palatka's Memorial Parkway affords a beautiful view of the St. Johns River.

Palatka lived for its steamboats. Everyone had favorite ships, so it was natural that there was competition among them. A certain race was described by a young man in the dockside crowd watching expectantly through the nighttime. At last one ship appeared: "Her funnels were blazing with sparks from her furnace," he wrote. "They were firing rockets from the decks—a beautiful sight, but no one could tell which boat it was that had showed up. She had hardly rounded the corner as it were before the second boat showed up . . . blazing, sparks flying and rockets also."

Tension gripped the crowd, for many bets had been placed. And when the winner became clear, pandemonium broke out.

Many thought the steamboats would always be there. But some realized they could not compete with the railroads that began snaking though the countryside in the 1880s, as a steamboat could carry only a fraction of the freight that a train could. The boats also had a disquieting tendency toward boiler explosions. In addition, they were subject to delays from storms or high winds, and their circuitous routes following the river bends made them far slower than a train on tracks that bridged over or cut through physical obstacles. Although the steamboats died slowly, by the early 1900s they were little more than nostalgic memories.

But Palatka revived. Cypress trees, plentiful in the swamps bordering the St. Johns, kept the town alive. Hauled to the river bank, they were formed into rafts more than 150 feet long and guided by tugboats to the Wilson Cypress plant, which, during its heyday, boasted being the second largest cypress mill in the world. The company had two piers, each protruding 1,800 feet into the river, and on certain occasions so many logs were stored between them that a person could walk from one to the other as if on a wooden floor. Yet by 1944 the cypress were gone and the mill closed.

Fortunately, just three years later the Hudson Pulp and Paper Company opened a large plant on Palatka's northern outskirts. At first Hudson employed only 279 persons, but within three decades the work force had risen to 2,400 persons whose annual payroll brought $23 million into cash-starved Palatka and Putnam County. Then in 1979 Hudson was bought by the even larger Georgia-Pacific Corporation, which modernized and expanded the already substantial facilities. Yet with increased automation Georgia-Pacific reduced the work force by more than half. This hit the town hard and in 1990 the population was actually more than a thousand below what it had been thirty years earlier.

With this background, you may want to explore Palatka. The Putnam County Courthouse on Fourth Street anchors the business section. Although it was constructed in 1909, it was extensively remodeled in 1963, at which time it lost its dome and its individuality to become a rather bland structure. On the grounds is the obligatory Confederate statue containing the inscription that some of the few who bother to read it find embarrassing: "The principle for which they fought will live eternally."

But it was not embarrassing when the statue was dedicated in 1924. At this time thousands of Southern war veterans still lived, and stories of battle heroism were told and retold whenever a vet could find an audience. The installation of the statue was a major event attended by nearly every citizen of Putnam County. It began with a festive parade down St. Johns Avenue. Then speeches were given by prominent persons at the veiled statue. At last the veil was dropped, and the statue stood proud and noble.

A reporter for the local newspaper wrote of the emotional scene. A veteran waved a faded Confederate flag that had thirty-two bullet holes. Thereupon, wrote a reporter, "one grizzled old veteran of the [eighteen] sixties [who] saw, for the first time in sixty years, the shrapnel-torn banner under which he fought [during] four long bloody years. Many wept with him when he fell upon his knees and kissed the flag he had followed across the sanguinary fields of Missionary Ridge, Lookout Mountain, and around Resaca. More persons wept before the statue." Now the heroes would be remembered forever. But "forever" has passed, and hardly anyone nowadays pauses to even acknowledge the statue.

From the courthouse, walk down St. Johns Avenue. Once a mule-drawn rail trolley rattled down the middle of the street. A popular stop was Hubbard Hart's rambling Putnam House at the northwest corner of Second Street. The hotel had a spacious verandah from which the distinguished guests could savor their juleps while they watched the passing panorama along the bustling avenue.

St. Johns became Palatka's first paved street when bricks were laid in 1907. People came from miles around just to have old Dobbin clatter over them. Some popped around town in one of those noisy Ford Tin Lizzies. Almost immediately sidewalks were added. Then St. Johns really shone.

Today the city is attempting to keep St. Johns appealing by adding trees shrubbery as well as installing bricks at the street corners. This has been done as part of Florida's Main Street program whose purpose is to revitalize central business districts devastated by the move to the suburbs. There is still a long way to go, but Palatka is on the way.

St. Johns ends at Memorial Parkway on the waterfront. In the old days this was called Water Street and along it crowded steamboat docks, warehouses, cheap hotels, and whiskey dives.

Turn onto Memorial Parkway and go a few blocks south to a rather large park directly on the river. Twin piers once reached far into the water. It was here that cypress rafts were broken up and fed to the screeching Wilson Cypress Mill to the south. The park offers a sweeping view of the river, of the soaring US 17 bridge, and of Hart's Point on the other side. A few blocks farther up the river is the Florida Furniture Company, one of Palatka's major employers.

Now backtrack on Memorial Parkway, which across US 17 becomes First Street. On the corner is the Holiday Inn, with rooms directly on the river and a restaurant with one of the best water vistas in Florida. Nearby is the Northside Historic Neighborhood with scores of picturesque old houses, among which is the officers' quarters of Fort Shannon at 100 Madison Street. Built when Palatka was a frontier post during the Seminole War, it is now the Putnam Historic Museum. If you're lucky enough to be here Tuesday, Thursday, or Sunday between 2 and 5 P.M., you can get inside. I have never been so blessed. Nearby, at 409 N. First Street, is the formidable former residence of the Wilson lumber barons.

Timber trucks are a familiar sight on the roads leading to the Georgia-Pacific mill in Palatka.

But enough of yesterday. Palatka is alive and active today. Anyone who doubts it should follow US 17 three miles north to the great Georgia-Pacific plant off of CR 216. This is the destination of most of the high-stacked timber trucks you probably encountered on the highway leading to town. There is an excellent view of operations from CR 216. A constant procession of timber trucks streams to the weight station, since the price paid for the timber depends on its weight. Then each truck proceeds to the unloading area where you can watch a towering crane move toward it with a claw so massive that the truck seems to shrink to the size of a child's toy. The claw grasps the entire load and swings it effortlessly to a conveyor belt for transportation to the debarking drum. Here a big chain knocks off the bark, which is saved to help fuel the power plant.

Although Georgia-Pacific only offers tours inside the plant to groups of ten or more, much can be observed just from driving through the grounds. As you enter through Gate One, you'll see on your right the piles of bark that are going to be carried by a conveyor to the power plant, which you can identify because it is the tallest structure on the grounds. The power plant's machinery is temperature-controlled by water, and the water thus used is routed to the three cooling towers on the right, where the excess heat is dissipated as steam.

Meanwhile the timber has been chopped into chips, which another conveyor has transported to the pair of buff-colored, cylindrical bins to the immediate right of the power plant. At the proper time the chips will be moved to the digesters: sixty-foot tanks beside the cooling towers. In the digesters, which act like pressure cookers, the wood is broken down into pulp and a liquid called black liquor. The pulp moves on to be dried and pressed into paper. The liquor is routed through silver pipes to the large black storage tanks on your left. Much of this liquor will be used to make such products as shampoos, toothpaste, and even paint.

Observing the huge operation, one wonders how many forests are being destroyed in order to provide us with the Angel Soft toilet paper that is one of the plant's most important products (along with Coronet and Sparkle towels and napkins). G-P, as the company

The public can drive through the grounds of the large Georgia-Pacific mill in Palatka.

is familiarly known hereabouts, maintains it is not destroying any forests at all. "For every tree that has been removed," a spokesman told me, "we plant three to five seedlings." Loblolly pines are the main tree used and are ready for harvest in as few as twelve years.

The G-P mill means everything to Palatka. One old-timer reminded the local newspaper that before the mill was built Palatka was just a country town largely confined to St. Johns Avenue. G-P has become such a highly regarded part of the community that there hasn't been a strike for almost forty years, and the head of the Putnam County Commission was a long-time electrician at the plant. "It would be hard to find any portion of life in Putnam County that has not been influenced by G-P and G-P people," wrote the *Palatka Daily News*.

A State of Happiness: San Mateo

From Palatka take the US 17 bridge over the St. Johns and continue south toward San Mateo. After passing beneath some high-tension wires, watch for an historical sign on your right indicating that this roadway is dedicated to William Bartram, the young British explorer-botanist we met in previous chapters. Behind the sign is a small park looking out on an electrical substation. It is not the kind of place you'd usually visit. But do so, and take a moment to read the weathered plaque that was once gold lettering on a green background, but now is pale dirt against dark dirt. The plaque tells an interesting tale.

During the British era Denys Rolle, a former member of Parliament, wheedled a 20,000-acre land grant from the king. In 1767 he brought the first forty-nine persons to the colony he was establishing here on the banks of the St. Johns. Rolle believed his mission was to work toward mankind's economic salvation, and Rollestown was to be the model that would change the world. The town would be parklike, with live oaks intermingled with such bountiful trees as oranges, bananas, peaches, and cherries. The streets were to be as much as eighty-two feet wide, with the central avenue, dominated by a church, an expansive 130 feet wide. Each settler would have his own five-acre garden. Contentment and moral uplifting would prevail, for "the very Fineness of the Climate disposes the Mind to a State of Happiness," claimed an English newspaper.

But the "State of Happiness" was to be a rare commodity at Rollestown. The motley assortment of criminals and prostitutes that Rolle intended to transform into noble humans rebelled when Rolle set them to clearing out the skin-piercing saw palmettos. Nor was the "Fineness of the Climate" apparent to them as they sweated beneath the torrid Florida sun. Shortly they all stomped off in disgust to ply their trades in lucky St. Augustine.

So Rolle gave up his idealism, stocked the plantation with slaves, and used the bullwhip to forge a rather prosperous export business based, not on the "State of Happiness," but on the exportation of orange wine and cotton. However, it all ended abruptly when Britain was driven from America as a result of the Revolutionary War. Rolle abandoned the site and resettled, with his slaves, in the Bahamas.

Although US 17 through San Mateo is not far from the river, there is so much hodgepodge that viewing the water is virtually impossible. Three miles south of town the road passes over Dunns Creek on a bridge several stories high. The original bridge put up in 1912 was a shaky wooden structure that required a toll to cross—a woefully small portion of which went the underfed collector, who received just $1.33 a day.

The Fruitland Peninsula begins across Dunns Creek. Many of the early settlers here had vineyards encompassing as many as fifty acres. But after the great freeze of 1894–95 killed all the vines, the financially ruined families deserted the peninsula.

A couple of miles beyond Dunns Creek is Satsuma, a mere fork in the road named for a peculiar type of tangerine-orange that once grew here. The sleepy hamlet gained notoriety in 1928 when Henry Hodges' place was pounced on by federal agents, who thereby wrecked one of the most successful counterfeiting rings in the history of Florida. Nothing that exciting has happened in the last seven decades, nor will such excitement probably ever reappear in Satsuma.

Calling All Tourists and Shad: Welaka

At Satsuma turn on CR 309 and follow it to the village of Welaka, five miles south. Welaka is what the Timucuans called the St. Johns River—it meant "Chain of Lakes." One of the most rewarding places to view the river is from the Bass Haven Lodge (904-467-8812), which, in addition to having $44 to $68 rental cabins on the water, features an attractive little restaurant that opens at 7 A.M. for breakfast and closes at 9 P.M. every day except Wednesdays. Fishing boats are for rent at $49 per day. The river is known for its bass—many coming indirectly from the state hatchery, conveniently just down the road. The fact that the river is much narrower here, and studded with forested islands, gave rise to one of the Civil War's oddest actions.

The Union navy operated in the St. Johns, where its gunboats coordinated the interception of Confederate supplies with the Union army, which had 5,000 soldiers at Palatka. The hard-pressed Confederacy's main defense against the Yankees in this area was Captain John Dickison, a brilliant cavalry tactician who kept the Yankees off balance even though he rarely had more than a few hundred troops under his command. Dickison could strike anywhere, and usually fought only when the odds were in his favor.

In late May 1864 Dickison learned that the armed ship *Columbine* had sailed through the narrows around Welaka and was headed up the St. Johns on a mission similar to that which had resulted in the capture of the *Hattie Brock* steamboat, which we saw earlier. Realizing that the *Columbine* must return the same way, Dickison dismounted the twenty sharpshooters riding with him and, reinforced by a small detachment of artillery, waited patiently along the thickly forested riverbank. At three in the afternoon, scouts reported the *Columbine* approaching. The ship slowed, wary that the passage had been mined. When it was just sixty yards away, Dickison let loose. A lucky artillery shot cut the *Columbine*'s wheel chains, causing the helmsman to lose control and the vessel to plow onto a sandbar, where it became stuck. Although the Yankees returned the fire, Dickison's force was obscured by foliage, and soon the *Columbine*'s decks were littered with dead and dying men. The Yankees had no choice except to surrender. This exploit has been called the only instance in North American history where cavalry captured a warship.

But the victory cost the citizens of Welaka dearly: for Union soldiers soon came calling and burned most of the town to the ground.

After the war, shad fishing thrived in the waters around Welaka. The operations eventually expanded until fishermen were using nets that could span nearly the entire river. Then the shad were fished-out and ultimately vanished entirely. With their demise went Welaka's prosperity.

Yet some people remained, worshiping at the Episcopal and the Methodist churches, both of which still grace CR 309. Even with this stubborn core, Welaka's revival has been slow, and the population has not yet reached 700. Front Street is quiet except for the Welaka Landing Boat Shop, put up in 1990 by Rand Speas, who builds and repairs boats. Speas believes the day is approaching when Welaka's scenic location and picturesque old buildings will make it a natural tourist attraction.

If the shad do return, it will probably be due to research done by the National Fish Hatchery, one of twelve such facilities in the Deep South. The hatchery is beside CR 309 on Welaka's southern outskirt. A free aquarium for the public is on the left side of the road, and on the right are some of the forty-one hatchery ponds. The aquarium is open seven days a week from 7 A.M. to 3:30 P.M. and consists of twenty-one tanks, each displaying St. Johns River fish. The room is dimly lit, allowing the tanks to be highlighted so that you get the eerie feeling you are actually underwater. Thus it is something of an anticlimax when you walk among the hatchery ponds across the road and know the fingerlings are down there but you can't see them. Nevertheless, this is an important operation where up to five million fish are raised and released annually.

For the Trip, Not the Destination: The Fort Gates Ferry

The sign for the Fort Gates Ferry is off of CR 309 a few miles south of Welaka. The mile-long ferry drive is down a mostly sand road to the Gateway Fishing Camp, where 1920s-style cabins look out on a small marina and the ferry dock. The first ferry pulled out of here before the Civil War, and the current tugboat is more than a hundred

Genial Don Yale runs the Fort Gates ferryboat.

years old. The ferry consists mainly of a simple steel platform capable
of transporting only two cars at a time. It runs between 7 A.M. and 5
P.M. every day except Tuesdays. The half-hour round trip is quite agreeable, if you don't mind standing all the way. The ferry master,
Don Yale, who retired from the Coast Guard, charges $9 to trans-
port a vehicle across the river to a country road in the Ocala National
Forest near where inconsequential Fort Gates once stood. But he
charges travelers who come to enjoy the forty-minute round-trip boat
ride without their cars just a dollar, which certainly makes it not only
the best deal on the river but probably in the entire Western
Hemisphere. Yale is also happy to rent you one of his rustic fish
camp cabins for $30 to $45 a night—just don't expect the Hilton.

Your experience on the river will be far different from that of
Harriet Beecher Stowe on a St. Johns voyage in 1872.

> One annoyance on board the boat was the constant and
> pertinacious firing kept up by that class of men who think
> that the chief end of man is to shoot something. . . . All the
> way along is a constant fusillade upon every living thing
> that shows itself on the bank. Now a bird is hit, and hangs,
> head downward, with a broken wing; and a coarse laugh
> choruses the deed. Now an alligator is struck; and the
> applause is great. . . . Now and then these sons of Nimrod
> in their zeal put in peril the nerves, if not the lives, of
> passengers. One such actually fired at an alligator right
> across a crowd of ladies.

"An Inexpressible Air of Grandeur": Mount Royal

From the ferry take Fort Gates Road back to a fork, then turn
right toward the Mount Royal home development. It is not an
auspicious setting for one of the most ancient sites in Florida. Upon
reaching Indian Mound Road, follow it to the mound, where there is
an informative roadside display.

Now try to block out the buzz from the private airstrip and let your
mind wander back nearly a thousand years. You are in a Timucuan
village composed of large dome-shaped huts framed with poles and
thatched with palmetto leaves. Perhaps a deer carcass is roasting over
a fire, from which the fragrant smoke curls upward. The men and
women are tall and well built. Children play with wooden figurines,
and squeal with delight when their mothers tickle them. Towering

over everything is a huge ceremonial mound. This is Mount Royal.

On festival days the scene would be different. Then shamans would chant their incantations to the spirits of the mound to make the tribe prosper. Mount Royal was undoubtedly a sacred place redolent with Big Medicine.

Much of what we know about the mound comes from William Bartram, who explored the mound in 1774, not long after the Timucuans were gone, having been killed by European diseases and slave-hunting tribes from Georgia. Bartram felt "an almost inexpress-ible air of grandeur" about the mound. He was impressed as much by the wide processional pathway leading to it as with the mound itself. He admitted to a sensation of reverence, perhaps akin to what the men and women who lived here so long ago must have experienced.

The mound is not as mysterious today as when Bartram mused about it, for science has allowed us to determine that the building of Mount Royal began around 1050 a.d. and that it was similar in style and in function to the huge sacrificial pyramids in Mexico. Sometime later Mount Royal was capped with a thick layer of deep-red ocher-colored sand, reconfirming that it may well have been used for bloody sacrifices.

Today Mount Royal is only a fraction of what it once was, for erosion and human activities have greatly diminished its size. Nonetheless, it is still an important portal to Florida's past.

Decorations of Indian Scalps: Georgetown

South from Mount Royal CR 309 parallels the St. Johns, out of sight to the west. Signs for fish camps pop up here and there. In three miles you'll reach Georgetown, which is mainly a restau-rant, some boat rental docks, and a few recently built motel units. The restaurant is not fancy, but the food is adequate for its patrons, mainly fishermen and casual tourists. Furthermore, you can eat directly on the river with Drayton Island across the water.

Drayton Island once belonged to Zephaniah Kingsley, a wealthy and ruthless slaveowner, who lived here in baronial splendor. In 1812 a visitor to Kingsley's home found it "handsomely decorated with Indian scalps." The island can be reached by means of a ferry which leaves from the public boat ramp off of CR 309 a few hundred yards south of the restaurant. The ferry is mainly a steel platform similar to that at Fort Gates. Today Kingsley is hardly more than a bad memory, and Drayton Island has become a seldom-visited place, for it has a lot of tranquility and little else.

A fishermen's tavern in Georgetown provides modest dining beside the St. Johns River.

Yet tranquility is not always in fashion, even in this little corner of the world. Incongruous as it seems, the entire eastern third of Lake George has been set aside for bombing practice. If a boater should stray into the buoy-marked restricted area at the wrong time, an air force jet will buzz him. Otherwise anyone is free to watch as a target is dropped into the lake, then planes roar overhead and try to hit it with smoke bombs.

Although CR 309 continues south from Georgetown for a mile to terminate near the shore of Lake George, the trip is not worth it, for the point of land is private and fenced off.

Tales From the Old Sprague House: Crescent City

From Georgetown drive back north two miles to CR 308, which will take you eight miles east to Crescent City. When you see Lake Stella, turn right on Grand Rondo for a shoreline drive to Central Avenue, which leads east to Crescent Lake, whose gentle curve indicates it was probably once a meander of the St. Johns River. There is a public boat ramp, a fishing pier, and a nice view of one of Florida's larger bodies of fresh water. But of most interest is the Sprague House Inn and Restaurant at 125 Central Avenue.

The Sprague House was constructed in the days when steamboats frequented Crescent Lake, carrying passengers and cargo down Dunns Creek and the St. Johns to the bustling piers at Jacksonville. The Sprague House reflects this era in its colorfully garish architecture known as steamboat Gothic.

Aside from its award-winning food and nineteenth-century ambience, the Sprague House is known for the pair of eight-foot-tall, stained-glass windows fronting Central. One window displays a riverboat with smoke streaming behind and its hull riding on a river of deep blue glass. The other shows a stagecoach drawn by four horses prancing over brilliant ocher flagstones.

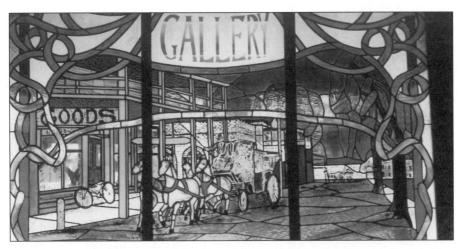

Stained-glass windows add to Sprague House's old-time atmosphere in Crescent City.

The windows were the work of the building's former owner, a Dutchman named Barry Nord, who had a gallery on the ground floor. Barry and his wife ran the business together for many years. But there came a time when the glow was gone, so they sold. After that, they split up, with Barry returning to Amsterdam. All that remained of their dream was the pair of beautiful windows made when they were young, and the future seemed as bright as the colored glass.

The new owners, Terry and Vena Moyer, entertained dreams of their own. They had already enjoyed successful careers, he as an anesthetist and she as a operating-room nurse. But both yearned to run a country inn, so when they found the building for sale in Crescent City, they snapped it up. "Running this is an eighteen-hour-a-day job, seven days a week," Terry told me, "but we love it." They serve lunches from 11 A.M. to 3 P.M. and dinners 5 to 9 P.M. Room rates run from $50 to $115 for the deluxe suite. The Sprague House can be reached at 904-698-2430.

The Moyers are keeping alive a tradition established by Guilford and Kate Sprague, who opened the first inn shortly after the building was constructed in 1892. Guilford was busy as the town's doctor as well as its mayor for sixteen years, so it was Kate who managed the inn. Her patrons were fishermen, steamboaters, and tourists, who rode into town by stagecoach or on the paddle wheelers. The inn was Kate's life, and over the decades she became a fixture in the small town. Although she has long since passed on to that great inn in the sky, perhaps some part of her still dwells in the building she loved so much.

The Silent War in Fern Country

Driving south on US 17 from Crescent City, you'll start seeing many fields surrounded by black screening. If you park at the side of the road and peer through one of the openings, you'll discover row after row of bushy green ferns thriving in a shady, dank environment so different from the hot, bright world outside. You are now in the fern belt, which continues for the next thirty-three miles as far as DeLand. Although it is quiet, even serene, within the acres of sheltered greenery, appearances can be deceiving, for there is a war being fought here. Armies of worms are attacking the leaves, and hordes of fungus are devouring the chlorophyll. Combating these enemies is a full-time task. The counterattack is led by sprayers, alert as infantrymen for their enemies. But the forces arrayed against them are powerful and sometimes the heavy artillery must be called in. Then entire sections of the greenhouses are chemically drenched. When even this is not sufficient, the buglers sound retreat and the rear guard burns the entire field. Aside from bugs and diseases, the fern growers must also battle the weather: a wet season can cause the ferns to rot, and a high wind can rip the saran screening to shreds.

If the ferns survive, they must be harvested by hand—and it is backbreaking work. Many of the laborers are Mexicans, each of whom cuts about four hundred bunches a day when the harvest is at its height in the spring. Mother's Day is to the fern growers what Christmas is to toy makers, since the fern background is an important element in the bouquets that make moms across the nation turn sentimental. While moms gush over the flowers, they hardly notice the ferns which set the colors off. "After all our work," a grower complained, "our ferns are ignored. People don't realize it's the ferns that make the bouquet. It's frustrating as hell!"

Just a *Little* Hype: Seville

Continuing south, you'll see the fern fields are on one side of US 17 and Amtrak rails on the other. When the original tracks were laid, this was the Jacksonville, Tampa, and Key West Railway, designed to be the state's mainline before Henry Flagler gobbled it up. In 1885 the J, T, & KW put out a booklet that extolled the virtues of the land along its route, which reached only as far as Sanford, not Key West. Although the booklet promised to paint a realistic picture of the communities, woe to the settler who believed it. There is, for example, the case of Seville.

As you drive through Seville, a half-deserted crossroads hamlet, it is difficult to believe that the railroad assured everyone it was destined to be a "model town" with fine avenues lined with large homes. "It seems reasonably certain," the railroad booklet declared, "that before long the town will number a very large population." Already there was a "very handsome station" and, nearby, a fine hotel with accommodations for fifty guests. Furthermore, Seville's prosperous orange groves and lumbermills would insure the town's continued prosperity.

Because the groves were too far north, they were destroyed by freezes, and the mills soon devoured the timber and moved on. So today Seville houses mostly fern pickers who shop at an old building on US 17 where Spanish is spoken.

Fire!

The railroad's forecast for Pierson, six miles south of Seville, did better. Peter Pierson had settled here in 1876, giving the community his name, and a group of hard-working Swedes followed him. Although the orange groves and sawmills at Pierson met the same fate as those at Seville, today the town of around 4,000 calls itself the Fern Capital of the World. It is an imperious title, but the fact is that the three hundred ferneries around Pierson account for eighty percent of the ferns sold in the United States. That's not exactly the world, but it's an awful lot of ferns, nonetheless.

There was danger that Pierson would not be the capital of anything during the devastating brush fires of 1998. Although the state suffered through a series of separate outbreaks, those that exploded in the dry pines around Pierson were among the most serious. The fear was that if they were not brought under control quickly, they would combine to form one immense firestorm whose updrafts of intense heat

Fire roared through woodlands near Pierson in the summer of 1998.

would create its own wind, which in turn would fan the flames into an inferno utterly beyond human control.

During early July, US 17 was thronged with firefighting equipment hurrying to the trouble areas. One problem was that some places were so inaccessible that live trees had to be felled and crude roadways cut through the forest just to get there. Once on location, firefighters encountered many unforeseen perils, among them that of displaced rattlesnakes. There was also danger from red-hot ashes landing on heads and clothing. The weather was scorching, so drinking water was in short supply. So too were other undreamed-of necessities such as lip balm and eyedrops.

Most of the work involved forming obstructions to the fires' spread. Thus bulldozers cleared firebreaks while wood choppers felled trees along highways. Often a crew would work the entire day and never even see a fire. But smoke clouded the air, and the danger was always present that a fire would suddenly materialize and they might be cut off. Such was the experience related to an *Orlando Sentinel* reporter:

Ultimately, a firefighter's senses rule on the front lines, where a wind-fanned wall of flames can seem to barrel out of nowhere with frightening menace. There is a second of calm, like the eerie silence before a storm. Debris starts falling from the sky like snow. Then the

This stack of timber will soon be loaded onto a truck and hauled to Palatka.

thick gray smoke begins to glow orange. "You hear the crackling sounds, and it breaks out into flame," said Tom McIsaac, a Montana firefighter describing his recent visit to the front lines in Volusia County. "The energy and intensity is something to respect. All your senses are maximized." McIsaac and the crew on Hunting Camp Road off of State Road 44 abandoned their efforts at the spot to save themselves—sometimes that's the only strategy left.

All is quiet now along US 17 around Pierson, for dozers have cleared out the dead wood, much of which was hauled off to the Georgia-Pacific mill at Palatka. Within weeks after the fire the fields were green with grasses and the leaves of saw palmettos emerging from their charred stalks. Then pine saplings began sprouting. Gradually the drama will be forgotten and the forest will return. So the cycle goes.

Gun Fight on the Bridge! Volusia-Astor

When you come to Barberville just south of Pierson, turn west on SR 40 and drive seven miles to Volusia and Astor, twin hamlets on opposite banks of the St. Johns River. The road is nothing special, going through pine flatlands where about the only activity is the procession of timber trucks.

Once tiny Volusia was the most important settlement for miles—giving its name to the modern county that extends all the way to Daytona Beach on the Atlantic. Its general store supplied farmers from miles around. It was immortalized, in all its grubbiness, by Marjorie Kinnan Rawlings in *The Yearling*. As for Astor, it was the site of an important British trading post known to William Bartram as the Upper Store. The post vanished when the British left, but in the 1870s the grandson of John Jacob Astor, powerful New York millionaire, built a hotel here to accommodate the steamboat traffic. Although the hotel was successful for a while, when the railroads displaced the steamers, it declined and eventually burned to the ground.

There was sometimes bad blood between the pair of settlements. Guns actually came into play when a new drawbridge was built in 1926. At this time the position of tender was taken from the ruffian who had held it for many years. Fuming, he met the new man in the middle of the bridge. Guns were drawn and shots were fired. When the smoke cleared, the former tender lay dead.

Today the excitement consists mainly of two activities: fishing and eating. For fishing, you can rent a boat and cruise along the river

The St. Johns bridge between Astor and Volusia was the scene of a deadly gun battle in 1926.

much as Marjorie Kinnan Rawlings and a female friend did in a small motorboat in the 1930s. "The river life was indeed the finest of lives," she mused in *Cross Creek*, "and there was no hurry left in the world. We put up in a golden-brown deep creek and fished all afternoon. A white egret fished companionable with us a few yards away, and water turkeys flapped their wings lazily from high cypresses."

For eating, William's Landing is a surprisingly good restaurant from which there is a marvelous second-floor view of the river, including the modern drawbridge that is a descendant of the bloody one of local notoriety. It is open 11:30 A.M. to 9 P.M. Tuesday through Sunday. For more sumptuous dinners the Blackwater Inn, on the ground floor of the same building, is open Tuesday through Friday from 4:30 to 9 P.M. and weekends 11:30 A.M. to 9 P.M.

The Fountain of Youth? DeLeon Springs

Activity of a far different sort can be found at DeLeon Springs State Park. Watch for the park sign when you enter the town of DeLeon. You'll find that the road to the spring passes through land that has suddenly become rather hilly. This is the DeLand Rise, a low, sandy ridge that helps define the St. Johns valley.

Locals like to believe that Ponce de Leon marched over this ridge searching for the elusive Fountain of Youth. There is no evidence that the aging explorer was ever here, but, if he was, he would have found a spring of immense size, but, alas, without that magic elixir for which he yearned. Nonetheless, the spring is still clear and refreshing, ideal for the swimmers, who change in the bathhouses that have been built in a tasteful, quasi-Spanish style.

The spring did not exist when the first Indians came to this area 8,000 years ago. At that time Florida's water level was much lower and the aquifer circulated far underground, where it gouged a deep cavern in the limestone bedrock. When the overlying rocks collapsed, a wide sinkhole was created, which, as the water level rose, became the spring pool.

The park is open from 8 A.M. to sunset seven days a week. Admission is $4 per car, although if you are just one or two persons, you can leave your car just outside the park, pay $1 each to enter, and walk a few minutes to the spring. Here you can use the changing rooms to put on your bathing suit and use the large, spring-fed pool, where you can rent a tube for $5 for the day. Or you can rent a canoe or kayak for $8.48 per hour and paddle through the spring run to Lake Woodruff, passing on your way nonchalant alligators and birds of many varieties, all colorful, for Lake Woodruff is a national wildlife refuge. More ambitious paddlers can reach the St. Johns River beyond.

If you don't have the time or the inclination for dunking or rowing, you can just admire the old story-and-a-half mill wheel turned by runoff water from the spring. There has been a mill at or near here from the Spanish era two hundred years ago. John James Audubon may have painted birds from this location when he was a guest of Colonel Orlando Rees, who built a mill here to grind cane from his sugar planta-

There has been a mill in DeLeon Springs for about two hundred years.

Live oaks form a cool, green canopy at DeLeon Springs State Park.

tion. This was probably the same Orlando Rees later killed by Seminoles and for whom many believe the town of Orlando was named. Other owners followed Rees, and such relics as roller gears and a kettle used to boil water from the sugar juice are displayed beside the mill.

Inside the mill house is a souvenir shop, bakery, and restaurant. The highlight of a meal here is to cook your own pancakes on the grill inset at your table. The pancake batter is made from grain that was stone-ground on site. The restaurant is open Monday through Friday from 9 A.M. to 4 P.M. and weekends from 8 A.M. to 4 P.M.

For persons who enjoy picnics, the park furnishes tables beneath the gnarled arms of some of the most graceful live oaks you'll see anywhere.

The Owl and the Buzzard: Hontoon Island

Returning to the town of DeLeon Springs, pick up CR 4053, also called Grand Avenue, which leads due south over the DeLand Ridge. After crossing SR 44, you will come to Old New York Avenue and the 1918 railroad station, which is still used by Amtrak. One reason the railroad located here, rather than in the nearby town of DeLand, was because the land was flat and, therefore, cheaper to build on than the more difficult terrain of the DeLand Rise. Earlier, the British found these damp St. Johns flatlands ideal for raising indigo, and on a plantation just south of here sixty slaves once toiled their lives away in the unmerciful sun.

Now turn west on Old New York and follow the signs, which will soon lead you south on Hontoon Road for two miles past meadows and country homes. Watch for the Safari River Tours sign on the east side of the road. Safari pontoon boats sail on two-hour narrated excursions along the St. Johns to Blue Spring State Park, which is next on the list of places to visit. On the way you'll see alligators and possibly manatees, if you are there in the winter, plus birds and miscellaneous critters of many descriptions. The trips cost $14 for adults and $8 for kids six through ten (younger are free.) Shove-off time is 10 A.M. and 2 P.M. every day of the week. The boat holds only forty-two passengers, so reservations are strongly advised: 904-740-0333. You can also enjoy a meal at the Sunset Restaurant and Tavern beside the Safari docks—but don't expect anything gourmet.

A sign will have you turn left on River Ridge Road, which parallels a canal where small boats slumber contentedly. It ends at a parking lot beside the St. Johns River across from which is Hontoon Island State Park, open from 8 A.M. until sunset seven days a week. You'll have to leave your car in the lot, since no automobiles are allowed on the island, and wait for the ferry. It won't be long, for the river is not wide here and the ferry's only mission in life is to shuttle constantly back and forth. Once across you'll pay an admission fee of $2 per group of up to eight persons. There is a small shop at the landing where ice cream, soda, and other refreshments can be purchased, but it is only open on the weekends. Otherwise the island is kept in a rather primitive state. There is a secluded location for camping and six of what the park warns are "rustic" cabins for rent. There is also a nature trail through a dense hammock to an ancient Indian shell mound—allow two hours. But the main interest for casual tourists is the owl totem and the eighty-foot observation tower.

The totem is a few hundred feet left from the landing. It is a careful replica of one of the largest wooden carvings ever discovered in Florida and was found in the muck during the excavation of the marina across the river. The totem represents an owl, with upright ears, a beak, and large eyes that are almost hypnotic. Carved out of a tree trunk by Timucuans using shells and sharks' teeth around six hundred years ago, the totem probably stood close to the river, perhaps to propitiate the water spirit, perhaps to warn hostile tribes from the area, or perhaps for some purpose that we cannot even fathom.

Near the totem is a picnic area ideal for its view of the river in which Timucuan dugouts once splashed. William Bartram got caught in a violent storm near here and hurriedly put to shore, drenched and a little frightened. During the early American era, steam-driven paddle wheelers churned past. But the river is quiet now, except for an occasional pleasure craft or fishing boat.

The observation tower is at the end of a short path from the picnic area. You may want to think twice about a climb of eight stories, but there are regularly-spaced resting platforms, and the view from the top is inspiring. As you look north, on the left is the St. Johns, with piers fringing its banks and, beyond, only trees and blue infinity. On the right is a portion of Lake Beresford. Some radio towers can be seen on the horizon, but they barely prick the immensity of the scene.

The birds around here believe that the tower was built for them, and regard humans as intruders. When dusk falls, the birds flock to the tower, which is a natural roost. Here they squawk and chatter before settling down for the night. They are off at dawn, leaving their feathers and down and further contributions of the guano that has turned most of the metal girders bird-white. During the daytime the tower makes an excellent lookout for buzzards, who perch imperiously on the topmost railing. Sometimes a buzzard resists human intrusions; I encountered one such individual. I got to within six feet of him, shouting and waving my hat, before he became disgusted and soared into the ether with a grace that made me envious.

From this lofty vantage point it is clear why the St. Johns is one of only fourteen streams to be selected as a Heritage River. This puts it in a special category that makes it available for federal environmental protection funds. The river's beauty makes it doubly surprising that many persons see it more as a dump than a natural treasure. In 1996 concern for this practice materialized in the form of a weekend cleanup sponsored by the St. Johns River Water Management District and environmental groups. At this time 50,000 volunteers in fourteen counties pulled from the river such items as barbecue grills, grocery carts, car parts, washing machines, broken toilets, and, of course, the usual treasure of rusted beer cans. When it was over, the river was

The observation tower at Hontoon Island State Park presents a view of the St. Johns valley.

relieved of 400,000 pounds of gunk, goo, and garbage! The operation was deemed such a success that it has since become an annual event.

Once you return to the mainland, drive back past the Amtrak station and on to SR 44, which leads east to DeLand, the seat of Volusia County. DeLand, a delightful community of nearly 20,000, is the home of highly regarded Stetson University. It has a thriving downtown with many first-class restaurants, most of which cater to students as well as to the general public. The 1927 county courthouse is a refurbished master work, with a pleasing rotunda encircled by a balcony that displays large murals depicting events in DeLand's history.

At DeLand pick up US 17, which has now been joined by US 92, and drive six miles south to Orange City, from where a sign points to Blue Spring State Park two miles west.

The Manatee Boardwalk: Blue Spring State Park

Blue Spring is one of central Florida's most popular state parks. It is open from 8 A.M. until sunset seven days a week, and admission is $4 per car. The spring is another of the large sinkholes that have caved into the underlying aquifer, from which water churns to the surface.

You can do about any activity at Blue Spring. There are changing rooms where you can don your bathing suit and swim either in the spring itself or in the spring's massive outflow that helps feed the nearby St. Johns River. If you like to snorkel, you can rent the equipment for $4 for the first hour and $2 each additional hour. If you just want to float around, tubes rent for the same price. More ambitious persons can rent a three-person canoe for $10 for the first hour and $5 each additional hour. If you just want to picnic, grills are provided for steaks, chicken, or what have you. A concession store sells burgers, chips, and like items. The park also features the two-hour narrated Safari cruise along the St. Johns already mentioned under Hontoon Island.

Of course none of this jingle-jangle was here when William Bartram, consumed with curiosity, arrived more than two hundred years ago. He was accompanied by the British owner of the indigo plantation near Hontoon Island. The two rowed their boat through the rustling quietude to the spring.

Today most people use the elevated boardwalk for an easy ten-minute stroll to the spring. The way is through a dense hammock, with plaques providing information about the trees, the animals, and how the spring was formed. Because the boardwalk is elevated, there is a surprisingly long view, with the bushy plants below and a palm filament above. Most walkers take their time while the subtle majesty of the hammock grows on them. The boardwalk ends on a low bluff from which there is a good view of the spring and the dark heart from which the water issues.

Bartram found the vegetation around the spring to be coated with the pale bluish substance that gave it its name. The spring itself smelled like bilge water. Alligators were everywhere. It was, all in all, not a place he considered agreeable. Such is not the case today. For some reason the spring has lost both its blue luster and its repellent fragrance. Now the water is clear as green-tinted glass. Neither is the water hot, as in Bartram's day, but maintains a refreshing temperature of seventy-two degrees.

Considerable numbers of manatee are attracted to Blue Springs during the winter, when manatee-watching consumes nearly everyone. During these times such crowds flock to the park that it often closes before noon. Sometimes up to seventy or eighty manatees winter here. Weighing around a ton and being about ten feet long, the animals are easy to see in the crystalline spring flow. Because they live in the water and consume sea grasses and river vegetation, it is difficult to realize that they are actually related to the elephant.

Returning to Orange City, you can reach Interstate 4 via CR 472 just north of town. From there it is ten miles to the turnoff to Sanford, from where these explorations began not so long ago.

Here I'll bid you farewell. I'm sure we'll meet again. Watch for me on some backroad.

The clear waters at Blue Spring State Park are as appealing to human swimmers as they are to manatees.

Index